PENGUIN HANDBOOKS

THE FARMHOUSE KITCHEN

Mary Norwak was trained on technical fashion-trade magazines and first edited a magazine at the age of twenty. After working on *Vogue* and *House & Garden*, she left a week before her first baby was due and decided to switch to food writing as it fitted better into a freelance life, and food was an over-riding passion. She has written on food for the *Daily Express*, *The Times*, the *Guardian* and dozens of magazines, has been food writer for *Farmers Weekly* for some fifteen years, and currently contributes to the *Lady*, *House & Garden* and edits two magazines on freezing.

Mary Norwak has written more than forty cookery books, together with one on kitchen antiques and another for children, and also parish and company histories. She developed an interest in food-freezing when it was still confined to farmers' wives with surplus produce and space for a large freezer, and has continued to write on all aspects of freezing and other methods of food preservation. Her real love, however, is good traditional British food and historical recipes, and she has a collection of about 1000 cookery books, including many fascinating old hand-written ones. Gardens, antiques and 'digging into history' are other obsessions, and all somehow seem to tie up with food and the kitchen.

Mary Norwak lives looking over the marshes of the north Norfolk coast with three children who enjoy eating.

MARY NORWAK

THE
FARMHOUSE
KITCHEN

PENGUIN BOOKS

Penguin Books Ltd, Harmondsworth, Middlesex, England
Penguin Books, 625 Madison Avenue, New York, New York 10022, U.S.A.
Penguin Books Australia Ltd, Ringwood, Victoria, Australia
Penguin Books Canada Ltd, 2801 John Street, Markham, Ontario, Canada L3R 1B4
Penguin Books (N.Z.) Ltd, 182–190 Wairau Road, Auckland 10, New Zealand

—

First published by Ward Lock Ltd 1975
Published in Penguin Books (with the omission of the last chapter) 1979
Reprinted 1981

—

—

Made and printed in Great Britain by
Richard Clay (The Chaucer Press), Ltd, Bungay, Suffolk
Set in Monotype Ehrhardt

CONTENTS

ACKNOWLEDGEMENTS

The author and publisher would like to record their sincere thanks to the many people and institutions who have helped to provide the material for this book. Notable among them are the following:

Mrs Daphne MacCarthy for the use of copyright material.
HER (Home Economists on Request) and Miss Sally Ashworth for obtaining test material.
Mrs Lylie Crowe for testing recipes.
The many eighteenth- and nineteenth-century cooks who recorded their recipes for modern cooks to use.
The many suppliers who have patiently sought and obtained unusual ingredients for making the dishes.
The author's family and others for eating them.

The line illustrations are from various works by Thomas Bewick.

NOTES ON FARMHOUSE COOKING

Fats

BUTTER was an expensive commodity in the past, so lard and dripping were mainly used by country families. Lard was obtained from the cottage pig, and dripping saved from roasting beef, pork or lamb joints.

Lard was obtained by cutting up the surplus pig fat into small pieces and 'rendering' it or 'doing it down' over a low heat. As it melted the fat was poured off until it ceased to give, and this resulted in pure and delicious lard, often flavoured with a sprig of rosemary. Throughout the nineteenth century, country children had lard spread on their bread instead of butter. When the lard had been extracted, there remained crisp crunchy pieces of fat, called, variously, 'scratchings', 'cracklings' or 'fritters'. These were often eaten rolled in salt, or added to a mixture of apples, dried fruit, brown sugar and spice in a delicious pie, or added to a cake mixture.

Dripping, the strained fat recovered after roasting meat, was kept in separate containers, according to whether it came from roast beef, lamb or pork. It was a particular teatime treat when spread on hot toast, but was also a traditional ingredient in puddings and cakes. Before using in recipes, dripping should be clarified.

Clarified dripping   Make the dripping hot and pour it into boiling water. Stir it for 3 or 4 minutes and leave it to get cold. The impurities will sink to the bottom and should be removed with a knife.

Butter, when it came into general use, was heavily salted.

Unsalted butter went rancid very quickly. Today, most recipes (including the ones in this book) expect you to use slightly salted butter or to add a pinch of salt, except when frying or making cakes. For these, use unsalted butter if possible.

Fires

Many old country recipes specify the use of a bakestone or girdle, or recommend that dishes should stand by the side, or in front of the fire. These methods arose from traditional ways of cooking. Originally food in cottages and farmhouses was cooked on or in front of an open fire. Meat was cooked on a spit set just before the fire, and baked goods could be prepared on a flat suspended girdle or griddle. Meat, bread, pies and cakes were frequently taken to the village bread-oven for cooking, being baked on the floor of the oven when the fire had been lit and removed from it. A similar bread oven was built into larger farmhouses. Early enclosed ranges began to appear at the beginning of the nineteenth century, and these gradually developed with a hotplate at the side on which pans could stand. Subsequently an oven was fitted at the side of a range so that housewives could prepare baked savoury and sweet dishes as we know them today.

Sugar

Most less wealthy country homes did not have sugar until quite late. When sugar came into general use, it was in the shape of 14 lb blocks or 'loaves' which had to be cut or scraped with a sharp knife, and the sugar itself was coarse and granular. It had to be pounded to make it soft and fine, like modern sugar. Today, granulated sugar can be used for many recipes, but caster sugar should be used for cakes and custards.

Flavourings

Country meals which were often rather plain and monotonous were sometimes varied by the use of liquid flavourings, spices and herbs.

Liquid flavourings   Rose-water and orange-flower water were used to flavour creams, sweet cakes and biscuits in the more prosperous households. They are still obtainable today from the chemist and give a subtlety to many sweet dishes.

Robust meat, poultry and game dishes were flavoured with cider, wine or beer. Home-made cider was prepared and used on small farms and in cottages, and home-made wines were also widely used, the sweeter flower wines being particularly popular in sauces. Larger houses had their own brew-houses and ale or richer stout were both drunk and used for cooking. These alcoholic liquids not only flavoured dishes, but also helped to break up tough fibres and give succulence to slow-cooked meats.

Spices   A wide range of spices was used for all types of sweet and savoury dishes and for pickles and preserves, but they were too expensive for small farmers or cottage dwellers. Originally they served to disguise the ill-flavour of winter-salted meat, and stale materials, but they became popular in their own right. Ginger was a particular favourite, particularly used in the gingerbread eaten on so many festive occasions. The ground spice was employed and in richer households preserved stem ginger was used. Root ginger was most often used in chutney and pickles, but it needed breaking up with a heavy weight to release its flavour.

Herbs   Many of our favourite herbs were introduced by the Romans, including onions, rosemary and parsley, and they have been popular flavourings in this country for nearly two thousand years. About 200 herbs were in common use in medieval times, but the number dwindled to about forty by the mid nineteenth century, and we only use six or seven regularly today. Country-dwellers made use of such herbs as nettles and sorrel to flavour plain suet puddings, mint to flavour fruit dishes, and cottage geranium leaves to flavour jellies and cakes. Herbs to go with meat were originally chosen from the grazing herbs which the animals had eaten. Thus English lamb, grazed on the marshes, was normally served with mint; the Welsh prefer thyme for their mountain sheep; while Greeks and Italians prefer oregano (a member of the marjoram family) for lamb dishes.

Pastry and pies

Three types of pastry were most commonly used in farmhouse cooking. *Shortcrust pastry* which is a simple mixture of fat, flour and water; *puff pastry* which is a richer mixture of fat and flour; and *hot-water pastry* made with fat, flour and hot water. The latter was used for meat, game and a few fruit pies, and used to be moulded over a wooden shape or over a clenched hand, but is now more commonly cooked inside a metal mould or cake tin.

Huff paste was made as a covering for baking joints of lamb, pork, ham and venison, rather as we use foil today. It was usually made with flour and water, but venison huff paste also contained fat. This paste kept the meat moist, but it was not usually eaten, being discarded into the hen bucket.

Shaping pastry   Early pies were rarely baked in special moulds, but were formed into turnovers or pasties which could be baked directly on a bakestone or griddle, or on the floor of a bread oven. When saucers came into general use, old ones were often used for baking little pies, particularly those made with fruit.

Pastry which covers a deep pie needs a tidy edge, and this is best achieved by *knocking-up*. This keeps shortcrust pies neat and decorates them, and it helps richer pastries to rise during cooking by opening up the edges. When the pastry is trimmed off, the knife should be held horizontally and the sides of the pie tapped with a slight upward movement forming a series of shallow cuts. This edge can be *crimped* or pinched between finger and thumb, or it can be *fluted* by holding the pastry lightly with the forefinger and thumb of one hand, pressing the pastry between them with the forefinger of the other hand.

Forcemeat

Many old recipes include forcemeat, either as a stuffing, or in the form of small balls which are fried. Forcemeat balls add savour to poultry and game dishes, and may be included in pies. Apart from adding flavour, they obviously extended portions in the days when meat was in short supply. The basic mixture includes suet, breadcrumbs, seasoning and herbs, and the flavourings can be varied to suit the dish. Sometimes minced meat, liver or bacon was added to the basic crumb stuffing. For the recipes in this book, a good basic forcemeat can be made from 50 g/2 oz shredded suet, 100 g/4 oz fresh breadcrumbs, 2 teaspoons chopped parsley, 1 teaspoon chopped thyme, grated rind of $\frac{1}{2}$ lemon, salt, pepper and 1 egg. This may be used for stuffing a bird or joint of meat, or can be formed into small balls (about 5 cm/2 inches diameter) to roast in the surrounding fat, or to fry in deep fat.

Servings

All recipes will serve 4–6 people, according to appetite.

WEIGHTS, MEASURES AND
USEFUL TABLES

Deep fat frying temperatures

Food	Bread browns in	Fat temperature	Oil temperature
Raw starchy foods: doughnuts, fritters, chips (1st frying)	1¼ minutes	325°-340°F 170°C	340°F 170°C
Fish in batter	1¼ minutes	325°-340°F 170°C	340°F 170°C
Fish in egg and crumbs	1 minute	360°F 185°C	360°F 185°C
Scotch eggs	1 minute	350°F 180°C	350°F 180°C
Reheated foods: potato straws, chips (2nd frying)	40 seconds	380°F 190°C	390°F 195°C

Sugar boiling temperatures

	°F	°C
Soft ball	237	114
Hard ball	247	119
Soft crack	280	140
Hard crack	310	154
Caramel	340	171

Domestic oven temperatures

	Electric °F	Celsius °C	Gas
Very cool	225	110	$\frac{1}{4}$
Very cool	250	130	$\frac{1}{2}$
Very cool	275	140	1
Cool	300	150	2
Warm	325	170	3
Moderate	350	180	4
Fairly hot	375	190	5
Fairly hot	400	200	6
Hot	425	220	7
Very hot	450	230	8
Very hot	475	240	9

U.S. equivalents

FLUID OUNCES	U.S. STANDARD
1	2 tablespoons
2	4 tablespoons
$2\frac{1}{2}$	5 tablespoons
3	6 tablespoons
4	$\frac{1}{2}$ cup
6	$\frac{3}{4}$ cup
	1 cup
10	$1\frac{1}{4}$ cups
12	$1\frac{1}{2}$ cups

SPOONS

Tablespoons

U.K.	U.S.
$\frac{1}{2}$	$\frac{3}{4}$
1	$1\frac{1}{2}$
$1\frac{1}{2}$	$2\frac{1}{4}$
2	3
$2\frac{1}{2}$	$3\frac{3}{4}$
3	$4\frac{1}{2}$
4	6
5	$\frac{1}{2}$ cup (scant)
6	$\frac{1}{2}$ cup + 1 tablespoon
10	1 cup (scant)

SPOONS

Dessertspoons

U.K.	U.S. teaspoons
1	$2\frac{1}{2}$
2	5

Teaspoons

U.K.	U.S.
$\frac{1}{8}$	$\frac{1}{8}$
$\frac{1}{4}$	$\frac{1}{4}$
$\frac{1}{3}$	$\frac{1}{3}$
$\frac{1}{2}$	$\frac{1}{2}$
$\frac{3}{4}$	1
1	$1\frac{1}{4}$
$1\frac{1}{4}$	2
2	$2\frac{1}{2}$
$2\frac{1}{2}$	3
3	4
4	5
6	$7\frac{1}{2}$

All spoon measures are normally level; where recipe calls for heaped or rounded spoons heap or round U.S. equivalent.

PINTS

Imperial (British) pints	U.S. standard
$\frac{1}{8}$	5 tablespoons
$\frac{1}{5}$	$\frac{1}{2}$ cup
$\frac{1}{4}$	$\frac{1}{2}$ cup + 2 tbsps
$\frac{1}{3}$	$\frac{3}{4}$ cup (generous)
$\frac{3}{8}$	1 cup (scant)
$\frac{1}{2}$	$1\frac{1}{4}$ cups
$\frac{5}{8}$	$1\frac{1}{2}$ cups (generous)
$\frac{2}{3}$	$1\frac{3}{4}$ cups (scant)
$\frac{3}{4}$	$1\frac{3}{4}$ cups (generous)
1	$2\frac{1}{2}$ cups
$1\frac{1}{4}$	3 cups (generous)
$1\frac{1}{2}$	$3\frac{3}{4}$ cups
2 (1 quart)	$2\frac{1}{2}$ pints
$2\frac{1}{2}$	3 pints (generous)
$2\frac{3}{4}$	$3\frac{1}{2}$ pints (scant)
3	$3\frac{3}{4}$ pints
4 (2 quarts)	5 pints
$4\frac{1}{2}$	$5\frac{1}{2}$ pints (scant)
5	6 pints (generous)
8 (4 quarts/ 1 gallon)	10 pints
12	15 pints
16 (2 gallons)	20 pints

CHAPTER I
BREAKFAST

MANY farmers have two breakfasts because they start work so early in the morning. A modern farmer may only begin his day, at first light, with a cup of tea and some toast or cereal, and then eat his full breakfast meal about nine o'clock. But in the past, those who had to start the day's work at some distance from their homes would begin it with porridge and then return later to breakfast. Those whose work was nearer home would begin with a hearty breakfast, and come back for 'ten o'clocks'.

Either way, a farm breakfast usually starts with a cereal or porridge. After this comes a cooked dish of two or three 'fries', such as bacon, eggs, tomatoes, mushrooms and fried potatoes; sometimes there may be kidneys, sausages or fish. In warmer weather, cold ham, brawn or boiled bacon is popular. After this comes plenty of new bread, oatcakes or toast, accompanied by honey or home-made marmalade.

Porridge to start on

OATMEAL PORRIDGE

200 ml/8 fl oz cold water   1 saltspoon salt
1½ tablespoons coarse oatmeal

Use the quantities above for each person. Bring the water to the
boil and start stirring it while you run the oatmeal in from your
hand. Stir very well to prevent lumps forming. Season with the
salt, and bring to the boil. Cover with a lid and simmer for 30
minutes.

CROWDY

Fine oatmeal   Butter
Salt   Milk
Boiling water

Crowdy differs from porridge in that it is made from finely-ground
meal and no cooking is needed if boiling water is used. For one
person, put 3 tablespoons fine oatmeal into a bowl and add salt to
taste. Pour in boiling water and stir briskly until it is as wet as you
want it. Leave the crowdy to stand for a minute or two, and it will
have swollen. Put a knob of butter in the centre of the bowl.

The crowdy should be eaten by taking a little on a spoon and
dipping it into a mug of cold milk.

Savoury cooked dishes

POTATO HOTCAKES

900 g/2 lb potatoes   2 eggs
2 tablespoons flour   Salt and pepper
2 teaspoons powdered mustard Fat or dripping for frying
2 tablespoons finely-grated onion

Peel the potatoes and soak in cold water for 30 minutes. Grate them and drain away any liquid. Add the flour, mustard powder, onion and beaten eggs. Mix thoroughly and season with salt and pepper. Melt a little fat or dripping in a pan and drop in the mixture in spoonfuls. When brown on one side, turn over and brown the other side. Serve with bacon or sausages.

FLODDIES

1 large potato	Flour
1 tablespoon grated cheese	Herbs and seasoning as in recipe
1 egg	Fat for frying

Peel the potato and grate the raw flesh. Mix this with the cheese and egg. Add enough flour to make a soft dropping consistency like a thick pancake mixture. Season to taste with salt and pepper and a pinch of mustard powder. Add some chopped fresh herbs such as chives, thyme, sage or parsley. Fry in spoonfuls in hot fat, and serve very hot.

KIPPER CAKES

225 g/8 oz cooked kippers	Salt and pepper
225 g/8 oz mashed potato	2 tablespoons browned bread-
25 g/1 oz butter, softened	crumbs
2 eggs	Fat for frying
1 teaspoon chopped parsley	

Remove bones from the kippers and flake the flesh. Mix with the mashed potato, softened butter and one of the eggs. Add the parsley and salt and pepper to taste and mix thoroughly. Divide the mixture into six pieces and form into cakes about 2·5 cm/1 inch thick and 6·25 cm/2½ inches across. Beat the other egg and dip the kipper cakes into it. Coat them in the breadcrumbs and fry in hot fat until golden-brown on both sides. Serve hot.

HERRINGS FRIED OR GRILLED IN OATMEAL

4 herrings	½ teaspoon salt
2 tablespoons oatmeal	Fat for frying

Scale and clean the herrings and wash and dry them well. Mix the oatmeal and salt and use this to coat the herrings. Fry in hot fat for 5 minutes each side. Grilled herrings can be coated likewise before cooking.

BUTTERED BLOATERS

4 bloaters	2 tablespoons lemon juice
50 g/2 oz butter	Salt and pepper

Cut off the heads, tails and fins of the bloaters and remove the backbones. Put into a greased ovenware dish and dot them with butter. Sprinkle on the lemon juice, salt and pepper. Cover and bake at 350°F, 180°C, gas mark 4 for 10 minutes.

Bloaters are a speciality of East Anglia. They are whole fresh herrings which are dry-salted and lightly smoked. They were very popular in Victorian times and were often made into a strongly-flavoured paste.

BLOATERS GRILLED WITH MUSTARD

4 bloaters	2 tablespoons browned bread-
25 g/1 oz butter, melted	crumbs
2 teaspoons made mustard	

Clean and trim the bloaters and make three slashes along one side of each fish with a sharp knife. Brush with melted butter and grill the bloaters on both sides very lightly. Fill the slashes with mustard and sprinkle the breadcrumbs on bloaters. Pour on any remaining butter and brown the bloaters under a hot grill.

SMOKED HADDOCK IN MILK

1 large smoked haddock   Butter
500 ml/1 pint milk

Skin the haddock and remove the main bones. Put into a shallow
heatproof buttered pan and cover with the milk. Cook gently for
10 minutes until the fish is tender. Drain, and serve with knobs of
butter.

SCRAMBLED EGGS WITH KIPPERS

2 kippers   1 tablespoon butter
6 eggs   4 slices buttered toast
Pepper

Grill the kippers and discard the bones and skin. Flake the flesh
and keep warm. Beat the eggs lightly with a fork and season with
a little pepper but no salt. Melt the butter in a pan and add the
beaten eggs. Add the kipper flesh and cook over a low heat,
moving the mixture constantly from the bottom of the pan but
not stirring. While the eggs are still creamy, put them on the
toast, and serve at once.

CREAMED EGGS

4 eggs   Salt and pepper
125 ml/¼ pint single cream   Buttered toast

Break the eggs into a thick pan and stir with the cream, salt and
pepper. Stir over a low heat until thick. Serve on buttered toast.

RUMBLED EGGS

4 eggs and 2 egg yolks   Toast or cooked bacon or kidneys
175 g/6 oz butter   Salt and pepper
1 tablespoon water

Put the eggs, egg yolks, butter and water into a thick saucepan.

Season with salt and pepper. Stir over a low heat until thick.
Serve on toast, or with bacon or kidneys.

SAUSAGE-MAKING

Sausage-making was part of a housewife's duty when the family
pig was killed. Today it is a useful way of getting the type of
sausage you like, either finely or coarsely ground, with or without
added bread and herbs. A mincer attachment to an electric mixer
speeds up the mincing process, and a skin-filling attachment is
also available.

Sausage mixtures are traditionally 'cased' or stuffed into a
casing or skin. If this is not possible, sausages are wrapped in *caul
fat* obtained from a butcher. This fat should be soaked in tepid
water, with 1 tablespoon vinegar added to 1 litre/2 pints water.
When the fat is soft, it can be cut into any shape and size and the
meat rolled in it with the edges well overlapped, and this gives a
firm casing for the meat (the same method can be used for pâtés
and faggots).

Sausage casings can be obtained from a butcher in small
quantities, and synthetic casings are easier to handle than natural
ones. Natural casings must be rinsed to free them from the salt in
which they are processed, and then have to be opened by fixing
them to a cold water tap, with the water running, pushing them
on to the tap in lengths. They can then be fitted to the sausage
filler and the meat pushed in. Synthetic casings must be handled
with dry, grease-free hands or the skins will not fill evenly and
will be understuffed. When the skins are filled evenly, they should
be moistened to make it easier to twist them into lengths.

CUMBERLAND SAUSAGES

675 g/1½ lb lean and fat pork   Pinch of marjoram
175 g/6 oz bread   Sausage skins (optional)
Salt and pepper

Mince the pork twice. Soak the bread in cold water until very wet, and mix this with the pork. Add the salt and pepper and the marjoram. Put into skins, or form into sausage shapes for frying. The water in these sausages will form a good gravy when the sausages are fried.

GLAMORGAN SAUSAGES

150 g/5 oz soft breadcrumbs
75 g/3 oz grated cheese
Pinch of mixed herbs
A little chopped onion
Salt and dry mustard
1 egg, separated
Lard for frying

Combine the dry ingredients, season, bind with egg yolk and form into sausage shapes. Roll in flour, dip in egg white and crumbs, and fry in lard.

SUFFOLK SAUSAGES

2·7 kg/6 lb pork sausage meat
50 g/2 oz salt
Pinch of mace
Pinch of cloves
8 g/¼ oz pepper
Pinch of nutmeg
150 g/5 oz soft breadcrumbs
125 ml/¼ pint hot water
Sausage skins

Mix thoroughly and put into skins. Boil these sausages before frying them.

OXFORD SAUSAGES

450 g/1 lb lean veal
450 g/1 lb pork
450 g/1 lb shredded suet
225 g/8 oz soft breadcrumbs
Rind of ½ lemon
8 g/¼ oz nutmeg
6 sage leaves
1 teaspoon pepper
2 teaspoons salt
Sprigs of thyme, marjoram and savory
Sausage skins

Mince all the meats together. Add all the other ingredients and mix thoroughly. Fill skins.

SPICED PORK SAUSAGES

1·35 kg/3 lb bread
4 kg/9 lb lean pork
1·35 kg/3 lb firm fat from fat
  bacon
75 g/3 oz salt

25 g/1 oz white pepper
15 g/½ oz ginger
20 g/¾ oz mace
Sausage skins

Soak the bread in cold water and wring out. Put lean meat and fat through a coarse mincer. Mix in seasonings, then add the bread and run the whole lot through a fine mincer. Fill sausage skins.

GRILLED KIDNEYS

8 lamb's kidneys
Salt and pepper

Butter, melted
Parsley, chopped

Skin the kidneys and split them in half without quite detaching them. Fasten them flat on skewers and season lightly with salt and pepper. Brush over with melted butter and grill on both sides for 5 minutes. Place on buttered toast and pour over a little melted butter and chopped parsley.

TOSSED KIDNEYS

8 lamb's kidneys
Butter
Salt and pepper
1 teaspoon flour

250 ml/½ pint stock
Juice of 1 lemon
1 teaspoon chopped parsley
Fried bread

Skin the kidneys and slice them. Heat a little butter in a pan and fry the kidney slices for 1 minute. Season, and stir in the flour. Add the stock, lemon juice and parsley; heat, but do not boil. Serve with fried bread.

BACON FRAZE

8 eggs
50 ml/2 fl oz single cream
25 g/1 oz plain flour

225 g/8 oz thin rindless bacon
rashers
Made mustard

Beat the eggs with the cream and flour to make a batter. Fry the bacon crisply, and remove from the pan. Pour half the batter into the pan and when it is just set, lay the bacon rashers on top, and cover with the remaining batter. When this is set, turn and brown the other side. Serve very hot with mustard.

JOLLY BOYS

2 heaped tablespoons flour
Pinch of salt
1 egg

Milk
Bacon fat left from frying bacon

Mix the flour, salt, egg and enough milk to make a thick batter. When the bacon has been fried, bring the fat left in the pan almost to boiling point. Put in the batter in tablespoonfuls. Spoon hot fat on top as they cook. The batter forms oval shapes and rises when fried. These can be served with the bacon when eggs are scarce, or can be eaten with marmalade afterwards in the old style.

OATMEAL BREAKFAST CAKES

100 g/4 oz oatmeal
250 ml/½ pint milk
2 tablespoons flour

75 g/3 oz shredded suet
Salt and pepper
Bacon fat for frying

Soak the oatmeal in the milk. Add the flour, suet, salt and pepper, and mix well together. Shape into small round flat cakes on a floured board. Fry on both sides in hot bacon fat and drain well. Serve very hot like scones.

WINTER OATMEAL CAKES

25 g/1 oz bacon fat, dripping or butter
125 ml/scant ¼ pint water

100 g/4 oz coarse oatmeal
¼ teaspoon salt
¼ teaspoon bicarbonate of soda

Heat the fat with the water until the fat melts. Stir the oatmeal with the salt and bicarbonate of soda. Add the liquid and stir well to make a stiff paste. Form into eight balls and squash these flat, pressing more oatmeal into each side. They should be about 3 mm/ ⅛ inch thick. Cook on both sides on a lightly greased griddle, hotplate or frying pan, or bake at 350°F, 180°C, gas mark 4 for 30 minutes. Eat hot or cold with butter, cheese or marmalade. These may be kept in a tin, or more traditionally buried in oatmeal in a meal-chest. If not freshly-baked, they should be reheated before serving.

POTATO CAKES

225 g/8 oz cold mashed potato
25 g/1 oz butter
50 g/2 oz plain flour

65 ml/2½ fl oz milk
Pinch of salt

Mash or sieve potatoes, work in butter and add flour and salt, working the mixture until the flour is well blended into the potatoes. Blend to a stiff dough with the milk. Roll out lightly on a floured board and cut into rounds or squares. Bake on a lightly greased hot griddle until golden-brown on both sides. Split and butter and serve while hot.

POTATO GRIDDLE CAKES

675 g/1½ lb potatoes
150 g/5 oz plain flour
1 egg
500 ml/1 pint milk

1 level teaspoon sugar
1 level teaspoon salt
Dash of pepper

Peel and grate the potatoes into a bowl. Mix in the flour, egg, milk and seasonings and leave the batter to stand for 2 hours or overnight. Grease a griddle or frying pan, and put on mixture in dessertspoonfuls. Cook until deep golden in colour on both sides. Serve hot with curls of crisp bacon, or spread with cranberry sauce or marmalade.

SAUTIE BANNOCKS

100 g/4 oz plain flour
100 g/4 oz fine oatmeal
1 tablespoon syrup
¼ teaspoon salt

½ teaspoon bicarbonate of soda
1 small teaspoon cream of tartar
1 egg
175 ml/7 fl oz milk

Mix dry ingredients, add syrup, beaten egg and enough milk to make a dropping consistency. Drop in spoonfuls on a hot, greased griddle. Cook until brown on either side. Cool on a towel. Serve with syrup.

COTTAGE CHEESE GRIDDLE CAKES

1 tablespoon melted butter
100 g/4 oz cottage cheese
2 eggs

50 g/2 oz self-raising flour
1 tablespoon milk

Add butter to cottage cheese and gradually whisk in eggs. Stir in flour and milk and mix to a smooth thick batter. Drop spoonfuls on to a hot greased griddle or frying-pan and turn several times. Serve freshly cooked with crisp hot bacon, honey, jam or jelly. These scones are very light and digestible, and particularly good for anyone who does not want much starch in his diet.

KENTISH FLEAD CAKES

350 g/12 oz flead
800 g/1¾ lb plain flour
15 g/½ oz salt

50 g/2 oz butter
Cold water

The flead (sometimes known as 'flair' or 'flare') is the fat which lines the abdominal wall and is packed round the kidneys of a pig.

Sift the flour and salt. Rub the butter into the flour. Remove the skin from the flead, and shred the flead finely. Mix with the flour and butter, and form into a smooth pliable dough with cold water. Turn on to a floured board and beat with a rolling pin until the flead is thoroughly mixed with the flour. Roll out 1·75 cm/ ¾ inch thick and cut into rounds. Bake at 350°F, 180°C, gas mark 4 for 20 minutes until golden-brown.

– and marmalade to end with

MARMALADE-MAKING

Citrus fruit for marmalade must be sliced, simmered in water until tender, and then boiled rapidly with sugar to setting point. The fruit and peel need not be soaked overnight, but it must be thoroughly soft when simmered. The water in this first cooking will evaporate, and the contents of the pan will reduce to about half.

The pips and white pith contain pectin which helps to set the marmalade. They should be tied into a piece of muslin or clean white cloth (an old handkerchief will do well) and suspended in the pan when the peel is cooked in water. Take out the bag when the water is added and squeeze it well to extract all liquid. When the sugar has been added, the marmalade should be stirred gently to dissolve it, and then the mixture must be boiled quickly to setting point. This can be most easily tested by pouring a little marmalade on to a cold plate. If it starts to set after a few seconds, and wrinkles when pushed with a finger, the marmalade is ready. Take it from the heat at once and leave to cool for 15 minutes. Stir well so that the peel is evenly distributed and pour into clean warm jars. Fill them right to the top and put on a waxed paper circle. Cover with a transparent paper top or screwtop lid.

OLD-FASHIONED SCOTCH MARMALADE

900 g/2 lb Seville oranges   1·8 kg/4 lb sugar
2 litres/4 pints water

Remove the rind from the oranges as thinly as possible and cut it into small pieces (not shreds). Put the pips into some of the water allowed in the recipe and leave for 12 hours. Cover the fruit and the peel with the rest of the water brought to the boil. Leave to stand for 12 hours. Add the liquid from the pips and simmer for 2 hours. Stir in the sugar until dissolved. Bring to the boil and boil to setting point. Cool slightly and stir well. Pour into hot jars and cover.

OXFORD MARMALADE

900 g/2 lb Seville oranges   2 litres/4 pints water
1 lemon   1·8 kg/4 lb sugar

Wash and wipe the fruit. Cut in half and squeeze out the juice and pips. Cut the peel into thick shreds and put into a pan with the pulp, juice and water. Tie the pips into a piece of muslin and put into the pan. Boil gently for about 2 hours, until the mixture is reduced by half. Take out the bag of pips and squeeze it well so that the liquid goes back into the pan. Add the sugar and stir until dissolved. Simmer for 1½ hours until the marmalade is dark and has reached setting point. Leave to stand for 15 minutes, stir, and put into warm jars. Cover with lids.

DARK ORANGE MARMALADE

1·35 kg/3 lb Seville oranges   2·7 kg/6 lb sugar
1 lemon   1 tablespoon black treacle
2·5 litres/5 pints water

Cut the oranges in half and squeeze out the juice. Put the pips into a muslin bag. Cut the fruit into thick shreds. Put into the pan with juice, the juice of the lemon, water and the bag of pips.

Simmer for about 2 hours until the peel is tender. Take out the bag of pips, and squeeze out the liquid. Stir in the sugar and black treacle until dissolved and boil quickly to setting point. Cool slightly, stir well, pour into hot jars and cover. If liked, 4 tablespoons rum or whisky can be added just before pouring into pots.

ORANGE SHRED MARMALADE

900 g/2 lb Seville oranges	2·5 litres/4½ pints water
Juice of 2 lemons	1·35 kg/3 lb sugar

Peel enough thin rind from the oranges to weigh 100 g/4 oz, and cut into thin strips. Cut up all the fruit and put into a pan with 1·25 litres/2½ pints water and the lemon juice. Cover and simmer for 2 hours. Simmer the peel in 500 ml/1 pint water with a lid on until the shreds are soft. Strain the liquid into the fruit pulp. Strain the pulp through a jelly bag and leave to drip for 15 minutes. Simmer the pulp in the remaining water for 20 minutes, and then leave to strain through a jelly bag overnight. Put the two liquids together and stir in the sugar until dissolved. Add the peel and boil hard to setting point. Cool slightly and stir well. Pour into hot jars and cover.

ORANGE MARMALADE WITH HONEY

Sweet oranges	Honey

Peel the oranges and shred the peel finely. Cook the peel in a little water until tender, and then drain. Remove the pith and pips from the oranges and measure the orange pulp. To each 500 ml/1 pint of orange pulp, allow 450 g/1 lb honey and 225 g/8 oz prepared rinds. Simmer pulp, honey and rinds together gently for 40 minutes, stirring often. Cool slightly, stir well, pour into hot jars and cover.

THREE FRUIT MARMALADE

2 grapefruit	3 litres/6 pints water
2 sweet oranges	2·7 kg/6 lb sugar
4 lemons	

Cut all the fruit in half. Put the pips, and the pith and membranes from the grapefruit into a muslin bag. Shred all peel finely and cut up the flesh roughly. Put the peel, flesh, water and bag of pips into a pan and simmer for 1½ hours. Take out the bag of pips and squeeze to extract the liquid. Stir in the sugar until dissolved, and boil rapidly to setting point. Cool slightly and stir well. Pour into hot jars and cover.

GINGER MARMALADE

5 Seville oranges	225 g/8 oz crystallized ginger,
2·5 litres/5 pints water	diced
1·35 kg/3 lb cooking apples	15 g/½ oz ground ginger
3 kg/6½ lb sugar	

Cut the oranges in half and squeeze out the juice. Shred the peel finely and cut up the flesh. Put the pips and trimmings into a muslin bag in the pan with orange peel and flesh, juice and water. Simmer for 1½ hours, and remove the bag of pips, squeezing all the liquid out. Peel and core the apples and cut them into slices. Simmer in 4 tablespoons water until pulped. Add the apples to the oranges and stir in the sugar until dissolved. Add the ginger cut in pieces and the ground ginger. Boil rapidly to setting point. Cool slightly, stir well, pour into hot jars and cover.

LEMON MARMALADE

8 large lemons	Sugar
4·5 litres/8 pints cold water	

Peel lemons very thinly and cut peel into very fine shreds. Put pith and pips into muslin, and cut up the flesh of the lemons. Put fruit, peel and pips into a pan with water and boil until the contents of the pan are reduced by half. Remove pips. Weigh the contents of the pan and add an equal weight of sugar. Bring to the boil, boil for about 20 minutes until setting point is reached, and put into pots.

GRAPEFRUIT MARMALADE

1 grapefruit	1 orange
1 lemon	1·8 kg/4 lb sugar

Cut all fruit up finely, removing pips. Pour over 2 litres/4 pints of cold water and let it stand for 20 hours or more. Tie pips in a piece of muslin and put in with the fruit. Boil until it is tender, then add sugar (remove pips bag first). Stir until dissolved, then boil up again until it sets when tested.

CHAPTER 2
FARMER'S ORDINARY

IN the past, the 'ordinary' was the meal traditionally served to farmers in the market town on market day. Each eating-house offered a meal at a fixed rate for all comers; sometimes the place itself was called an 'ordinary'. These meals were great favourites with the farmers. They usually started with a hearty soup, followed by a pie or savoury pudding, roast meat or poultry. The meal would finish with a sweet pie or pudding and plenty of cheese. With the main course, there would be an abundance of vegetables; creamed vegetables were particularly popular in the winter. In addition to potatoes, a variety of savoury, starchy puddings were prepared to eat with the meat and soak up the gravy. These were also made at other times, in the home, to quell appetites, and so eke out frugal portions of meat. Although cooked with the meat, they were often served first with the gravy so that the family would eat less meat.

Soups

PEA SOUP

450 g/1 lb dried green peas	100 g/4 oz swede
2 medium-sized onions	1 ham bone
2 carrots	Salt and pepper
1 small turnip	2 litres/4 pints water

Soak the peas overnight. Put soaked peas and prepared vegetables into a large saucepan, add the ham bone, salt and pepper, and water. Bring to the boil, cover the pan and simmer until the peas are soft. Sieve the vegetables. Return the pulp to the liquid and reheat.

BARLEY SOUP

40 g/1½ oz patent barley	25 g/1 oz butter
250 ml/½ pint milk	½ teaspoon meat extract
1 litre/2 pints well-flavoured stock	Salt and pepper
	Grated nutmeg

Blend the barley with the milk. Boil the stock with the fat and the meat extract, stir it into the barley and milk, return all to the pan and simmer until the barley thickens and becomes clear. Stir all the time, as the barley easily forms lumps. Season very carefully, adding the merest trace of nutmeg.

Serve with small cubes of fried bread, handed separately.

COWHEEL SOUP

1 cowheel	Salt and pepper
1·5 litres/3 pints water	25 g/1 oz fine tapioca or sago
1 onion	Lemon juice
1 carrot	Grated nutmeg
1 stick of celery	Chopped parsley
A bunch of herbs	

Scrape, clean and blanch the cowheel; divide it into convenient pieces. Put it in a pan with the water, bring to boiling point, add the vegetables (cut in small dice) and herbs, and simmer for 3–4 hours. Strain, remove some of the meat from the bone and cut into small dice. Season the soup, reboil it and sprinkle in the sago or tapioca. Cook till the grain is quite clear and soft. Add the pieces of meat, a little lemon juice, nutmeg and parsley, and serve.

COCK-A-LEEKIE

1 boiling chicken	1 onion
900 g/2 lb veal knuckle	2 cloves
Salt	4 leeks
1 carrot	50 g/2 oz rice
1 turnip	

Put the chicken in a deep pan with the veal knuckle and cover with water, adding a pinch of salt. Bring to the boil, remove scum, then add the carrot, turnip and the onion which has been peeled and stuck with the cloves. Continue simmering till the chicken is tender and remove the bird. Clean the leeks, removing outer leaves, and cut into short lengths. Strain the broth and add the leeks and the rice. Boil for a further 30 minutes and season to taste. Cut half the chicken meat into small pieces (use the remainder for another dish) and put into the soup. Just before serving add a teaspoonful of chopped parsley.

OXTAIL SOUP

1 oxtail	1 litre/2 pints water or bone stock
25 g/1 oz beef dripping	1 teaspoon salt
1 onion	A bunch of herbs
1 carrot	6 peppercorns
1 piece of turnip	25 g/1 oz flour
1 stick of celery	

Cleanse the oxtail, remove outside fat and cut into joints. Make the dripping hot and in it fry half the meat till brown, then remove it. Slice the vegetables and fry them till golden-brown, then remove them. Put the fried and raw meat and the fried vegetables into a deep pan, cover with the liquid, and bring very slowly to boiling point. Add the salt, herbs and peppercorns and simmer very gently for 3–4 hours. Meanwhile fry the flour in the dripping until golden-brown. Strain the soup, return to the soup some of the thinner pieces of meat and small rounds of carrots. Whisk in the browned flour. Whisk till boiling, season and serve. The thicker pieces of meat may be served as stewed oxtail. A little sherry can be added to the soup just before serving.

OATMEAL SOUP

1 leek
25 g/1 oz butter
50 g/2 oz fine oatmeal
500 ml/1 pint beef stock

250 ml/½ pint milk
50 ml/2 fl oz single cream
Salt

Slice the leek finely and cook gently in the butter until the leek is soft but not coloured. Add the oatmeal and stock and stir until it comes to the boil. Simmer for 1 minute. Add milk and cream, and salt to taste, and reheat without boiling.

BEEF BROTH AND PARSLEY DUMPLINGS

225 g/8 oz shin beef
1 litre/2 pints vegetable stock
Salt and pepper
1 carrot

1 onion
1 small turnip
1 stick of celery
25 g/1 oz dripping

Parsley Dumplings:
100 g/4 oz self-raising flour
50 g/2 oz shredded suet

Salt
2 teaspoons parsley

Cut the meat in cubes and cook with the stock, pepper and salt for 1 hour. Dice the vegetables and fry in dripping for a few minutes.

Add to the meat and simmer for 1 hour. To make the dumplings, mix the dry ingredients and form into a soft dough with water. Add the dumplings to the broth 20 minutes before the soup is ready. Sprinkle with a little extra chopped parsley before serving.

GAME SOUP

Carcass and trimmings of 2 partridges *or* equivalent amount of any game
25 g/1 oz lean bacon
25 g/1 oz butter
1 onion
1 carrot
½ parsnip
1 stick of celery
25 g/1 oz flour
1 litre/2 pints stock
A bunch of herbs
1 clove
Some neat pieces of breast of bird
Salt and pepper

Put the pieces of carcass, the trimmings, and the bacon, with the fat in a saucepan and fry them till brown. Remove the game and fry the sliced vegetables till brown. Add the flour and fry it till golden-brown. Stir in the stock, bring to the boil, add the herbs, return the game to the pan and simmer for 1½–2 hours. Meanwhile cut the pieces of breast meat into small dice. Strain the soup, and reheat the diced game in it. Season carefully and serve.

PHEASANT SOUP

1 pheasant
1 medium-sized onion
2 leeks
1 medium-sized carrot
1 stick of celery
Bunch of fresh herbs
25 g/1 oz brown breadcrumbs
1 egg yolk
25 ml/1 fl oz single cream

Using a sharp knife, remove the meat from the breast and wings of the pheasant and keep them to one side. Put the remaining carcass in a pan with sliced onion, leeks, carrot, celery and the herbs. Cover with water and simmer for 4–5 hours. Mince the breast meat and pound it finely. Mix with the breadcrumbs and egg yolk and shape the mixture into small balls. Strain the soup, and put the liquid into a clean saucepan. Add the meat balls and bring to the boil. Simmer for 20 minutes, stir in the cream and serve at once.

IPSWICH PARTRIDGE (OR HARE) SOUP

2 partridges	100 g/4 oz lean ham
1·5 litres/3 pints beef stock	50 g/2 oz butter
6 medium-sized onions	50 g/2 oz plain flour
12 cloves	125 ml/¼ pint double cream
1 carrot	Cayenne pepper

Roast the partridges until they are just cooked. Crush the meat and bones very thoroughly and add to the stock. Stick 2 cloves in each onion, and add the onions and carrot to the stock, together with the ham. Cover and simmer very gently for 4 hours. Strain the liquid. Mix the softened butter and flour together and add a little of the hot soup. When the mixture is like thick cream, add it to the rest of the soup and bring it to the boil, stirring well. Simmer for 10 minutes, then stir in the cream and a little Cayenne pepper and serve at once. This soup may also be made from cooked hare.

POACHER'S SOUP

1–2 kg/2–4 lb venison	1 blackcock or woodcock
225 g/8 oz shin beef	1 pheasant
450 g/1 lb mutton with bones	½ hare or 1 rabbit
1 head celery	2 partridge or grouse
2 carrots and turnips	6 small onions
4 onions	6 peeled potatoes
Bunch of parsley	1 small white cabbage
8 g/¼ oz peppercorns	2·5 litres/5 pints water

If liked:

Red wine	Forcemeat balls
Mushroom catsup	

Cut up the venison, beef, mutton, celery, carrots, turnips, onions, and put into the water with parsley and peppercorns. Simmer for 3 hours and strain the stock. Cut up the game, dust with flour and brown. Add to the stock with small onions, some more sliced celery, potatoes, and the cabbage cut in quarters. Season to taste with some black pepper, allspice and salt, and simmer 2 hours. Remove bones. Add some red wine, mushroom catsup and forcemeat balls if liked.

KIDNEY SOUP

1 ox kidney
Seasoned flour
25 g/1 oz dripping
2 small onions

2 carrots
A little beef extract
Salt and pepper

Remove fat from the kidney and cut the meat into slices. Roll them in the seasoned flour and fry them deep brown in the dripping. Slice the onions and carrots and put into 3 litres/6 pints boiling water. Simmer for 3 hours, skimming off the fat from time to time. Season to taste with beef extract, salt and pepper, and serve very hot.

Main dishes

ROAST BEEF WITH YORKSHIRE PUDDING AND HORSERADISH SAUCE

2·25 kg/5 lb sirloin of beef   Black pepper

Yorkshire Pudding:

100 g/4 oz plain flour
½ teaspoon salt
2 eggs

250 ml/½ pint milk
1 tablespoon cold water

Horseradish Sauce :

50 g/2 oz grated horseradish	½ teaspoon salt
125 ml/¼ pint double cream	½ teaspoon white pepper
1 teaspoon sugar	2 teaspoons white wine vinegar
½ teaspoon dry mustard powder	

Put the beef into a roasting tin without any fat. Sprinkle beef with pepper. Roast in a hot oven, 425°F, 220°C, gas mark 7, for 15 minutes. Lower heat to 375°F, 190°C, gas mark 5 for the rest of cooking time, allowing 15 minutes to the pound. Baste meat frequently with pan juices. Beef should be served underdone, and should be transferred to a heated dish and left to rest for 15 minutes before carving.

To make the Yorkshire Pudding, sieve flour and salt together into a mixing bowl. Add the eggs and stir into the flour. Add half the milk slowly, and stir until the mixture is smooth. Add the remaining milk slowly and beat batter well, and then beat in the cold water. Fifteen minutes before the beef is cooked, pour 2 tablespoons of its fat into a 25 cm/10 inch square tin. Put tin into the oven, and when fat is sizzling hot, pour in the pudding batter. Bake at the top of oven for 30 minutes (the meat is removed 15 minutes earlier to rest before carving). The pudding should be well-risen, puffy, crisp and brown on top and bottom, and should be served straight from the tin in which it is baked, cut in squares.

If fresh horseradish is to be used for the Horseradish Sauce, the root should remain in cold water for 1 hour, then be washed well, and scraped into very thin shreds with a sharp knife. If bottled horseradish is used, it must be drained and squeezed dry in a kitchen towel. To make the sauce, whip the cream to stiff peaks, and fold in the horseradish, sugar, mustard, salt, pepper and vinegar. Serve cold.

STUFFED SHOULDER OF LAMB

1 shoulder of lamb, boned	50 g/2 oz butter
2 onions, skinned and chopped	Rosemary or parsley to taste

Stuff meat with onions and rosemary or parsley. Skewer and tie well in round shape. Put in tin, brush melted butter over joint. Roast at 350°F, 180°C, gas mark 4 for 25 minutes per pound and 25 minutes over. Remove the skewers and string, and serve in wedges. A shoulder of lamb is also excellent if lamb's kidneys are used in place of the onions. Three or four will be needed.

ROAST LAMB WITH MINT SAUCE

1 shoulder or leg of lamb	Juice of 1 lemon
Salt and pepper	Sprig of rosemary

Mint Sauce:

2 teaspoons chopped fresh mint	Pinch of salt
1 teaspoon sugar	2 tablespoons wine vinegar
2 teaspoons hot water	

The meat on a shoulder of lamb is succulent and sweeter than on a leg. It can be boned and rolled for easy carving. Remove any thick pieces of fat from the joint, chop small, and put them in the roasting tin to cook with the lamb. Rub the joint with salt and pepper and squeeze on the juice of a lemon. Put a sprig of rosemary under the joint. Put the meat into a hot oven for 10 minutes, 425°F, 220°C, gas mark 7, then reduce heat to a moderate level, 350°F, 180°C, gas mark 4, and continue cooking for about 1½ hours according to the size of the joint. Lamb tastes best if it is still slightly pink near the bone. Place meat on a hot serving dish. Drain off excessive fat from the roasting tin, and add a little vegetable water to the pan drippings to make thin gravy. Serve with roast potatoes and vegetables in season, together with Mint Sauce.

To make the sauce, put the freshly-chopped mint into a bowl with sugar and hot water. Stir until sugar dissolves, and add salt and vinegar.

ROAST PORK WITH SAGE AND ONION STUFFING AND APPLE SAUCE

1 leg or loin of pork
Oil

Salt and pepper

For the stuffing:

2 large onions
50 g/2 oz fresh white bread-
    crumbs

75 g/3 oz butter
2 teaspoons chopped fresh sage
Salt and pepper

Apple Sauce:

4 large cooking apples
40 g/1½ oz sugar
Juice of ½ lemon

4 cloves
25 g/1 oz butter

The skin of pork should be scored by the butcher with a sharp knife. A little oil rubbed into the skin, and a sprinkling of salt and pepper will give crisp crackling. Cook in a fairly hot oven, 375°F, 190°C, gas mark 5, allowing 30 minutes per pound. Pork should be well cooked and not pink when served. Drain off excess fat, and use a little vegetable water with the pan juices to make a thin gravy.

The stuffing may be put into the pork if it has been boned, or cooked separately in the same oven. Peel the onions, chop them coarsely and simmer until soft in enough water to cover them. Add breadcrumbs, butter, sage, and plenty of salt and pepper. When stuffing is well mixed, pack it into the joint before roasting. To cook separately, put into a greased ovenware dish and dot with butter. Cook for 1 hour with the joint.

To make the sauce, use apples which become fluffy when peeled. Peel, core and slice them. Put into a saucepan with the sugar, lemon juice, cloves and a little water. Simmer until soft, and then beat apples to a pulp. Remove cloves, and stir in butter. Serve hot.

ROAST MICHAELMAS GOOSE

1 goose	2 slices bread soaked in milk
100 g/4 oz pork	1 egg yolk
100 g/4 oz veal	Parsley, thyme, sage
1 large onion	75 ml/3 fl oz red wine
15 g/½ oz butter	

Chop the pork, veal, onion, and the goose liver very finely and brown them in the butter. Squeeze the milk out of the bread and mix together all the ingredients, chopping the herbs finely, and using only a little of the wine to moisten. Season with salt and pepper to taste. Stuff the goose and put into a very hot oven, 450°F, 230°C, gas mark 8, for 15 minutes. Reduce heat to 350°F, 180°C, gas mark 4 and cook for 15 minutes per 450 g/1 lb, basting with the remaining wine.

ROAST CHICKEN STUFFED WITH HERBS

1 chicken	Salt and pepper
40 g/1½ oz butter	100 ml/4 fl oz white wine or
1 tablespoon chopped onion	cider (optional)
2 tablespoons chopped carrot	1 teaspoon parsley
25 g/1 oz flour	1 teaspoon chervil
375 ml/¾ pint stock	1 teaspoon tarragon

For Herb Stuffing:

2 tablespoons breadcrumbs	Salt and pepper
1 teaspoon chopped shallot	Liver from chicken
1 teaspoon chopped tarragon	25 g/1 oz melted butter
1 teaspoon chopped parsley	(approximately)
1 teaspoon chopped chervil	

Remove gall bladder, wash and chop the liver finely. Mix the chopped liver with breadcrumbs, herbs, seasoning and sufficient oiled butter to moisten. Stuff the bird with stuffing, truss for roasting. Roast in moderately hot oven (350–375°F, 180–190°C, gas mark 4–5) until tender, 1–1½ hours, basting frequently.

Melt butter in saucepan, fry onion and carrot lightly, stir in flour, cook gently until lightly browned. Stir in stock, boil until cooked, add seasoning and wine (if used) together with 1 teaspoon each of parsley, chervil, tarragon or other herbs, as liked. Simmer sauce gently for ¼ hour. Remove trussing string from bird.

Serve with a little sauce poured round, and remainder of sauce in a sauceboat.

CHICKEN CASSEROLE

1·8 kg/4 lb chicken	225 g/8 oz sausage meat
Seasoned flour	Salt and pepper
100 g/4 oz bacon	375 ml/¾ pint stock
450 g/1 lb potatoes	Dripping
225 g/8 oz onions	

Cut the chicken into large pieces, and coat lightly with seasoned flour. Cut the bacon into small pieces and put them into a thick frying pan. Heat them until the fat runs out, and then remove the bacon. Fry the chicken pieces in this fat until golden. In a casserole, put a layer of sliced potatoes and the bacon pieces. Place on top a layer of onion slices and then chicken, potato, onion, and sausage meat. Continue in layers until all the ingredients are used, seasoning lightly with salt and pepper. Finish with a layer of potato slices and dot lightly with pieces of dripping.

Pour in the stock and cover with a lid. Bake at 325°F, 170°C, gas mark 3 for 2 hours. Take off the lid and leave in the oven for 25 minutes to brown the potatoes.

COUNTRY CHICKEN BAKE

225 g/8 oz mashed potato	225 g/8 oz leeks
175 g/6 oz plain flour	225 g/8 oz cooked chicken
50 g/2 oz butter	3 eggs
50 g/2 oz lard	125 ml/¼ pint milk

Sieve the flour, rub in the fats, add the mashed potato and mix to a fairly stiff dough. Roll out half this pastry and line a shallow dish. Roll out the remaining pastry, cut out rounds about 4.5 cm/ 1¾ inches diameter, and place them overlapping round the top edge of the dish. Prick the base and leave in a cool place for about 30 minutes. Wash the leeks and cut into thin slices, and cook in boiling salted water for 10 minutes, then drain. Slice the chicken and place in the pie shell. Add the leeks, reserving some to decorate.

Whisk together the eggs and milk, season and pour into the pastry shell. Arrange leek slices on top. Brush the pastry with a little egg and milk. Bake at 350°F, 180°C, gas mark 4 for 35–40 minutes until set. Serve with vegetables or a salad.

BOILED HAND OR SHOULDER OF PORK AND PEASE PUDDING

1·35 kg/3 lb shoulder (or hand) pork	3 carrots
	1 large onion
3 sage leaves	½ turnip
6 peppercorns	2 or 3 stalks celery

Pease Pudding:

450 g/1 lb split peas, soaked overnight	25 g/1 oz butter
	1 egg
Sprig mint	Salt and pepper

Prepare the vegetables and tie the sage and peppercorns in a muslin bag. Put the pork in a large pan, cover with warm water and bring to the boil. Skim, boil for 15 minutes, then add the quartered carrots, sliced onion, turnip, chopped celery, peppercorns and sage. Boil steadily for 1½ hours with the pease pudding.

To make the pudding: Tie the peas in a pudding cloth with the mint, allowing room for the peas to swell. Suspend the bag in a pan with boiling pork and boil for 1 hour. Then take out, rub peas through a sieve, mix in the butter, egg and seasoning. Replace in a clean cloth and boil with pork again for a further

30 minutes. Lift out pudding and unroll from the cloth on to a hot dish. Serve with the pork and vegetables.

COLLARED BEEF

1·35–1·8 kg/3–4 lb fresh
  silverside *or* brisket
Salt and pepper
A sprinkling each of ground
  cloves, ground mace and
  ground ginger

A few drops of red colouring
¼ teaspoon each of whole allspice,
  peppercorns, sage and thyme
1 bay leaf

Lay out the meat in a flat strip; if thick, cut it through horizontally, and lay the two pieces end to end. Season it with salt and pepper and the sprinkling spices, and rub with red colouring. Roll it up tightly, and tie it with string at each end and in the middle. Wrap it in one thickness of butter muslin, to keep it moist. Place it in a stewpot with water to cover, and bring gently to the boil. Remove the scum, add the remaining spices and herbs, and simmer very gently for 3–4 hours, or until tender. Serve hot with a savoury suet pudding such as Herb Pudding, and pickles, or press and serve cold with a salad which includes herbs and pickled mushrooms or gherkins.

BOILED BEEF AND CARROTS WITH DUMPLINGS

1·8 kg/4 lb salt beef brisket or
  silverside
1 bay leaf
Parsley and thyme

10 peppercorns
4 onions
12 carrots

Dumplings:

100 g/4 oz self-raising flour
Water to mix

50 g/2 oz suet

Tie the meat into a neat shape and put in a large pan with enough water to cover. Add the bay leaf, thyme, parsley and peppercorns, and bring to the boil. Skim, then simmer for $1\frac{1}{2}$ hours. Add the whole onions, and the carrots cut in pieces, and cook for 15 minutes. Make the dumplings by mixing the flour, finely-chopped suet and water into a firm paste, and rolling with the hands into eight round balls. Drop the dumplings into the liquid with the meat and vegetables and continue cooking for 30 minutes. Remove the meat to a serving dish, surround with the vegetables and dumplings, and serve some of the cooking liquid.

OVEN BEEF AND BAKED HERB DUMPLINGS

1·35 kg/3 lb salt brisket
225 g/8 oz carrots
225 g/8 oz onions

4 celery sticks
2 bay leaves
6 peppercorns

Dumplings:

175 g/6 oz plain flour
$1\frac{1}{2}$ teaspoons baking powder
1 level teaspoon salt

1 level teaspoon mixed herbs
75 g/3 oz shredded suet

Soak the meat in cold water overnight, and drain. Line the inside of a roasting tin with foil and put the joint in the centre. Cut onions, carrots and celery in large pieces, put round the joint, add bay leaves and peppercorns, and pour 125 ml/$\frac{1}{4}$ pint water over the meat. Cover the tin with a second piece of foil, tucking the edges well under the tin. Cook in the centre of the oven, 400°F, 200°C, gas mark 6, for 1 hour and 50 minutes.

Make the dumplings by sifting flour, baking powder and salt into a bowl with herbs and suet, mixing to a fairly stiff dough with cold water and dividing into eight pieces. Form each piece into a ball. At the end of cooking time, take foil off the meat, put the dumplings on vegetables round the joint and re-cover with foil. Continue baking for 40 minutes until dumplings are well risen and cooked.

BOILED BACON WITH PARSLEY SAUCE

1·8 kg/4 lb bacon joint	6 peppercorns
1 bay leaf	1 tablespoon brown sugar

Parsley Sauce :

50 g/2 oz butter	250 ml/½ pint bacon stock
50 g/2 oz plain flour	Salt and pepper
250 ml/½ pint milk	1 tablespoon chopped parsley

Soak the bacon joint for 4 hours. Put into a saucepan with fresh cold water, bay leaf, peppercorns and sugar. Bring to the boil, then reduce heat and simmer for 2 hours. Drain bacon and strip off skin. Sprinkle fat surface of bacon with a little oatmeal or browned breadcrumbs.

To make the sauce, melt the butter and stir in the flour gradually, away from the heat, until the mixture is smooth. Add milk and stock gradually, beating well, and stir over low heat until boiling. Simmer gently, stirring often, and add parsley, salt and pepper to taste.

STUFFED LAMB ROSETTES

2 breasts of boned lamb

Stuffing :

100 g/4 oz lamb's liver, chopped	1 teaspoon finely-grated lemon peel
1 small onion, skinned and chopped	2 teaspoons chopped parsley
25 g/1 oz butter	Salt and pepper to taste
4 tablespoons soft, white breadcrumbs	Milk to bind stuffing

Vegetables :

900 g/2 lb thinly-sliced potatoes	2 level teaspoons flour
225 g/8 oz tomatoes, skinned and thinly sliced	250 ml/½ pint stock
1 onion, skinned and thinly sliced	

Put the lamb breasts on a board, skin side down. Mix the stuffing and spread it on the lamb. Roll and tie each breast in four places; cut to make eight rosettes. Arrange vegetables in layers in an ovenproof dish, sprinkling each layer with flour. Add rosettes and stock. Cover with foil. Cook on the centre shelf of the oven for 30 minutes at 375°F, 190°C, gas mark 5. Take off the foil and cook for further 45 minutes. Remove the string before serving.

IRISH STEW

1·35 kg/3 lb lean neck of lamb chops
900 g/2 lb potatoes
450 g/1 lb onions

Sprig of thyme
Sprig of parsley
375 ml/¾ pint water
Salt and pepper

Make sure the meat is trimmed of fat and gristle. Keep the bones in the chops as this adds flavour. Peel the potatoes and slice one third thinly, leaving the rest whole. Slice the onions, and chop the thyme and parsley. Put the sliced potatoes into a pan, then a layer of onions and the meat. Add the herbs and remaining onion, and top with the whole potatoes. Add water and salt and pepper. Cover tightly. Cook in a warm oven, 325°F, 170°C, gas mark 3, for 2½ hours. The stew may be cooked on the top of the stove, very gently, for the same time.

WILTSHIRE MARKET DAY DINNER

6 pork chops
2 pigs' kidneys
450 g/1 lb onions
1 apple

1 teaspoon sage
Salt and pepper
450 g/1 lb potatoes

Put the chops into a casserole. Cover with sliced kidneys and onions. Peel, core and slice the apple and put this on top. Sprinkle on the sage and season well with salt and pepper. Peel and slice the potatoes and cover the top of the dish with them. Pour on 125 ml/

¼ pint water. Cover and cook at 325°F, 170°C, gas mark 3 for 3 hours.

BEEF IN BEER

1·8 kg/4 lb brisket of beef	250 ml/½ pint beef stock
6 rashers lean bacon	125 ml/¼ pint wine vinegar
450 g/1 lb onions	Salt and pepper
250 ml/½ pint brown ale	Bay leaf

Have the beef rolled and tied. Cut bacon into thin strips and put into casserole. Put in the meat. Slice the onions thinly and put round the beef. Add salt and pepper, depending on possible saltiness of bacon; add bay leaf. Heat together ale, stock and vinegar and pour over the meat. Cover tightly and cook at 300°F, 150°C, gas mark 2 for 3½ hours. The gravy is rich and delicious, and the meat has a good flavour when eaten cold or in sandwiches.

BACON AND BEER CASSEROLE

1 kg/2½ lb bacon collar	1 bay leaf
1 carrot	500 ml/1 pint ale
1 onion	25 g/1 oz butter
Pepper	25 g/1 oz flour
1 tablespoon black treacle	

Soak the bacon for 6 hours (2 hours if unsmoked). Put in a casserole, and add sliced carrot and onion, a shake of freshly ground black pepper, treacle, bay leaf and beer. Bring to the boil, skim, and simmer for 1 hour (or cook in the oven at 350°F, 180°C, gas mark 4). Remove the bacon, take off the skin, and keep the joint hot. Blend the butter with flour and thicken the strained liquid. This is very good with baked parsnips.

SCOTCH COLLOPS

450 g/1 lb fresh minced beef	1 tablespoon oatmeal
1 large onion	200 ml/8 fl oz water
25 g/1 oz butter or dripping	Mashed potato
Salt and pepper	Poached eggs (if liked)

Brown the beef and finely-chopped onion in the fat. Season with salt and pepper, and add the oatmeal and water. Cover with a lid and simmer for 30 minutes. Put into a serving dish and surround with mashed potato. Poached eggs may be served on top.

TRIPE AND BACON

450 g/1 lb pre-cooked tripe	125 ml/$\frac{1}{4}$ pint water
225 g/8 oz bacon rashers	2 teaspoons tomato sauce
15 g/$\frac{1}{2}$ oz plain flour	Salt and pepper

Fry the bacon slowly so that the fat runs. Put the bacon on a warm dish. Slice the tripe and fry it until golden in the bacon fat. Put the tripe with the bacon in the dish. Sprinkle the flour into the fat and cook for 1 minute, stirring well. Add the water, sauce, salt and pepper, stirring all the time. When hot and thick, pour over the tripe and bacon.

LANCASHIRE HOT-POT

10 large potatoes	Salt and pepper
6 onions	Water
3 lamb's kidneys	Pickled red cabbage
900 g/2 lb neck of mutton chops	

Peel and slice the potatoes and onions, skin and slice the kidneys. Place the chops in the bottom of a casserole, cover with alternate layers of potatoes, onions and kidneys, seasoning well. Cover with a layer of potatoes, and brush well with melted butter. Add a little water, and cook with a lid on in a hot oven, 425°F, 220°C, gas mark 7, for 30 minutes, then in a cool oven, 300°F, 150°C, gas mark 2, for 2 hours. Remove the lid for 30 minutes before serving to brown the top. Serve with pickled red cabbage.

LAMB AND MUSHROOM HOT-POT

675 g/1½ lb best-end lamb cutlets	375 ml/¾ pint stock
25 g/1 oz plain flour	Salt and pepper
50 g/2 oz butter	Pinch of rosemary
1 onion	450 g/1 lb potatoes
175 g/6 oz button mushrooms	

Trim fat from the cutlets and coat them with flour. Melt the butter and fry the cutlets and sliced onion until golden. Put into a casserole with the mushrooms, stock, salt and pepper and rosemary. Peel the potatoes and cut in 0·5 cm/¼ inch slices. Arrange the potatoes on top of the meat, cover and bake at 300°F, 150°C, gas mark 2 for 1½ hours. Take off the lid and continue baking for 30 minutes.

STOVED CHICKEN

1·35 kg/3 lb chicken joints	500 ml/1 pint giblet stock
2 large onions	Salt and pepper
1 kg/2½ lb potatoes	Chopped parsley
50 g/2 oz butter	

Wipe the chicken joints. Cut the onions in slices, and the potatoes in medium-thick slices. Brown the chicken pieces in half the butter. In a casserole, put a thick layer of potatoes, then onions and chicken pieces. Season well with salt and pepper and add small pieces of butter. Put on another layer of potatoes, then onions, chicken and finally potatoes.

Season again and pour on the stock. Put on a piece of buttered paper and a lid. Cook at 300°F, 150°C, gas mark 2 for 2½ hours, adding a little more stock or water if needed. If an iron casserole is used, this dish may be simmered gently on a low heat on top of the stove. Sprinkle with parsley before serving.

BACON WITH CIDER SAUCE

500 ml/1 pint cider	4 eating apples
1–1·35 kg/2½–3 lb bacon joint	25 g/1 oz plain flour
8 small onions	1 tablespoon redcurrant jelly

Put the cider into a large casserole with the bacon joint, which should have been soaked overnight in cold water if necessary. Add the peeled onions and cover with a lid. Cook for 1½ hours at 325°F, 170°C, gas mark 3. Remove from the oven and turn the bacon over. Core the apples but do not peel them. Arrange round the bacon, baste and return to the oven for a further 30 minutes.

Transfer the bacon to a heated serving dish and arrange the onions and apples round it. Pour the cider into a pan, add the flour mixed to a smooth paste with cold water and the redcurrant jelly. Bring to the boil, stirring continuously, and boil for 3 minutes. Serve in a sauceboat.

BRAISED PORK WITH APPLE RINGS

1 loin of pork	Squeeze of lemon juice
450 g/1 lb breadcrumbs	4 tablespoons olive oil
50 g/2 oz chopped suet	6 tablespoons cider
1 tablespoon thyme	3 eating apples
2 tablespoons parsley	2 tablespoons butter
1 cooking apple	Salt and pepper
1 egg	

Combine the breadcrumbs with the suet, herbs and chopped cooking apple, and add salt and pepper to taste. Add the egg and lemon juice and mix well, adding a little milk if necessary. Slice the pork down to the bone and place stuffing between the cuts. Use long skewers to keep the joint together. Heat 2 tablespoons oil in casserole, and toss pork in this until golden. Pour cider over, cover and cook at 375°F, 190°C, gas mark 5 for 45 minutes. Core the eating apples but do not peel them. Slice and fry them in butter and the remaining oil until golden. Put pork on to a very hot dish and garnish with the apples.

FAGGOTS

675 g/1½ lb pig's liver	75 g/3 oz shredded suet
175 g/6 oz bacon	2 teaspoons sage
2 onions	1 teaspoon basil
200 g/7 oz white breadcrumbs	Salt and pepper

Mince the liver, bacon and onions. Place all the ingredients together in a bowl and mix well. Form the mixture into eight balls and roll in flour. Pack closely together in a baking tin. Bake in the centre of the oven at 350°F, 180°C, gas mark 4 for 30 minutes. When cooked, divide with a knife and serve with a rich brown gravy and pease pudding.

LIVER AND BACON CASSEROLE

450 g/1 lb pig's liver	1 tablespoon chopped parsley
4 rashers lean bacon	1 teaspoon salt
2 cooking apples	¼ teaspoon pepper
2 large onions	250 ml/½ pint stock or water
100 g/4 oz breadcrumbs	

Slice the liver, and cut the bacon into small pieces. Peel and chop apples and onions. Grease a casserole, put in a layer of liver, then bacon. Top with a layer of breadcrumbs, onions, parsley, salt and pepper, then apple. Repeat the layers, finishing with breadcrumbs, and pour in the stock or water. Bake at 375°F, 190°C, gas mark 5 for 2 hours, removing the cover for the last 30 minutes.

LIVER AND POTATO CASSEROLE

350 g/12 oz liver
675 g/1½ lb potatoes
6 rashers bacon
250 ml/½ pint stock or water

15 g/½ oz flour
4 medium-sized onions
Salt and pepper
Dripping

Cut the liver into small pieces. Dip into flour seasoned with salt and pepper, and brown on each side in hot dripping. Remove from the pan, and fry the sliced potatoes. Put layers of potatoes, onions, and liver in a casserole, seasoning well, and put the rashers of bacon on top. Pour in stock to come half way up the dish. Bake in a moderate oven, 375°F, 190°C, gas mark 5, for 1 hour.

KIDNEY CASSEROLE

450 g/1 lb lamb's or veal kidneys
2 medium-sized onions
2 tablespoons dripping
4 bacon rashers

Flour
Salt and pepper
125 ml/¼ pint stock

Clean the kidneys, skin and remove cores, and cut in slices. Chop the onions finely and fry until golden in melted dripping. Put the onions in a casserole, arrange the kidneys on top, then pieces of chopped bacon. Season with salt and pepper and dust lightly with flour. Pour over stock and cook at 350°F, 180°C, gas mark 4 for 40 minutes.

BROWN OXTAIL

1 jointed oxtail
4 carrots
2 onions
1 turnip
25 g/1 oz dripping
25 g/1 oz flour
4 rashers bacon

375 ml/¾ pint stock
4 tablespoons red wine
Salt and pepper
1 bay leaf
Sprig of parsley
Sprig of thyme

Slice the carrots, onions and turnip and brown in the melted dripping. Remove from the pan and put into a casserole. In the same fat, brown the oxtail pieces, and stir in the flour. Blend well, then put into the casserole. Add the chopped bacon, stock and wine, herbs, salt and pepper. Cook at 325°F, 170°C, gas mark 3 for 4 hours. Remove the herbs before serving, and skim off excess fat.

POTTED BEEF

450 g/1 lb chuck steak
175 g/6 oz bacon rashers
125 ml/¼ pint stock
1 bay leaf

1 sprig of parsley
1 sprig of thyme
Salt and pepper
Nutmeg

Slice steak and bacon in very small pieces, and arrange in a small casserole in alternate layers, sprinkling each layer with a dash of salt, pepper and nutmeg. Put the herbs halfway up the dish, and pour on the stock. On top of the casserole, put the rinds cut from the bacon. Cover tightly and cook in slow oven, 300°F, 150°C, gas mark 2 for 3 hours. Remove the bacon rinds and herbs before serving. Serve hot, or leave until cold when the gravy will form a clear pink jelly.

BRAISED MUTTON

1 shoulder of mutton
Salt and pepper
2 carrots
4 onions

1 garlic clove
1 clove
Bunch of mixed herbs
Stock

Have the mutton boned, and season it with salt and pepper. Roll and tie the meat, and brown it in its own fat on all sides. Put into a casserole with the sliced carrots and onions, crushed garlic, clove and herbs. Add stock to come halfway up the meat. Cover and cook at 325°F, 170°C, gas mark 3 for 4 hours.

Just pudding and pie

STEAK, KIDNEY (AND OYSTER) PUDDING

225 g/8 oz suet
450 g/1 lb self-raising flour
Water to mix
900 g/2 lb rump steak

2 veal kidneys
Oysters or mushrooms if liked
Salt and pepper
1 bay leaf

Chop the suet finely and rub into the flour, then add enough water to make a stiff paste which can be rolled out on a floured board. Roll out 0·5 cm/¼ inch thick, giving enough paste to line and cover a 1 litre/2 pint pudding basin. Line the basin with the paste, and fill with alternate layers of steak and kidney cut in small pieces. If oysters are added, they should be raw; mushrooms should be sliced and tossed for 2 minutes in a little butter. Season the layers with salt and pepper, and insert the bay leaf halfway up. When the basin is full, put in enough water to reach within 2·5 cm/1 inch of the top, moisten the edges of the lining paste and put on the top, cutting off the surplus and pinching the two edges together. Wring out a cloth in hot water, flour it, and tie over the top of the basin with string. Bring up the ends of the cloth and knot on top of the pudding, and then put the basin in a pan of boiling water and boil for 4 hours. The water in the pan must be topped up with boiling water from time to time. When ready for serving, untie the cloth and make a small cut in the top paste to let the steam escape. Serve in the pudding basin with a table napkin wrapped round it.

CHICKEN PUDDING

350 g/12 oz self-raising flour
175 g/6 oz suet
1 old chicken
1 chopped onion

Bay leaf
Salt and pepper
2 teaspoons chopped parsley

Make up a suet pastry with enough water to give a firm paste. Cut the flesh from legs, wings and breast of bird. Line a 1 litre/2 pint basin with suet pastry. Fill with alternate layers of meat and onion, with some seasoning and parsley. Put bay leaf in the centre. Just cover meat with stock or water, and top with pastry. Steam for 4 hours. Serve with gravy made from chicken stock, using carcass of bird, or with parsley sauce.

KENTISH PORK AND APPLE PUDDING

225 g/8 oz self-raising flour	Salt and pepper
100 g/4 oz shredded suet	Sage
225 g/8 oz lean pork	Stock or water
1 cooking apple	

Prepare pastry with flour, suet and enough water to make a firm paste. Line a 500 ml/1 pint basin with pastry, and put in pork, cut in squares, the chopped apple, salt and pepper, a good pinch of chopped sage and stock to cover. Put on pastry lid, cover and boil for 4 hours.

NORFOLK PLOUGH PUDDING

225 g/8 oz self-raising flour	1 large onion
100 g/4 oz shredded suet	2 teaspoons chopped sage
450 g/1 lb pork sausage meat	15 g/½ oz Demerara sugar
100 g/4 oz bacon	Fresh tomato sauce

Mix together the flour and suet with a pinch of salt and enough cold water to make a firm dough. Roll out the dough, and use two-thirds to line a 1 litre/2 pint pudding basin. Press the sausage meat into the pastry all round the basin. Chop the bacon and onion and mix together with the sage and sugar. Put this mixture into the centre of the pudding and cover with the remaining pastry. Cover with greaseproof paper and a piece of foil or a pudding cloth. Steam for 4 hours, and serve with a hot tomato sauce.

BACON LAYER PUDDING

175 g/6 oz self-raising flour   2 onions
75 g/3 oz shredded suet   2 carrots
225 g/8 oz chopped bacon

Make a suet pastry by adding the suet to the flour with a pinch of salt, and enough water to make a firm dough. Roll out the pastry thinly and cut out a round to fit the bottom of a greased 1 litre/ 2 pint basin. Put in a layer of bacon pieces. Grate the onions and carrots, and put a little of the mixture on top of the bacon. Continue until the basin is full, and cover with a layer of pastry. Cover and steam for 2 hours. Serve with gravy.

DUCK PUDDINGS

75 g/3 oz bread without crust   1 teaspoon flour
200 ml/8 fl oz milk   1 onion
1 egg   ½ teaspoon chopped sage
50 g/2 oz shredded suet   Salt and pepper

Pour the milk over the bread and leave for 10 minutes, then beat well with a spoon. Stir in the egg, suet, flour, finely-chopped onion, sage and seasoning. Grease and warm some small patty tins, and put in the mixture. Bake for 15 minutes at 425°F, 220°C, gas mark 7. Take out of the tins and put round a roasting duck or pork for the last 15 minutes' cooking time. Cut into slices to serve.

SALT BEEF PIE

350 g/12 oz cooked salt beef   1 potato
1 onion   Pepper
1 carrot   175 g/6 oz shortcrust pastry

Mince the meat and vegetables. Put meat and vegetables on a 17·5 cm/7 inch pie plate, moisten with a little water and season with pepper. Cover with the pastry. Brush with beaten egg or milk. Bake for 20 minutes at 400°F, 200°C, gas mark 6 then reduce to 350°F, 180°C, gas mark 4 for a further 20 minutes.

FARMHOUSE PLATE PIE

1 onion	2 teaspoons flour
1 carrot	125 ml/¼ pint beef stock
50 g/2 oz mushrooms	450 g/1 lb mashed potato
2 tablespoons oil	50 g/2 oz grated cheese
350 g/12 oz cooked meat	

Dice the onion and carrot, and slice the mushrooms. Gently fry the vegetables in the oil until just cooked. Add chopped or minced meat with seasoning to taste. Stir in the flour then the stock, bring to the boil and cook for a few minutes. Press just under half the potato on to a 20 cm/8 inch greased ovenproof plate, rather like pastry. Pile the meat mixture into the centre. Press the remaining potato flat over the top or roll out on a floured surface and lift on. Press the edges well together, brush the top with a little melted butter and sprinkle the cheese on top. Bake at 400°F, 200°C, gas mark 6 for 30 minutes.

BEEF AND COWHEEL PIE

350 g/12 oz shin beef	Salt and pepper
½ cowheel	175 g/6 oz self-raising flour
1 onion stuck with cloves	75 g/3 oz shredded suet

Cut up the beef and cowheel, cover with water and add the onion, salt and pepper. Simmer for 3 hours. Strain, and keep the liquid. Remove the bones and onion and cut the meat into neat pieces. Put into a greased pie dish, moisten with cooking liquid, and taste for seasoning. Mix the flour and suet with a pinch of salt, and mix to a soft dough with cold water. Roll out and put on top of the meat. Bake at 400°F, 200°C, gas mark 6 for 1 hour. Make gravy with the remaining cooking liquid, and serve the pie with gravy, mashed potatoes and a green vegetable.

PORK AND KIDNEY PIE

450 g/1 lb pork shoulder or hand of pork
3 pig's kidneys
2 teaspoons basil
250 ml/½ pint stock

Pinch of nutmeg
1 onion
2 carrots
175 g/6 oz shortcrust pastry

Cut the pork and kidneys in pieces and put them into a pie dish with basil, stock, nutmeg, chopped onion and carrots. Cover with a lid or piece of foil and cook at 325°F, 170°C, gas mark 3 for 1 hour. Cover with pastry lid and bake at 400°F, 200°C, gas mark 6 for 30 minutes.

STEAK AND KIDNEY PIE

675 g/1½ lb beef skirt
175 g/6 oz ox kidney
25 g/1 oz seasoned flour
50 g/2 oz dripping
125 ml/¼ pint dry red wine if liked

125 ml/¼ pint stock
½ teaspoon dried thyme
1 bay leaf
225 g/8 oz puff pastry

Trim the meat and cut it into 2·5 cm/1 inch pieces. Cut the kidney into pieces of about the same size. Discard the core. Dust the meat and kidney with well-seasoned flour. Heat the fat and brown the meat very slowly. Remove from the heat, pour over the red wine and the stock (or omit the wine and make up the total amount of liquid in stock). Add the thyme and the crushed bay leaf and additional salt and pepper if necessary. Allow to cool, and if possible stand for 2 to 3 hours (covered). Transfer to a pie dish with a centre cone. Cover with the pastry supported in the centre; seal the edges of the dish. Cut slits in the pastry cover. Decorate if wished and brush with a little milk or beaten egg to glaze. Place on a low shelf in the oven at 400°F, 200°C, gas mark 6 and cook for about 20 minutes or until the pastry is golden-brown. Cover the pie completely with greaseproof paper, then reduce the oven heat to 300°F, 150°C, gas mark 2 and continue cooking for a further 3 hours or until the meat is tender. If necessary, additional stock may be added through the slits in the pastry during or after cooking.

BEEF AND BACON PIE

1 onion	125 ml/¼ pint water
225 g/8 oz bacon	Pinch of fresh mixed herbs
225 g/8 oz minced raw beef	Salt and pepper
1 tablespoon plain flour	225 g/8 oz shortcrust pastry

Chop the onion and bacon in small pieces, put in a heavy pan, and cook gently until the fat runs from the bacon, and the onion and bacon are soft and golden. Add the mince and cook until mince browns. Stir in flour mixed with a little water, and the rest of the water, herbs and seasonings, and cook until mixture is thick and well blended. Roll pastry into two rounds and line a 20 cm/8 inch pie plate with one. Put in filling, and cover with second round of pastry. Bake at 400°F, 200°C, gas mark 6 for 30 minutes.

CHICKEN PARSLEY PIE

1 chicken	225 g/8 oz shortcrust or puff
500 ml/1 pint basin full of	pastry
washed parsley	125 ml/¼ pint double cream
500 ml/1 pint milk	Salt and pepper
Stock made from chicken giblets	

Joint the chicken and place the pieces in a pie dish. Scald the parsley in milk. Season and add to the chicken with the stock. Cover with pastry, leaving an air hole in the middle and bake for 1½ hours, starting at 425°F, 220°C, gas mark 7 but reducing to 350°F, 180°C, gas mark 4 when the pastry has risen. Cover the pastry with foil if it begins to get too brown. When baked, pour the cream through the air hole and shake gently to mix with the other liquid inside the pie.

SAVOURY HERBED PUDDING

175 g/6 oz stale bread	3 eggs
250 ml/½ pint milk	Salt and pepper
50 g/2 oz shredded suet	Cayenne pepper
50 g/2 oz fine oatmeal	Thyme, sage and marjoram

Soak the bread in hot milk and leave it to get cold. Mix the dry ingredients with the bread. Beat the eggs and mix in well. Over heat, melt some dripping in a flameproof ovenware dish to boiling point. Spread in the mixture with a fork. Bake from 30–40 minutes in the oven with a joint. Serve in squares with the meat and gravy.

YORKSHIRE SAVOURY PUDDING

225 g/8 oz bread without crust	25 g/1 oz oatmeal
4 large onions	75 g/3 oz shredded suet
2 teaspoons chopped sage	Salt and pepper

Pour some boiling water over the bread and leave it to stand for 30 minutes. Drain well but do not squeeze out moisture. Chop the onions finely and mix with the bread and other ingredients. Put into a greased baking dish and bake at 375°F, 190°C, gas mark 5 for 1 hour until well browned. Cut into slices to serve with thick gravy and vegetables.

SEASONING PUDDING

2 large onions	1 tablespoon melted butter
225 g/8 oz fresh breadcrumbs	Salt and pepper
2 teaspoons chopped sage	Gravy
1 egg	

Boil the onions and chop them finely. Mix with the breadcrumbs, sage, egg, melted butter, salt and pepper. Put into a greased oven tin, and spread about 1·25 cm/½ inch thick. Bake at 425°F, 220°C, gas mark 7 for 30 minutes until crisp and brown. Serve with gravy.

POTATO DUMPLINGS

7 potatoes, peeled
2 onions
12 slices white bread
¾ teaspoon salt
½ teaspoon black pepper

¾ teaspoon dried dill seeds
3 eggs
175 g/6 oz plain flour
Boiling water or light stock

Grate the potatoes coarsely, squeeze out as much water as possible, then press between paper towels to squeeze out any further liquid. Grate or mince the onions, put in a fine sieve, and press out all juices with the back of a spoon. Mix the onion juice and 3 tablespoons onion pulp with the grated potatoes; keep the rest of the onion pulp for another dish.

Soak the bread in water until soft. Squeeze out as much water as possible and place the bread in a bowl. Add the salt, pepper and dill, stir in the grated potato and onion mixture, and mix in the eggs. Blend all ingredients thoroughly. Form the mixture into dumplings. Bring 3·5 litres/7 pints of salted water or stock to a full boil. Spread a good quantity of flour on a pastry board, and roll the dumplings in it until thickly coated. Drop into the water or stock, and lower the heat. Cook gently for 15–17 minutes. Remove with a perforated spoon and serve very hot.

NORTH COUNTRY TASTY BATTER PUDDING

25 g/1 oz shredded suet
100 g/4 oz plain flour
2 eggs

500 ml/1 pint milk
Pinch of salt

Mix the suet and the flour with salt. Beat the eggs, and add to the mixture, and make into a batter with the milk. Put into a greased pie dish and bake at 350°F, 180°C, gas mark 4 for 1½ hours. Serve with meat, or make it into a sweet pudding by adding 2 tablespoons sugar and a few currants.

Vegetables

CREAMED CABBAGE

1 large white cabbage	250 ml/½ pint creamy milk
25 g/1 oz butter	Salt and pepper
25 g/1 oz plain flour	

Shred the cabbage and put into boiling water. Boil for 10 minutes and drain very well, pressing out moisture. Melt the butter in a saucepan and work in the flour. Cook for 2 minutes and then gradually add the milk and seasoning. Heat and stir for 5 minutes, and then stir in the drained cabbage. Cook gently for 10 minutes.

BASHED 'NEEPS'

6 large turnips	1 teaspoon plain flour
25 g/1 oz butter	
125 ml/¼ pint single or thin cream	

Peel the turnips and cut them into slices. Boil them in salted water until tender. Mash the turnips and sieve them. Return the sieved turnips to the saucepan with the butter and cream. Scatter in the flour and stir over the heat until the mixture is thick and creamy.

SAVOURY LENTILS

450 g/1 lb lentils	1 small onion
3 rashers streaky bacon	1 bay leaf
1 small carrot	1 sprig of thyme

Rinse the lentils and leave them soaking overnight in cold water. Drain them and put them in a saucepan with chopped bacon, carrot and onion, and the bay leaf and thyme. Just cover with cold water, and bring slowly to the boil. Reduce the heat and continue simmering until the lentils are soft, adding more liquid if necessary during the cooking. (The lentils can be left to simmer in a low oven if preferred.) Serve them with bacon, pork or ham.

CREAMED HARICOT BEANS

450 g/1 lb haricot beans   25 g/1 oz plain flour
1 onion   250 ml/½ pint stock
25 g/1 oz butter

Soak the beans overnight in cold water and drain them. Chop the onion finely and cook it in the butter until lightly browned. Work in the flour and stock and simmer until the liquid thickens. Add to the beans and simmer until they are soft.

BRAISED ONIONS

6 large onions   Flour
100 g/4 oz dripping   Salt and pepper
250 ml/½ pint stock   Juice of ½ lemon

Peel the onions and put into a pan with the dripping. Cover with a tight lid and cook the onions gently until golden. Drain off the excess fat and cover the onions with stock. Simmer until the onions are soft but unbroken. Thicken the liquid with a little flour, and season with salt, pepper and lemon juice before serving.

ONIONS IN THEIR JACKETS

6 large onions   Salt and pepper
Butter

Remove any loose outer skin from the onions, but leave as much skin as possible. Put on to a baking tin in the bottom of the oven in which the joint is cooking. Cook until the onions are tender, testing them with a skewer, which will easily go into the centre when they are done. Serve with plenty of butter, salt and pepper.

BAKED PUMPKIN

1 small, very ripe pumpkin   Milk as required
  (with a hard shell)

Slice the stem end from pumpkin, to form a cover with a handle. Scoop out the seeds and stringy fibres so that only the solid meat remains. Fill the shell with milk, cover with foil, and bake very slowly in the bottom of the oven for 6–7 hours when doing other baking.

To serve, add more milk to the brim and eat straight from the shell.

CHAPTER 3

SPORTING LIFE

UNTIL about thirty years ago, many country families never saw 'butcher's meat' except when they could barter it for the chickens they had reared. All kinds of game were eaten, however, particularly rabbits, hares and pigeons which were considered to be vermin. Occasionally, young game in season was roasted, but the older or badly-shot birds were mainly used for soup, casseroles, pies and puddings, with plenty of onions, herbs and root vegetables.

Pigeons have no close season. They need not be hung, but if they are hung downwards for an hour immediately after killing, they will bleed, and the flesh will be paler.

Rabbits have no close season. A plump rabbit feeds six people.

Hares are in season from the early autumn to the end of February. A young hare is best roasted, and a hare should feed eight to ten people easily. Often a hare can be served roast or jugged for a smaller number and the remains used for a casserole, soup or cold dish.

Partridges are in season from 1 September to 1 February. The grey partridge needs only three to four days hanging, but the red-legged birds need six to seven days hanging. One bird will usually serve two people, and if plainly roasted is good with watercress, wafer potatoes, and an apple and celery salad.

Pheasants are in season from 1 October to 1 February. Hen birds are smaller but less dry and more tender with good flavour. A good bird should serve four people. A pheasant is best hung for about seven days before cooking. Only young birds should be roasted; the others are fine for casseroles. When roasted, the bird needs additional fat such as butter or bacon for basting, and should be served with bread sauce, fried crumbs and wafer potatoes. Mushrooms, chestnuts and braised celery are all good accompaniments.

Grouse are in season from 12 August to 10 December. A good bird should serve three people, and is usually preferred roasted, but older birds are best in a casserole or pudding. The roast birds are best served on a piece of toast spread with the cooked liver mashed in a little stock, with bread sauce, buttered crumbs, wafer potatoes and watercress, and with rowanberry jelly.

Venison is in season from late June to January. It is best hung for eight to ten days, and needs larding and marinading before roasting. Large joints are best roasted, but venison is excellent in casseroles, soups, cottage pies and pasties. A sharp jelly, made with rowanberries, cranberries, or redcurrants is the most usual traditional accompaniment.

Game dishes

ROAST PHEASANT WITH GAME CHIPS AND BREAD SAUCE

1 pheasant	50 g/2 oz butter
4 rashers bacon	

Game chips:

4 potatoes	Deep fat for frying

Bread Sauce:

1 medium onion	100 g/4 oz soft white bread-
4 cloves	crumbs
250 ml/½ pint milk	15 g/½ oz butter
Pinch of mace	2 tablespoons cream
6 peppercorns	

Spread a plump young pheasant with butter and put some butter inside the bird. Cover with bacon rashers and roast in a moderate oven, 350°F, 180°C, gas mark 4, for 45 minutes. Remove to a warm dish and keep hot. Use the pan drippings with a little stock or vegetable water to make clear gravy, and serve the bird with Brussels sprouts or braised celery.

To make the Game Chips, cut peeled potatoes in wafer-thin slices across. Soak in ice-cold water and dry very thoroughly. Fry in a wire basket in deep fat heated to 395°F, 200°C. Shake the pan as they cook so that they do not stick together. They will float to the surface when ready. Drain on absorbent paper, sprinkle with salt and serve hot.

To make the Bread Sauce, stick the onion with cloves and put into a saucepan with the milk, mace and peppercorns. Bring to the boil, and then remove from heat and leave to stand for 30 minutes. Strain the milk into another pan and add the breadcrumbs. Heat until boiling, stirring gently. Stir in butter and cream, and season to taste with salt and pepper.

ROAST VENISON

1 joint of venison
250 ml/½ pint red wine
250 ml/½ pint vinegar

1 sliced onion
Parsley, thyme and bay leaf

Mix together the wine, vinegar, onion and herbs and put the venison in it to soak for 2 days, turning the meat from time to time. When ready to cook the meat, put the joint on a rack in a baking tin, with the marinade in the tin. Cook at 375°F, 190°C, gas mark 5 until meat is tender (for 15–20 minutes per 450 g/1 lb if young or well marinated); baste frequently. Strain the pan juices through a sieve, thicken with a little flour, and if liked 125 ml/¼ pint sour cream or yoghurt.

ROAST GROUSE WITH CRANBERRIES

2 grouse
100 g/4 oz butter

225 g/8 oz fresh cranberries

Hang the grouse to taste, until the feathers loosen easily. Pluck and truss them, and fill the cavities with the butter and cranberries. Roast at 450°F, 230°C, gas mark 8 for 25 minutes.

RABBIT PUDDING

1 jointed rabbit
225 g/8 oz self-raising flour
100 g/4 oz shredded suet
1 large onion

2 teaspoons sage
100 g/4 oz mushrooms
2 rindless rashers streaky bacon
Salt and pepper

Soak the rabbit joints in salted water for 2 hours and dry well. Mix together the flour and suet with a pinch of salt and enough cold water to make a firm dough. Roll out the dough and use two-thirds to line a pudding basin. Slice the onion and chop the sage, mushrooms and bacon. Arrange alternate layers of rabbit, onions, sage, mushrooms and bacon in the basin, adding a sprinkle of flour, salt and pepper to the layers. Cover with water and put on the remaining suet dough as a lid. Put on a piece of greaseproof paper and foil or a pudding cloth, and steam for 3 hours.

PARTRIDGE PUDDING

675 g/1½ lb self-raising flour
225 g/8 oz suet
100 g/4 oz rump steak
Brace of old partridges
½ teaspoon pepper
1 teaspoon salt

100 g/4 oz mushrooms
1 teaspoon each freshly-chopped
    parsley, thyme and tarragon
375 ml/¾ pint brown stock
125 ml/¼ pint sweet stout

Line a 1 litre/2 pint pudding basin with a suet crust made with the flour, suet and enough cold water to make a stiff dough, leaving enough crust for a cover. Cut the rump steak in thin slices and put on the bottom, cut the partridges into neat joints and season with pepper and salt, and put in the basin mixed with sliced mushrooms and herbs. Pour in stock mixed with stout, cover with suet crust and pinch the edges together. Tie a pudding cloth or foil over the basin, place in boiling water, and keep boiling for 3 hours.

GROUSE PUDDING

225 g/8 oz plain flour
1 teaspoon baking powder
½ teaspoon salt
100 g/4 oz shredded suet
1 old grouse

450 g/1 lb stewing steak
1 onion
25 g/1 oz butter
Salt, pepper, nutmeg

Sift together flour, baking powder and salt, and add the grated or chopped suet. Stir in enough cold water to make a pliable dough, and line a pudding basin with two-thirds of the pastry. Cut the flesh of the grouse into neat chunks, stewing the bones and trimmings in water to make a good stock. Brown the grouse and cubes of steak in the butter and put into the basin with salt,

pepper and a pinch of nutmeg, chopped onion, and enough stock
or water to half fill the basin. Cover with the top crust, put on
paper and a cloth, and steam for 3 hours, adding boiling water to
the saucepan to keep it almost to the top of the basin. Make a hole
in the top crust before serving and pour in hot stock or gravy.

GAME PUDDING

225 g/8 oz suet pastry
4 pigeons or 2 partridges or
  2 grouse
225 g/8 oz stewing steak

3 hard-boiled egg yolks
Salt, pepper and nutmeg
Stock made from game trimmings

If pigeons are used, the breasts only can go into the pudding, and
the rest can be simmered for stock. If partridges are used, they
can be split in half. A little bacon and chopped onion, and sometimes a few mushrooms, can be added to this pudding, but they
are optional. If appetites are very hearty, the quantity of suet
pastry may be increased so that the bowl can be lined as well.

Line the bowl with 1·25 cm/½ inch thick pastry if liked. Put in
pigeon breasts or halved partridges or halved grouse, chopped
steak, egg yolks, seasoning and gravy to come half way up
the bowl. Put on pastry lid and cover with cloth. Steam for
3 hours.

HARE PIE (COLD)

3 joints hare
1 teaspoon fresh herbs
Salt and pepper
3 tablespoons cider
225 g/8 oz plain flour

Pinch of salt
50 g/2 oz lard
65 ml/2½ fl oz milk and water
Stock
1 egg, beaten

Chop or mince the hare finely, season with herbs, salt and pepper,
and leave to stand overnight in cider. Sieve flour and salt in a
warm bowl. Bring lard, milk and water to boil together and pour
into the middle of the flour; stir until cool enough to handle.

Knead until smooth, adding more hot milk and water if necessary. Cover with a tea towel damped in hot water and wrung out, and stand bowl in warm water for 15 minutes, keeping dough only just warm. Roll out three-quarters of the pastry and line a pie mould or cake tin with a removable bottom. Mix hare meat well and stir in a spoonful of stock; put filling into pastry case to within 2·5 cm/1 inch of the top. Brush top edge with egg, cover with pastry lid, and glaze with beaten egg. Make a hole in the centre of the lid. Bake at 400°F, 200°C, gas mark 6 for 20 minutes, then reduce heat to 350°F, 180°C, gas mark 4 for another hour, covering the pastry with thick paper to prevent burning. When pie is cool, pour in a little cold jellied stock almost at setting point, using a funnel in the hole. Leave in tin until completely cold.

PARTRIDGE, VEAL AND BACON PIE (HOT OR COLD)

2 partridges
25 g/1 oz butter
225 g/8 oz lean veal
225 g/8 oz boiled bacon or ham
125 ml/¼ pint onion sauce
2 hard-boiled eggs
1 tablespoon chopped parsley

100 g/4 oz mushrooms
Salt and pepper
Pinch of nutmeg
225 g/8 oz puff pastry
Rich stock or gravy
1 egg, beaten

Cut the birds in halves and cook them lightly in butter until just coloured. In a pie dish put a layer of mixed chopped veal and bacon. Put in partridges. Add parsley, mushrooms and seasoning, and put on a second layer of veal and bacon. Pour on the onion sauce and cover with slices of egg. Cover with pastry, glaze with beaten egg and bake at 400°F, 200°C, gas mark 6 for 1 hour. When the pie is removed from the oven, pour in a little rich hot stock or gravy. Serve hot or cold.

RABBIT PIE (HOT OR COLD)

1 jointed rabbit
100 g/4 oz pork sausage meat
225 g/8 oz stewing steak
Salt and pepper

1 tablespoon chopped parsley
Ground nutmeg
225 g/8 oz shortcrust pastry

Soak the rabbit joints in salted water for 2 hours and dry well. Make the sausage meat into small balls and cut the stewing steak into cubes. Arrange layers of the steak, rabbit and sausage meat balls in a pie dish, sprinkling well with salt and pepper, parsley and nutmeg. Cover with stock or water. Put on a pastry lid, and bake at 450°F, 230°C, gas mark 8 for 20 minutes. Reduce heat to 350°F, 180°C, gas mark 4 and cook for 1 hour. This pie is delicious hot or cold.

ROOK PIE

6 young rooks
Seasoned flour
225 g/8 oz streaky bacon,
   chopped

Stock
225 g/8 oz shortcrust pastry

Only young rooks should be eaten, and then only the breasts and upper part of the legs. The skin should always be removed, the bird drawn, and the backbone removed since it has a bitter flavour. Prepare the rooks and stew them in water with a good pinch of salt for 15 minutes. Drain and remove the breasts and upper legs. Roll these in seasoned flour and arrange in a pie dish with chopped bacon. Fill the dish three-quarters full with stock. Cover with pastry and bake at 425°F, 220°C, gas mark 7 for 15 minutes. Reduce heat to 350°F, 180°C, gas mark 4 and continue cooking for 1¼ hours.

PIGEON PIE

3 pigeons	2 hard-boiled eggs
225 g/8 oz rump steak	Salt and pepper
100 g/4 oz ham or rindless lean bacon	375 ml/¾ pint beef stock
100 g/4 oz mushrooms	225 g/8 oz puff pastry
	1 egg yolk

Cut each pigeon into four pieces. Cut steak into squares, and ham or bacon into strips. Chop the mushrooms roughly, and cut eggs into quarters. Put steak into the bottom of a pie dish, and then add the pigeon pieces, ham or bacon, mushrooms and eggs. Season well with salt and pepper and pour in the stock. Roll out pastry and cover pie, using pastry trimmings to make decorative 'leaves' to finish the crust. Brush pastry with the egg yolk beaten with a pinch of salt. Bake in a hot oven, 425°F, 220°C, gas mark 7 for 15 minutes, then lower heat to 350°F, 180°C, gas mark 4 for 1¼ hours.

SQUAB PIE

2 squabs (young pigeons)	1 teaspoon mixed herbs
1 thick rindless bacon rasher	75 ml/3 fl oz red wine
Seasoned flour	Salt and pepper
1 onion	50 g/2 oz mushrooms
250 ml/½ pint stock	350 g/12 oz shortcrust pastry
2 teaspoons parsley	

Cut the birds in four pieces each, and the bacon in strips. Coat the birds lightly in seasoned flour. Cut up the onion and cook with the pigeons and bacon until golden. Add herbs, wine and seasoning to the stock, and simmer the pigeons, bacon and onion in this for 1½ hours, until the meat comes from the bones. Line a pie plate with half the pastry. Put in meat cut from the pigeons, onions, bacon, gravy and mushrooms. Cover with pastry and bake at 400°F, 200°C, gas mark 6 for 30 minutes. Serve hot or cold.

GROUSE PIE

2 grouse	1 egg, beaten
225 g/8 oz pork sausage meat	100 g/4 oz raw ham
Salt, pepper and herbs	225 g/8 oz puff pastry
4 hard-boiled egg yolks	

Cut up the grouse, each of them in five parts, and season with pepper and salt. Cover the bottom of a pie dish with a layer of sausage meat, on which place the pieces of grouse. Sprinkle over a few herbs. Fill the cavities between the pieces with the hard-boiled yolks, and place pieces of ham on top of the grouse; pour in good gravy to half the height, cover the pie with pastry and brush with egg. Bake at 350°F, 180°C, gas mark 4 for 1½ hours.

CAMBRIDGE HARE IN BEER

1 hare	40 g/1½ oz plain flour
2 large onions	250 ml/½ pint brown ale or stout
225 g/8 oz carrots	250 ml/½ pint stock

Joint the hare. Slice the onions thinly and the carrots rather thickly. Fry the onions in a little dripping until soft but not coloured and put them into a casserole. Coat the hare joints in a little of the flour seasoned with salt and pepper, and cook them in the dripping until golden. Put on top of the onions and add the carrots. Work the remaining flour into the fat in the pan and cook for 2 minutes. Gradually add the beer and stock and cook until smooth. Pour over the hare, cover the casserole, and cook at 350°F, 180°C, gas mark 4 for 2½ hours. Very good with jacket potatoes.

OCTOBER PARTRIDGE

2 partridges	1 small red cabbage
Salt and pepper	125 ml/¼ pint cider
Juice of ½ lemon	1 teaspoon vinegar
50 g/2 oz butter	6 chestnuts
2 rashers rindless bacon	25 g/1 oz butter
1 small onion	

Wipe the partridges inside and out, dust with salt and pepper and sprinkle with lemon juice. Melt 50 g/2 oz butter in a pan and brown the birds slowly all over. Cool slightly, then wrap each bird in a slice of bacon. Slice the onion and red cabbage very finely, season with salt and pepper and put into a saucepan with the cider and vinegar. Bring to the boil and simmer for 20 minutes. Put birds on top and put on lid, then simmer for 1½ hours. Peel the chestnuts, toss in butter and add to the dish 10 minutes before cooking is finished.

PARTRIDGE CASSEROLE WITH CABBAGE

2 old partridges	1 savoy cabbage
2 onions	250 ml/½ pint stock
2 carrots	Thyme and parsley
100 g/4 oz rashers streaky bacon	Salt, pepper
225 g/8 oz chipolata sausages	

Cut the vegetables into neat pieces and brown them in a little butter, together with the partridges. Cut the cabbage into quarters and cook in boiling water with the bacon for 5 minutes. Drain well. Cut bacon and cabbage into small pieces. Put half the cabbage into a casserole, season with salt and pepper, and lay the partridges on it. Cover with bacon and vegetables, chopped herbs, and the rest of the cabbage. Pour in stock, cover with a lid and cook at 300°F, 150°C, gas mark 2 for 3 hours. Grill the sausages lightly and add ½ hour before serving time. The addition of a glass of dry perry (using a little less stock) makes a good dish.

PHEASANT WITH APPLES AND ONIONS

1 old pheasant
450 g/1 lb cooking apples
225 g/8 oz onions
50 g/2 oz butter

250 ml/½ pint cider
1 garlic clove and mixed herbs
Salt and pepper

Wipe pheasant thoroughly inside and out. Cut apples in quarters after peeling, and put into casserole. Slice onions and cook in butter until soft and transparent. Put pheasant on top of apples and cover with onions. Pour in cider, and put in herbs and crushed garlic clove. Season with salt and pepper. Cover tightly and cook in the oven at 325°F, 170°C, gas mark 3 for 2½ hours.

PHEASANT WITH MUSHROOMS AND SHERRY

75 g/3 oz butter
225 g/8 oz mushrooms
1 pheasant
3 tablespoons flour

375 ml/¾ pint stock
75 ml/3 fl oz sherry
Salt and pepper
Watercress

Melt half the butter and cook the sliced mushrooms gently for 10 minutes. Season lightly and cool. Stuff the pheasant with three-quarters of the mushrooms. Brown the bird in the rest of the butter, and put in a casserole. Blend the flour into the pan juices, and gradually work in the stock and sherry. Season well and pour over pheasant. Cover tightly and cook in the oven at 325°F, 170°C, gas mark 3 for 1½ hours, but allow an extra 30 minutes for an old bird. Just before serving, add remaining mushrooms, and garnish with watercress. The sauce is rich and delicious.

PHEASANT WITH CELERY SAUCE

1 large old pheasant	500 ml/1 pint stock

Celery Sauce :

1 head celery	Salt and pepper
50 g/2 oz butter	25 g/1 oz butter
1 onion	25 g/1 oz flour
Parsley, thyme and bay leaf	125 ml/¼ pint cream
1 clove	

The stock for cooking the pheasant should include a carrot and onion, a couple of cloves, salt and pepper and a good sprig of parsley. Poach the pheasant in this until tender (this will depend on the age of the bird). Cut the bird into neat pieces for serving with the celery sauce.

Make sauce by cooking the chopped celery in butter with the onion, herbs, clove, salt and pepper until tender, then simmering in 250 ml/½ pint of the pheasant stock until really soft. Put the celery through a sieve and thicken with the butter and flour worked together. Finally, stir in the cream and pour over the pheasant. The sauce should be rather thick. If time is short and the celery young and without strings, the pieces may be left whole without sieving. If money is short, use a little top of the milk instead of cream for the sauce. The same recipe may be used for partridges and this quantity of sauce will be enough for two birds.

PHEASANT AND HERB CASSEROLE

1 pheasant	¼ teaspoon parsley
225 g/8 oz onions	375 ml/¾ pint chicken stock
Salt and white pepper	25 g/1 oz butter
¼ teaspoon thyme	

Cut the pheasant into eight pieces. Slice the onions and mingle with the pheasant, salt and pepper. Leave to stand for 3 hours or overnight in a cool place. Chop the giblets finely. Remove the onions from the pheasant and cook them in the butter until golden. Add the giblets, thyme and parsley, and stock, and simmer on a low heat. Carefully fry the pheasant pieces in a little cooking oil for about 5 minutes, turning occasionally. Put the pheasant and onion gravy together in a casserole and cook at 350°F, 180°C, gas mark 4 for 1 hour 20 minutes.

HAMPSHIRE RABBIT

1 rabbit	100 g/4 oz rindless streaky bacon
Seasoned flour	rashers
Poultry stuffing	Dripping
225 g/8 oz onions	Stock
225 g/8 oz tomatoes	Salt and pepper

Joint the rabbit and soak in salt and water until blanched. Dry joints and toss in seasoned flour. Put joints in a fireproof dish and surround with balls of poultry stuffing. Cover the rabbit with sliced onions and tomatoes and top with bacon rashers. Dot with dripping, and brown in a hot oven for 20 minutes. Add stock to come half way up the dish, season well with salt and pepper, and cover with a lid. Cook at 325°F, 170°C, gas mark 3 for 2 hours.

IRISH ROAST RABBIT

1 rabbit	50 g/2 oz butter
4 rashers rindless bacon	250 ml/½ pint scalded milk
2 onions	Pepper
1 tablespoon flour	2 teaspoons chopped parsley

Cut up rabbit and soak in vinegar and water. Dry pieces well and coat in flour seasoned with pepper. Brown in the butter and put into a casserole. Add chopped bacon, onions and parsley and pour over milk. Cover and bake at 375°F, 190°C, gas mark 5 for 1 hour. Serve with plenty of floury potatoes. Parsley sauce is also good with this.

RABBIT WITH LENTILS

100 g/4 oz lentils	125 ml/¼ pint cider
1 rasher rindless bacon	Bunch of mixed herbs
1 onion	Salt and pepper
1 rabbit	

Soak the lentils in water to cover overnight. Next morning, chop the bacon and fry till the fat runs, then add chopped onion, and soften without browning. Stir in the lentils and any water remaining, and simmer till soft, adding a little more water if necessary to prevent burning. When lentils are soft, put through a sieve. Put the jointed rabbit in a casserole with cider, herbs, salt and pepper. Cover and cook in a slow oven at 325°F, 170°C, gas mark 3 till rabbit is tender. Drain off the rabbit liquid and mix with the lentil purée. Pour over the rabbit and continue cooking for 15 minutes.

RABBIT IN CIDER

1 jointed rabbit	50 g/2 oz chopped bacon
4 large onions	225 g/8 oz peeled sliced tomatoes
1 bay leaf	250 ml/½ pint dry cider
Sprig of thyme	Salt and pepper

Soak the rabbit joints in salted water for 2 hours and dry well. Fry them until golden in a little fat (bacon fat if possible). Slice the onions and add them to the rabbit. Cook until soft. Add the bay leaf and the thyme, bacon and tomatoes, and simmer for 10 minutes. Pour on the cider and cover the pan. Simmer for 1 hour. Season with salt and pepper just before serving, and garnish with plenty of chopped parsley if liked.

JUGGED RABBIT

1 rabbit	Pinch of nutmeg
1 onion	1 teaspoon sugar
1 bay leaf	250 ml/½ pint dry cider
Salt and pepper	

Soak rabbit joints overnight in 500 ml/1 pint water with 2 tablespoons vinegar, together with chopped onion, bay leaf, salt and pepper and nutmeg. Drain joints, keeping the liquid, and dry joints well. Fry rabbit in dripping or bacon fat until golden, then cover with liquid and simmer very gently until tender (about 1 hour). Add sugar and cider to pan and continue cooking for 15 minutes. Thicken gravy with a little flour or cornflour, and serve with forcemeat balls and redcurrant jelly.

STEAMED AND BROWNED PIGEONS

2 pigeons	1 large onion
4 rashers rindless streaky bacon	Salt and pepper

This method can be used to make dry birds succulent. When they have been steamed, the birds can be browned under a grill or in the oven. Rub the pigeons with salt and pepper and tie two rashers of bacon over each bird. Steam them until tender together with the onion. When the birds are tender, brown them lightly under the grill or in the oven. Use the juices and pieces of onion in the steamer to make a rich gravy.

PIGEON AND MUSHROOM CASSEROLE

2 pigeons	50 g/2 oz mushrooms
25 g/1 oz butter	Salt and pepper
225 g/8 oz stewing steak	1 tablespoon redcurrant jelly
1 rasher rindless bacon	1 tablespoon lemon juice
250 ml/½ pint stock	1 tablespoon plain flour

Cut the pigeons in half and brown them lightly in the butter. Put into a casserole with the steak cut in cubes and the bacon cut in pieces. Cover with stock and sliced mushrooms, and season with salt and pepper to taste. Cover and simmer for 2 hours. Mix together the redcurrant jelly, lemon juice and flour with a little water and stir this into the casserole. Simmer for 15 minutes. Serve with plainly boiled or mashed potatoes.

SLOW-COOKED PIGEONS

4 pigeons	200 ml/8 fl oz rosé wine
12 small onions	25 g/1 oz butter
3 rashers rindless lean bacon	25 g/1 oz flour
225 g/8 oz mushrooms	1 teaspoon sugar
500 ml/1 pint stock	Parsley, thyme and bay leaf

Use an oven-to-table fireproof dish which will allow the pigeons to fit side by side. A cast-iron one is perfect as it can be started on top of the stove, then put into the oven. Peel the onions, cut the bacon into thin strips and wipe the mushrooms. Heat the butter and lightly fry the bacon. Put on a warmed dish, and reserve; cook onions until lightly golden, sprinkling with sugar. Remove to dish. Cook the mushrooms in the same fat, and remove to the dish. Brown the pigeons in the fat, very slowly and carefully, and lift out. Work the flour into the fat, cooking until brown. Gradually add stock and wine, bring to the boil and strain. Rinse out the pan, put back the sauce and bring to the boil. Add all the ingredients, cover with greased paper and well-fitting lid. Cook at 300°F, 150°C, gas mark 2 for 2½–3 hours. Remove bunch of herbs before serving.

JUGGED PIGEONS

2 pigeons
2 hard-boiled egg yolks
Pinch of nutmeg
Salt and pepper
Bunch of fresh herbs
200 ml/8 fl oz beer
75 g/3 oz soft white breadcrumbs

25 g/1 oz melted butter
A little grated lemon peel
500 ml/1 pint water
1 onion
25 g/1 oz butter
25 g/1 oz plain flour

Pluck and draw the birds. Boil the livers and chop them finely. Make a stuffing with the chopped livers, the yolks of hard-boiled eggs, nutmeg, pepper, salt, breadcrumbs, finely-chopped suet or melted butter, and grated lemon peel. Mix well together. Stuff the birds, and place them in the top of a double saucepan with the water, peeled and sliced onion, the sweet herbs, and the beer. Cover with a close fitting lid and place on the bottom pan, which should be kept three-quarters full with boiling water (and when refilling, fill from kettle of boiling water), and allow the pigeons to stew until tender. This will take 1½–2 hours.

Strain off the gravy. Melt the butter in a saucepan, add the flour, stir well and dilute with 500 ml/1 pint of the pigeon broth, and bring to the boil. Stir, and, when thickened, pour over pigeons.

PIGEON AND APPLE CASSEROLE

2 pigeons
25 g/1 oz butter
1 small apple
1 small onion
15 g/½ oz flour

250 ml/½ pint cider
250 ml/½ pint stock
Salt and pepper
Bay leaf, thyme and parsley

Brown the pigeons in the butter and then cut them in half. Peel and slice the apple and onion, and brown them in the fat drained from the pigeons. Sprinkle in the flour, and cook and stir well for 2 minutes. Add the cider and stock and bring to the boil. Season well with salt and pepper and add the herbs. Put the pigeons into a casserole and pour over the liquid from the pan. Cover and simmer for 2 hours. Put the pigeons on a serving dish. Strain the liquid and boil quickly to reduce by half. Pour this sauce over the pigeons and garnish with fried apple rings and crisp bacon.

RABBIT BRAWN

2 pig's feet	Salt and pepper
1 jointed rabbit	Mace

Put the pig's feet into a saucepan and cover with cold water. Bring to the boil and simmer for $1\frac{1}{4}$ hours. Add the rabbit and continue cooking for 2 hours. Remove the meat from the bones and cut it into small pieces. Season with plenty of salt and pepper and a pinch of mace and put into a pudding basin. Pour in enough cooking liquid to cover and leave until completely cold before turning out. Cold things tend to lose their flavour, so the seasoning can be strong.

DEVONSHIRE VENISON

1 roasting joint of venison	Stock
Seasoned flour	Fresh herbs
Butter or dripping	Stuffing using thyme and parsley

Soak the venison in cold salted water for 30 minutes, and then drain and dry it well. Cut the meat in thick slices and dust them with seasoned flour. Fry in butter or dripping until brown on both sides. Put the slices into a casserole and cover with stock which has been lightly thickened with flour. Add a good pinch of fresh herbs, cover and cook at 325°F, 170°C, gas mark 3 for 2 hours. Add small balls of any favourite stuffing flavoured with thyme and parsley and continue cooking for 30 minutes.

NEW FOREST VENISON ROLL

900 g/2 lb venison
225 g/8 oz fat bacon
1 onion
Salt and pepper
175 g/6 oz soft white bread-
    crumbs

1 tablespoon chopped parsley
2 eggs
Stock

Mince the venison, bacon and onion and add salt and pepper, breadcrumbs and chopped parsley. Beat the eggs and add to the other ingredients. Add sufficient stock to bind. Flour a pudding cloth or foil and place the mixture on it in a long roll, wrap up, tie the ends with string or twist to secure, and boil for 2½ hours. Serve with brown gravy and cranberry or quince jelly. Rowan-berry jelly is also good with this dish.

VENISON IN ALE

1·35 kg/3 lb stewing venison
225 g/8 oz Demerara sugar

2 tablespoons black treacle
500 ml/1 pint beer

Dissolve the sugar and treacle in the beer. Put the well-hung meat into a stewpan or casserole, cover with the liquid, put on the lid and bring to the boil. Simmer gently for 2 hours.

CHAPTER 4

FRESH FROM THE SEA
AND RIVER

UNTIL about a hundred years ago, fresh fish from the sea was rarely seen inland, and farmers' wives used smoked or salted sea fish. They did, however, get fresh fish from rivers, streams and ponds. It was abundant, from perch and bream to salmon, carp and pike. So were eels and freshwater shellfish.

Many housewives used estuary and coastal fish too. The coastal areas of the West Country and East Anglia in particular were rich in herring, mackerel and pilchard, as well as cockles, mussels and oysters. There are many traditional ways of preparing all these in cider or vinegar which make delicious dishes, and which also serve to preserve fish for a while.

HAMPSHIRE HADDOCK OR COD

900 g/2 lb whole haddock or cod
75 g/3 oz soft white breadcrumbs
40 g/1½ oz shredded suet
1 teaspoon chopped parsley
1 teaspoon chopped thyme
Grated rind of ½ lemon
Salt and pepper
Pinch of nutmeg
1 egg
25 g/1 oz butter or dripping

Use a middle cut for this dish. Clean the fish, removing the head, fins and tail. Mix together the breadcrumbs, suet, herbs, lemon rind, seasoning and egg and stuff the fish with this mixture. If preferred, the stuffing mixture may be spread over the surface of the fish instead. Dot the fish with pieces of butter or dripping and bake at 350°F, 180°C, gas mark 4 for 45 minutes. This is very good served with plenty of melted butter or with parsley sauce.

COD WITH BACON

675 g/1½ lb cod cutlets   4 rashers rindless streaky bacon
25 g/1 oz bacon fat   Salt and pepper

Dry the fish well. Put the bacon fat into a fairly deep ovenware dish which will hold half the fish. Put in half the cutlets and season well. Cut each bacon rasher in two pieces and put half the slices over the fish. Lay the remaining fish on top and then the remaining bacon rashers. Cover and bake at 350°F, 180°C, gas mark 4 for 30 minutes. Remove the lid and continue cooking for 10 minutes so that the top layer of bacon becomes crisp.

CORNISH MACKEREL

4 mackerel   1 teaspoon chopped onion
1 teaspoon fresh horseradish   125 ml/¼ pint cider
75 g/3 oz sour clotted cream, or
  cream cheese

If cream or cream cheese are not obtainable, nor fresh horseradish, the fish can be prepared with butter creamed with some bottled horseradish sauce, but the flavour is less good. Split and clean the fish. Work the horseradish into the cream or cream cheese together with the onion and just enough cider to make a soft spreadable cream. Spread this inside the fish and fold them back into shape. Place side by side in an ovenware dish and sprinkle with the remaining cider. Bake at 350°F, 180°C, gas mark 4 for 45 minutes. Serve very hot.

WEST COUNTRY MACKEREL (A COLD DISH)

8 mackerel	1 tablespoon brown sugar
8 bay leaves	250 ml/½ pint mixed cold tea
20 black peppercorns	and white vinegar

Clean the mackerel and put a bay leaf inside each one. Put the fish side by side in an ovenware dish. Sprinkle on the peppercorns and sugar, and add the mixed tea and vinegar. Cover and bake at 350°F, 180°C, gas mark 4 for 1 hour. Serve cold.

WELSH COCKLE PIE (HOT OR COLD)

1 litre/1 quart cockles in shells	75 g/3 oz streaky bacon, diced
225 g/8 oz shortcrust pastry	Salt and pepper
6 spring onions	

Cook the cockles in 250 ml/½ pint water until you can get them out of their shells. Line a pie dish with pastry, reserving some for a lattice decoration. Put a layer of the cockles in the dish. Sprinkle with chopped onions (chives can be used instead), and a layer of diced bacon, seasoning well. Repeat the layers until the dish is full and pour in the cockle liquid. Make a pastry lattice over the pie and bake at 400°F, 200°C, gas mark 6 for 30 minutes. Serve hot with new potatoes, or cold with salad.

YORKSHIRE HERRING PIE

4 herrings	Butter or bacon fat
6 potatoes	Salt and pepper
2 cooking apples, peeled, chopped and dipped in mild vinegar	

Clean the herrings and cut them into fillets. Peel the potatoes and cut them into thin slices like crisps. Arrange these potato slices round the sides and bottom of a greased ovenware dish. Put a layer of herring in the dish, and then a layer of peeled and finely-chopped apple, sprinkling each layer with salt and pepper. Put on another layer of herrings and apples, then herrings, and finish with pieces of potato as a top layer. Put one or two knobs of butter or bacon fat on top and cover with greased paper. Bake at 350°F, 180°C, gas mark 4 for 30 minutes. Remove the paper and continue cooking for 20 minutes.

SCOTTISH SALT FISH PIE

900 g/2 lb salt fish	Salt and pepper
900 g/2 lb potatoes	50 g/2 oz butter

This pie can be made with any salt fish, but cod is the most easily obtainable. Soak the fish for 24 hours, and then simmer until tender in enough fresh cold water to cover. Remove the bones, and flake the flesh into small pieces. Boil and mash half the potatoes with the butter, seasoning to taste. Parboil the remaining potatoes and cut them into slices. Put one layer of potatoes in an ovenware dish and season lightly. Put on a thick layer of fish, then the remaining sliced potatoes. Top with the remaining fish and cover with the mashed potatoes. Bake at 375°F, 190°C, gas mark 5 for 45 minutes. Mustard sauce is very good with it.

SCOTCH SALMON PUDDING

225 g/8 oz cooked salmon	Salt and pepper
3 tablespoons cooked rice	½ teaspoon mixed chopped
1 egg	chervil and tarragon
2 tablespoons milk	½ teaspoon chopped celery leaves

Flake the salmon and mix it with the rice, egg, milk, seasoning and herbs. Put into a buttered ovenware dish and cover with a buttered paper. Steam for 30 minutes. Turn out and serve with briefly-steamed cucumber marbles and with melted butter, which can be flavoured with a little anchovy essence or grated horse-radish.

NOTE: Make cucumber marbles by cutting out with a potato baller.

FISH STAND-BY

175 g/6 oz shortcrust pastry	125 ml/¼ pint milk
175 g/6 oz kipper fillets	225 g/8 oz mashed potato
1 hard-boiled egg	2 eggs
25 g/1 oz butter	1 tablespoon chopped parsley
25 g/1 oz plain flour	

Use the pastry to line a 20 cm/8 inch flan ring. To make the filling, cook the kipper fillets, skin and flake them. Chop and mix in the hard-boiled egg. Melt the butter in a small saucepan, stir in the flour, then remove from the heat and stir in the milk. Return to the heat, bring to the boil and simmer for a few minutes, stirring continuously. Mix in the kipper mixture, season to taste and pour into the pastry case. To make the topping, beat the egg yolks and parsley into the mashed potato. Stiffly whisk the egg whites and fold in. Pile this mixture on top of the filling and bake at 375°F, 190°C, gas mark 5 for 45 minutes until golden-brown.

TRELLIS PIE

225 g/8 oz mashed potato	225 g/8 oz tinned fish or cooked
175 g/6 oz plain flour	smoked haddock
100 g/4 oz butter	Milk
50 g/2 oz lard	1 heaped tablespoon flour
1 chopped onion	1 egg yolk
100 g/4 oz sliced mushrooms	

Sieve the flour with a pinch of salt, and rub in half the butter and all the lard. Add the potato and mix to a fairly stiff dough. Line the dish with this potato pastry, reserving the scraps. Fry the vegetables in the remaining butter, and when cooked, take out a few mushroom slices. Drain off the liquid from tinned fish if used and make it up to 250 ml/½ pint with milk, otherwise use 250 ml/ ½ pint milk. Add the flour, stirring continuously to make a smooth sauce. Add the flaked fish and egg yolk, and adjust seasoning. Spoon the mixture into the flan case. Decorate with a lattice of potato pastry and brush with a little milk. Bake the flan at 400°F, 200°C, gas mark 6 for 25–30 minutes until cooked through. Decorate with the reserved mushrooms before serving.

HADDOCK OR BREAM PUDDING

450 g/1 lb haddock or bream
1 chopped onion
2 eggs
250 ml/½ pint milk
75 g/3 oz butter

75 g/3 oz soft white breadcrumbs
Juice of ½ lemon
Salt and pepper
Grated Lancashire cheese

Poach the fish and cool it. Flake the flesh and mix with the finely-chopped onion, beaten eggs, milk, softened butter, breadcrumbs and lemon juice. Season well and put into a greased pie dish. Sprinkle with grated cheese. Bake at 375°F, 190°C, gas mark 5 for 40 minutes.

SUFFOLK TROUT

4 river trout
4 bay leaves

50 g/2 oz butter
Juice of 1 lemon

Clean the trout and remove their heads. Put a bay leaf inside each trout. Melt the butter in a thick frying pan, and put in the trout. Add the lemon juice and cover with a lid. Cook on a very low heat for 20 minutes, turning the trout once during cooking. Serve very hot with lemon slices, peas and new potatoes.

WELSH TROUT WITH BACON

175 g/6 oz rindless streaky bacon
  rashers
4 river trout

Salt and pepper
1 teaspoon chopped parsley

Line an ovenware dish with the slices of bacon. Split and clean the trout and put them on the bacon. Sprinkle with salt, pepper and parsley. Cover and bake at 350°F, 180°C, gas mark 4 for 20 minutes.

WEST COUNTRY BAKED PILCHARDS (HOT OR COLD)

8 pilchards	1 onion
Salt and black pepper	250 ml/½ pint pale ale
1 teaspoon ground cloves	250 ml/½ pint vinegar
1 teaspoon ground allspice	4 bay leaves

Clean and fillet the fish. Sprinkle salt, pepper and spices on the inside of the fish, roll them up and put them into an ovenware dish. Slice the onion finely and scatter the onion rings on the fish, together with the bay leaves. Pour over the ale and the vinegar. Cover and bake at 350°F, 180°C, gas mark 4 for 1 hour. Serve hot or cold.

HAMPSHIRE HERRINGS (HOT OR COLD)

6 herrings	175 ml/7 fl oz vinegar
1 large onion	175 ml/7 fl oz port
1 bay leaf	175 ml/7 fl oz water
6 peppercorns	

Clean the herrings and remove their heads, tails and side fins. Put them side by side in an oven dish, close together and head-to-tail. Cover with finely sliced onion, bay leaf and peppercorns. Pour on the mixed vinegar, port and water and bake at 350°F, 180°C, gas mark 4 for 45 minutes. Serve hot or cold.

STUFFED HERRINGS WITH GOOSEBERRY SAUCE

4 herrings	25 g/1 oz soft white breadcrumbs
1 tablespoon chopped parsley	Seasoned flour
1 tablespoon chopped thyme	25 g/1 oz browned breadcrumbs
½ teaspoon grated lemon rind	225 g/8 oz gooseberries
1 tablespoon lemon juice	Sugar to taste

Wash and dry the herrings, and clean them. Mix the parsley, thyme, lemon rind, lemon juice and soft breadcrumbs and stuff the herrings with this mixture. Roll the fish lightly in seasoned flour. Melt a little dripping in a baking pan and when it is very hot, put in the herrings.

Put into the oven and bake at 350°F, 180°C, gas mark 4 for 20 minutes. Sprinkle lightly with browned crumbs and return to the oven for 5 minutes. Meanwhile, for the Gooseberry Sauce simmer the gooseberries in very little water until they are soft. Rub them through a sieve and sweeten lightly. Add a little green vegetable colouring if the colour is pale. Serve the gooseberry sauce with the herrings.

Mackerel can also be cooked in this way, but omit the crumbs.

Sprats can be used if the stuffing is put between pairs of the little fish so that they remain flat.

SEFTON BLOATERS

2 bloaters	1 egg, beaten
25 g/1 oz grated Lancashire cheese	Lard
	Chopped parsley
75 g/3 oz breadcrumbs	

Put the lard in a pan. Fillet the fish and cut it into pieces. Dip them in flour, then in egg, and then roll in the breadcrumbs and cheese mixed together. When the lard smokes, put them in and fry until golden. Drain them well and serve with chopped parsley.

BAKED PIKE

1·35 kg/3 lb pike	Herb forcemeat
4 rashers bacon	50 g/2 oz butter

Clean the fish and discard the roe. Remove the scales. Stuff with the forcemeat, and sew up with soft darning thread. Cover with bacon. Grease a fireproof dish and put in the fish. Put knobs of butter on the top and cover with foil. Bake at 375°F, 190°C, gas mark 5 for 30 minutes, basting several times. Remove the thread and put the pike on a very hot dish. It is good served with a caper sauce.

MUSSEL PUDDING COOKED IN PAPER

225 g/8 oz self-raising flour	Water
75 g/3 oz finely-chopped suet	Mussels
Salt	Pepper and salt

Make a suet crust pastry. Roll out into a square and lift on to a piece of greased greaseproof paper. Open the mussels by heating gently in a dry, covered pan. Remove beards. Scoop them out on to one half of the dough, leaving an edge free all round. Season. Damp this edge and fold the pastry over, covering the mussels. Press the edges of the pastry 'envelope' together. Tie up in a cloth and steam for 1½ hours.

JAMAICA HERRINGS

12 herrings, or more	20–35 whole allspice
Salt	White wine vinegar as required

Clean the herrings, take off the heads and (only if necessary) run briefly under the cold tap. Wipe dry with soft kitchen paper. Scrape each fish on both sides with a blunt knife held almost parallel to the fish. Work from the tail downward, holding the tail in your left hand. Sprinkle your fingers with salt for a firm grip.

Lay a row of herring side by side in a deep square or loaf tin. Sprinkle well with salt. Repeat the layers until you have used all the herrings. Cover the container, and leave in a cool place for 24 hours.

Remove the herrings, wipe off the surface salt with soft kitchen paper, and lay them on paper to dry slightly. Drain and dry the container. Replace the fish, sprinkling each layer with whole allspice berries. Fill the container with white wine vinegar. Cover tightly with aluminium foil, and leave in the oven overnight at a very low heat (not more than 300°F, 150°C, gas mark 1–2).

Next day, skim off any fat floating on the surface of the vinegar, replace the foil cover, and leave in a cool place until required for use.

It is not worth pickling fewer then twelve herrings, nor is it effective. They should be used within 4–6 weeks.

CHAPTER 5
THE DAIRY

EGGS, milk, cream, butter and cheese have always been important to the countryman. Milk fresh from the cow has been used for a variety of puddings, notably, in the past, for junkets, 'creams' and syllabubs. The milk from a newly-calved cow, called beestings, was once used in many areas to make curds and cheesecakes (although, today, we usually make the latter with cottage cheese). Buttermilk was used likewise, and whey had many uses.

Soured milk was often made into the local cheese, either soft or semi-firm. In poorer households, a piece of cheese and slab of bread was often the complete meal; since butcher's meat was too costly to obtain, eggs and cheese might well be the only protein food available. These farmhouse cheeses were matured for a long time, and developed rich, strong flavours; so they were also used to make many nourishing, tasty dishes.

There used to be many different regional British cheeses, and each had its own characteristics and flavour. The ones which are still made have kept these.

Cheeses

Cheddar cheese is close-textured, golden or orange-red, with a clean, mellow and nutty flavour. It is excellent for cooking, or for eating with fruit, and cider or beer.

Cheshire is more crumbly, and may be orange-red or white. It is particularly good with fruit, or with a piece of cake or semi-sweet biscuits. A blue Cheshire is sometimes available.

Derby is a buttery open cheese, with a clean and tangy flavour and the colour of honey. It, too, is very good with fruit. Derby flavoured with sage leaves is sometimes available and is criss-crossed, if genuine, with thin green lines; a thick green line through the centre of the cheese indicates a synthetic Sage Derby.

Double Gloucester is also buttery and open, with a delicate, creamy flavour and an orange-red colour. It is good with beer, and is one of the most useful cooking cheeses.

Leicester has a mild flavour and buttery texture, and is reddish in colour. It is good for both eating and cooking.

Caerphilly is a white, close-textured cheese with a clean, mild and slightly salt flavour. It is nice with celery.

Lancashire is white, soft and crumbly with a mild flavour. It is particularly good for toasting and for crumbling on soups and hot-pots.

Wensleydale is generally white, and is moderately close with a mild, slightly salt flavour. A blue Wensleydale is also obtainable. It is good with apples or apple pie.

Stilton is the prince of British cheeses. It is a rich, creamy blue cheese with a soft, close texture. It is traditionally eaten after a meal with port and nuts, but it is superb with, or after, cold meats and game, apples and many other foods. It is also excellent cooked, and when potted.

Much more could be written about our cheeses; about the Scottish cheeses for instance, or the difference between present-day farmhouse cheeses, which still take long to mature, and our excellent but different creamery-made cheeses of the same types. For anyone who is interested in cheese, both well repay study by offering satisfying flavoursome foods.

COTTAGE CHEESES

There are several different ways to make even the basic, simple soft cheese we call Farmer's Cheese, Pot Cheese, Clabber Cheese, Cottage Cheese, Crowdie and so on. This is just one of them.

Put sour, whole or skimmed milk in a warm place until thick. Add ½ teaspoon salt to each 500 ml/1 pint of milk. Put into a muslin bag and leave to drain overnight. Press between two plates for an hour, then mix with a little fresh cream to serve. Keep refrigerated.

SOUR MILK SOFT CHEESE WITH HERBS

1 litre/2 pints thick sour milk   Salt and pepper
25 g/1 oz butter   Chopped fresh herbs
1 tablespoon salt

Scald the sour milk until the curd separates from the whey, but do not boil. Add all other ingredients except the herbs and beat well. Add herbs to taste.

HOME-MADE YOGHURT

Yoghurt can be made at home without elaborate equipment, but *unpasteurized* milk is essential, so milk must be obtained straight from the cow. For a family of four, a week's supply of yoghurt can be made from 2 litres/4 pints of milk. Besides the milk, a little *genuine live* yoghurt is needed, as a 'starter'.

Use a large casserole with a well-fitting lid, and be sure the dish retains heat well. Put the milk into a saucepan, and bring it just to the boil. Pour it immediately into the casserole and cover with the lid. Leave the milk until it is just cool enough to leave your finger in for a little while. Add a teaspoon of the live yoghurt and stir gently. Put on the lid, wrap the casserole in a blanket, and put it in a place which remains gently warm, such as an airing cupboard. Leave overnight, and the yoghurt should be set, in which case it will 'cut' like a junket. If it is not successful, it is probably because the milk was either too hot or too cold when the 'starter' was added. (A spoonful of this yoghurt when successful can be used to 'start' a new batch.)

Junket or renneted curd is very like yoghurt although it lends itself more to sweet flavours.

DEVONSHIRE JUNKET

1 litre/2 pints new milk	Grated nutmeg
3 tablespoons brandy	1½ tablespoons rennet
40 g/1½ oz Demerara sugar	

Heat the milk to lukewarm (about 104°F, 50°C). Put the brandy and sugar into a china serving dish with nutmeg to taste. Pour in the milk and stir well to blend the flavours. Stir in the rennet, and leave the milk in a cool place to set. This junket should be served with a covering of thick cream, topped with a sprinkling of Demerara sugar and a little more brandy.

Cheesecakes

The following cheesecakes are made with cottage cheese but by no means all cheesecakes contain cheese. Many traditional cheese-cakes were (and are) made with milk 'set' with rennet, eggs, herbs or other mildly acid products instead of using a cheese curd.

YORKSHIRE CHEESECAKE

100 g/4 oz plain flour	2 eggs
Pinch of salt	Grated rind of 1 lemon
65 g/2½ oz butter	2 teaspoons cornflour
Juice of 1½ lemons	2 tablespoons double cream
225 g/8 oz curd or cottage cheese	1 tablespoon melted butter
2 tablespoons caster sugar	25 g/1 oz raisins

Sift the flour and salt, rub in the butter, and add the juice of ½ lemon and enough water to bind. Roll out thinly and use to line a 25 cm/10 inch plate. Bake blind at 425°F, 220°C, gas mark 7 for 10 minutes. Sieve the cheese and mix with the sugar, eggs, lemon rind and the remainder of the lemon juice. Beat until smooth and add the cornflour mixed with cream to a smooth paste. Fold in the melted butter and blend well. Pour into the pastry case and sprinkle with raisins. Bake at 350°F, 180°C, gas mark 4 for 30 minutes. Serve cold.

LITTLE COUNTRY CHEESECAKES

225 g/8 oz puff pastry	50 g/2 oz butter
225 g/8 oz cottage cheese	Pinch of nutmeg and salt
175 g/6 oz sugar	Grated rind of 2 lemons
6 egg yolks	

Line small tart tins with the pastry. Sieve the cheese and mix with all the other ingredients, and put into the tart cases. Sprinkle the top of each with a mixture of chopped candied peel, currants and sultanas. Bake at 375°F, 190°C, gas mark 5 until pastry is golden, about 20 minutes.

LEICESTER CHEESECAKES

350 g/12 oz puff pastry
100 g/4 oz smooth curd (not cottage) cheese
50 g/2 oz butter, softened
1 whole egg
1 egg yolk
50 g/2 oz fine dry white bread-crumbs

50 g/2 oz granulated sugar
175 g/6 oz mixed currants and sultanas
1 tablespoon single cream
Grated nutmeg and lemon rind to taste
2 teaspoons brandy

Roll out the pastry to 3 mm/⅛ inch thick and line deep patty pans or small bun tins with it. Prick the bottoms to prevent rising, and chill. Mix the cheese with the butter then fork in the beaten eggs, breadcrumbs, sugar, fruit, cream and flavourings. The mixture will be fairly wet. Fill the pastry shells three-quarters full only. Bake for 15 minutes at 425°F, 220°C, gas mark 7, then lower the heat and bake at 325°F, 170°C, gas mark 3 for a further 15 minutes, or until the cheesecakes are firm in the centre. Eat warm or cold. You should have about twelve cakes.

FARMHOUSE CURD CAKES

225 g/8 oz shortcrust pastry
225 g/8 oz unsalted curd cheese from skimmed milk
50 g/2 oz caster sugar

2 eggs
100 g/4 oz mixed currants and candied chopped peel
1 teaspoon ground cinnamon

Roll out the pastry and use it to line 6·25 cm/2½ inch patty pans or bun tins, well greased. Leave to 'rest' in a cool place. Put the curd in a basin. Sift the sugar. Beat the eggs until frothy, then gradually beat in the sugar. When the mixture is pale and light, mix thoroughly with the curd, adding the dried fruit and spice dusted over it. Fill the pastry shells about two-thirds full. Bake for 30–35 minutes at 350°F, 180°C, gas mark 4.

HONEY CHEESECAKE

100 g/4 oz cottage cheese	2 beaten eggs
50 g/2 oz honey	175 g/6 oz shortcrust pastry
50 g/2 oz caster sugar	Cinnamon
½ level teaspoon cinnamon	Caster sugar

Blend together the sieved cottage cheese, honey, sugar, cinnamon and eggs. Line a pie plate with shortcrust pastry and fill with the cheese mixture. Sprinkle thickly with a mixture of cinnamon and caster sugar and bake at 375°F, 190°C, gas mark 5 for 35 minutes.

Other cheese dishes

CHEESE AND ONIONS

4 medium-sized onions	Salt and pepper
125 ml/¼ pint milk	100 g/4 oz grated cheese

Peel and slice the onions. Cook until tender in very little water. Add milk and seasoning. Bring to the boil and turn into an ovenproof dish. Cover with cheese and brown under the grill. Serve with bread and butter.

CHEDDAR CHEESE PUFFS

50 g/2 oz butter	Salt and Cayenne pepper
100 g/4 oz grated Cheddar cheese	Deep fat for frying
2 eggs	
225 g/8 oz soft white bread- crumbs	

Melt the butter and add the cheese. Mix well and add the beaten eggs, salt and pepper. Mix in the breadcrumbs to make a stiff consistency. Divide and form into balls. Fry in deep hot fat for 3 minutes. These are good served with baked tomatoes.

CHEDDAR FRITTERS

50 g/2 oz butter
125 ml/¼ pint water
100 g/4 oz plain flour

3 eggs
75 g/3 oz grated Cheddar cheese
Salt and pepper

Boil the butter and water together. Add the sieved flour to the boiled liquid, beating well until smooth. Add the eggs and beat well. Beat in the grated cheese, salt and pepper. Fry spoonfuls in hot fat, turning to brown on both sides.

LANCASHIRE CHEESE AND EGGS

25 g/1 oz butter
1 teaspoon olive oil
225 g/8 oz Lancashire cheese

4 eggs
Pepper

Melt the butter and oil in a shallow dish on top of the stove. Cut the cheese into slices, reserving about 25 g/1 oz for grating. Put the cheese into the dish and melt cheese gently. Break the eggs on top. Cook at 350°F, 180°C, gas mark 4 for 8 minutes. Sprinkle with pepper and grated cheese, and brown under the grill.

GLOUCESTERSHIRE POTATO CAKES

225 g/8 oz cooked potatoes
50 g/2 oz plain flour
50 g/2 oz grated Double
   Gloucester cheese

1 egg
A little butter

Mash the potatoes thoroughly with a little butter. Work in the flour and cheese. Beat the egg and add it to the mixture. Roll out and cut into small round cakes. Cook in the butter on a girdle or heavy frying pan until golden on both sides.

COTTAGE CHEESE AND HAM TART

175 g/6 oz shortcrust pastry	2 eggs
25 g/1 oz butter	50 g/2 oz chopped ham
1 large onion	Salt and pepper
450 g/1 lb cottage cheese	

Line a 20 cm/8 inch flan ring or pie plate with the pastry. Melt the butter and fry the finely-chopped onion until golden. Sieve the cottage cheese finely, and mix it with the beaten eggs, ham, salt and pepper. Pour into the pastry and bake at 375°F, 190°C, gas mark 5 for 15 minutes, and then reduce the heat to 325°F, 170°C, gas mark 3 for 45 minutes. Serve hot. Finely-chopped mushrooms or some chopped parsley may be used instead of the ham, or can be added to the recipe if liked.

CHEESE AND POTATO PIE

675 g/1½ lb potatoes	175 g/6 oz grated cheese
4 tablespoons milk	3 tablespoons chopped parsley
1 egg	Salt and pepper
1 teaspoon dry mustard	

Cook the potatoes until they are tender, and then drain them. Mash them with the milk, egg, mustard, half the cheese, the parsley, salt and pepper. Put into a greased ovenware dish and sprinkle with the remaining cheese. Bake at 425°F, 220°C, gas mark 7 for 15 minutes until golden-brown.

CHEESE BREAD AND BUTTER PUDDING

6 slices bread and butter	250 ml/½ pint milk
175 g/6 oz grated cheese	2 eggs

Butter a shallow ovenware dish. Line with bread and butter, and cover the bread thickly with cheese. Put on the remaining bread with the buttered side upwards. Beat the milk and eggs together and pour over the bread. Leave for 1 hour. Bake at 425°F, 220°C, gas mark 7 for 30 minutes; eat at once while very hot.

BAKED CHEDDAR PUDDING

175 g/6 oz grated Cheddar cheese
225 g/8 oz white breadcrumbs
1 litre/2 pints milk
2 onions, peeled and grated

50 g/2 oz butter
4 eggs
Salt and pepper
Butter

Boil the milk with the grated onions. Pour on to the cheese, breadcrumbs, butter, salt and pepper. Mix well with the beaten eggs. Pour into a buttered pie dish and bake at 375°F, 190°C, gas mark 5 for 30 minutes.

CHEESE AND PARSLEY CUSTARD PUDDING

2 eggs
250 ml/½ pint milk
75 g/3 oz grated cheese
50 g/2 oz soft white breadcrumbs

½ teaspoon dry mustard
½ teaspoon salt
2 tablespoons chopped parsley

Separate the eggs. Beat the yolks with lukewarm milk and cheese. Mix the crumbs with mustard, salt and parsley and gradually stir in the milk mixture. Leave to stand for 30 minutes. Beat the egg whites stiffly and fold them into the mixture. Put into a greased ovenware dish and bake at 400°F, 200°C, gas mark 6 for 30 minutes. (Instead of the parsley, 50 g/2 oz finely-chopped ham can be used.)

BAKED CHEESE AND CREAM

100 g/4 oz cheese
Salt and pepper

125 ml/¼ pint single cream

Butter an ovenware dish. Cut the cheese into matchstick slices and arrange them so that they are not packed together in the dish.

Season well and pour the cream over them. Bake at 350°F, 180°C, gas mark 4 for 15 minutes.

LEICESTERSHIRE RAREBIT

15 g/½ oz butter
100 g/4 oz Leicestershire cheese
2 tablespoons milk

Salt and pepper
1 teaspoon made mustard
Hot buttered toast

Melt the butter and add the crumbled cheese. Heat gently, stirring until melted, and gradually add the milk. This must be done carefully or the cheese becomes hard and lumpy. Season with salt, pepper and mustard and pour over hot buttered toast. The rabbit, rare-bite or rarebit was first made by soaking a toasted slice of bread in front of the open fire in red wine or beer. The thinly-cut cheese was then laid on top and left before the fire until the cheese was toasted and browned. If a fried or poached egg were added on top, the dish became Buckinghamshire Rare-bit, or Buck Rabbit.

'BOILED' CHEESE

100 g/4 oz mild cheese
50 g/2 oz butter

2 tablespoons double cream
1 egg

Cut the cheese in very thin slices and put it into a thick pan with the butter and cream. Stir the mixture over very gentle heat until it is smooth. Beat the egg lightly and stir into the mixture. Pour into a fireproof dish and brown under the grill. Serve with dry toast.

STEWED CHEESE AND ALE

100 g/4 oz Cheshire cheese   100 ml/4 fl oz ale

Cut the cheese into very thin slices and put into a thick-bottomed saucepan. Cover with the ale and heat very gently until the mixture is like custard. Serve very hot on toast.

The cheese and ale can, if you wish, be heated in a bowl over hot water or in an ovenware dish in a very low oven.

CHESHIRE SAVOURY

50 g/2 oz Cheshire cheese	1 hard-boiled egg yolk
25 g/1 oz butter	1 slice buttered toast

Crumble the cheese finely and mix with the butter and egg yolk until a smooth paste is formed. Spread on the buttered toast and put under a grill to brown.

POTTED CHEDDAR (NOT FOR KEEPING)

100 g/4 oz butter	225 g/8 oz Cheddar cheese
Salt and pepper	3 tablespoons milk
½ teaspoon made English mustard	5 drops Worcestershire sauce

Cream the butter and season with salt, pepper and mustard. Grate the cheese finely and mix it with the butter, gradually adding the milk and sauce. Chill before use.

MOCK CRAB

15 g/½ oz butter	1 egg
1 large tomato, skinned and	25 g/1 oz grated cheese
de-pipped	Salt and pepper

Melt the butter and add the tomato, skinned and de-pipped. Simmer for 5 minutes. Beat the egg with cheese and season well. Add to the tomato mixture and cook gently until thick. Use hot on toast, or cool for use as a sandwich filling.

Eggs

SLIPPERY JACK OR POTTED EGGS

6 eggs
100 g/4 oz butter, softened

1 teaspoon anchovy paste

Boil the eggs hard and cool them. Put the yolks through a sieve and chop the whites very finely. Mix with the softened butter and paste. Chill before use. This is very good on toast or in sandwiches.

YORKSHIRE BAKED EGGS

2 eggs
4 tablespoons creamy milk
1 teaspoon chopped parsley

Salt and pepper
15 g/½ oz butter

Beat the eggs and milk with the parsley, salt and pepper. Put the butter into an ovenproof dish and heat it in the oven until just melted. Pour in the egg mixture and bake at 375°F, 190°C, gas mark 5 for 10 minutes. Serve hot with toast.

Variations
A little crisp bacon or chopped ham, or a few shrimps, can be put at the bottom of the dish before the egg mixture is poured in.

EGG AND MINT PASTY

175 g/6 oz plain flour
Pinch of salt
75 g/3 oz clarified dripping
Cold water
1 tablespoon scratchings (see
  recipe)

9 eggs
1 tablespoon chopped fresh mint
Salt and freshly-ground black
  pepper

Make a dripping crust pastry first. Mix flour and salt to a firm dough with cold water. Roll out thinly, and dot with one-third of the dripping cut into flakes. Fold over, turn, and roll out again. Repeat the process twice more. Let the pastry 'rest' in a cool place before use.

Preheat the oven to 425°F, 220°C, gas mark 7. Grease a shallow 17·5 cm/7 inch pie plate and line with two-thirds of the pastry. Scatter on the scratchings which are crisp scraps of pork fat left after rendering lard. (Scraps of crisp fat from a roast joint serve quite well.) Break 8 eggs very carefully into the shell, taking care not to break the yolks. Sprinkle with the mint, salt and pepper. Separate the last egg, beat the yolk lightly in a bowl and glaze the edge of the pastry lining. Make sure the remaining one-third rolled-out pastry will cover the lining, and lay it gently on top of the eggs. Press down the edges of the pie to seal. Glaze the whole lid very gently with beaten egg yolk; the pie is very fragile. Bake for 20–30 minutes until the pastry is golden-brown and set; the eggs should then be half set but still moist. Serve hot with steamed spring greens or spinach and parsley sauce.

This old farm dish is clearly of peasant origin, using as it does the dripping and crisp fat which, being precious meat products, the farmer's wife dared not waste, and whose flavour she 'stretched' as far as possible. It was usually made in spring when the first fresh wild herbs appeared and the farm hens started laying, so although its many eggs make it seem quite a luxurious dish, it was a cheap one.

MARIGOLD EGG PIE

225 g/8 oz shortcrust pastry	Salt and pepper
4 tart eating apples	Thyme
2 eggs	Sage
250 ml/½ pint milk	Marigold petals

Grease a 17·5 cm/7 inch flan ring or pie plate with butter, and line it with pastry. Peel, core and slice the apples, and lay them in the dish; flake a little more butter over them, and bake the dish at

400°F, 200°C, gas mark 6 until the apple slices are tender and the pastry rim is set. This will take 15–20 minutes.

While the dish is baking, make a custard mixture with the eggs beaten in the milk, and season it strongly with salt, pepper, thyme and sage. Add about ½ teacup of marigold petals, or to your taste.

When the apple slices are done, pour this savoury custard over them, cover the pastry with a buttered paper or aluminium foil, and return the pie to the oven at a reduced heat of 325°F, 170°C, gas mark 3–4, until the custard is set. It will take 20–30 minutes. Serve with roast pork just as you would serve Yorkshire pudding with beef. The pungent marigold flavour is first class with it.

TO PRESERVE EGGS: THREE WAYS

1. *Waterglass method*
Make up the waterglass according to the instructions on the tin. Use a large stone jar, zinc pail or barrel with the top sawn off. Put in the waterglass and add the fresh eggs a few at a time when available. Store in a place where the container need not be moved. As many as one hundred eggs can be put into a container, and they will keep for up to fifteen months. The eggs should be examined carefully to see that the shells are not thin, rough or cracked before they are put in the waterglass.

The waterglass which is used makes a marvellous cleaner when the eggs have been used up, as it changes in composition during the storage period. Housewives once used it with the water for boiling clothes to give added brightness. It was also used as a scrubbing agent for kitchen tables, sinks and floors.

2. *Dry salt method*
Use kitchen salt, and dry it in the oven. This is most important, as if it is wet, it will flavour the eggs. When the salt is cold, cover the bottom of a crock or pail with a deep layer. Put the eggs in, standing them on their pointed ends. Cover with 2·5 cm/1 inch salt

between each egg and each row. Fill with layers of eggs and salt and complete the layer with salt.

3. *Dripping method*

Melt a little dripping and pour it into the palms of the hands. Take each egg and rub it carefully between the hands, so that the whole shell is covered. Store the eggs in tins, piling them up, but do not put on a lid. Tie a piece of brown paper over the top.

Buttermilk and whey

After making butter and cheese, a good deal of buttermilk and whey were left. These were never thrown away, for they were nourishing and flavoursome. They were used for various purposes, such as making curds for cheesecakes, for moistening bread and cakes, and for refreshing drinks.

CURDS AND WHEY

1 litre/2 pints unpasteurized milk
Setting agent as described in recipe (rennet, eggs or buttermilk)
Vanilla essence or rose-water to taste

Caster sugar to taste
½–1 teaspoon ground cinnamon or grated nutmeg

There are several ways to make curds. Bottled rennet has been widely used since the late nineteenth century when it replaced the prepared calf's stomach lining. A more extravagant method in eighteenth century use was to add 3 beaten eggs with 1 teaspoon salt to each pint of milk; the mixture was heated very gently until at simmering point, and the curds were then tipped into a cloth laid on a sieve over a basin, to drain. A more practical method for use now is to make 1 litre/2 pints milk scalding (not boiling) hot and tip them into 2 litres/4 pints commercial buttermilk. Let the mixture stand until cold and firm before tipping into a cloth to drain as above.

Sweeten and flavour both curd and whey with sugar and spice to suit your taste. Serve the curd chilled, either alone or with fresh stewed fruit, and pour some of the whey over it as a sauce, just before serving.

Variation

An older way to serve curds and whey is to add only a little salt to the curd and then to mix it lightly with 1 stiffly-beaten egg white. Place in a small mould or dish and chill. Unmould to serve, and offer the whey sweetened as above and single cream to pour over it.

BUTTERMILK CURD CREAM

500 ml/1 pint fresh milk
1 litre/2 pints buttermilk
Caster sugar
Single cream
Icing sugar
Salt
Vanilla essence or ground
   cinnamon

Make the milk scalding (not boiling) hot, and stir it quickly into the buttermilk. Let the mixture stand until cold and firm, then tip it gently on to a cloth laid over a sieve. Allow to drain until set and crumbly.

Turn gently out of the cloth on to a board, and pat square with the side of a knife. Cut into square individual helpings, and lift them with a spatula into serving bowls.

Sprinkle each lightly with sifted caster sugar. Then pour over a small amount of single cream flavoured with sifted icing sugar, a pinch of salt and vanilla essence or cinnamon to suit your taste. Flavour some of the whey like the cream, and serve it in a jug as a sauce.

GUERNSEY BUTTERMILK CAKE

225 g/8 oz currants
125 ml/¼ pint cider
450 g/1 lb plain flour
100 g/4 oz unsalted butter
1 teaspoon grated nutmeg
2 teaspoons cream of tartar

1 teaspoon bicarbonate of soda
225 g/8 oz caster sugar
2 eggs
125 ml/¼ pint buttermilk
2 teaspoons lemon juice or a few
    drops lemon essence

Steep the currants in the cider until plumped. Rub the butter into the flour until the mixture resembles fine crumbs. Sift together the nutmeg, cream of tartar, soda and sugar, and add to the mixture. Mix the eggs into the buttermilk with the flavouring. Make a well in the dry ingredients. Mix in the cider and the buttermilk alternately, adding about one-third each time. Mix thoroughly to blend. Place the mixture in a 20 cm/8 inch cake tin, lined and greased, and bake at 325°F, 170°C, gas mark 3 for 2 hours or until the cake is springy and brown. Cool well before cutting.

CHAPTER 6
HARVEST HOME

THE harvest was always important in corn-growing Britain, and was widely celebrated by a 'horkey' or party; it is still commemorated by autumn thanksgiving services in churches throughout the land. Even the poorest labouring families would glean enough corn from the fields to supply their flour for the winter months.

Wheat, barley and oats were the three grains used for home baking. Wheat predominated in East Anglia, barley in the north, and oats in Scotland and Wales. Bread was made in most farm and cottage kitchens, and so were a wide variety of scones, pancakes or bannocks. All these plain baked goods were first made on a hot hearthstone since ovens were not built in most small homes until the nineteenth century (meat, cakes and pies were taken to the local baker's oven). From the eighteenth century on, however, most farmhouses of any size had a brick bread oven in which the bread was baked on the hot floor after raking out the hot ashes of a fire. Later still, the bread came to be baked in tins, to make the shapes of loaves we know now; but many traditional small baked goods are still griddle baked.

Baking Day was busy, but the men and children could usually look forward to a special treat for tea. This was often a piece of bread dough left from the loaf-making, made richer and sweeter with fat and sugar. For extra special days, fruit and peel were added to make (among others) the still-popular Lardy Cakes.

Successful breadmaking

Flour and yeast   Ordinary plain flour, both white and wholemeal, is satisfactory for breadmaking, but the best kind is 'hard' or 'strong' flour. If a large quantity of flour can be bought direct from a mill for regular breadmaking, it can be stored for about three months in a small dust-bin. Fresh baker's yeast is cheap and will keep for about ten days in a covered bowl in a refrigerator. It can also be frozen in 25 g/1 oz cubes which are convenient to use; the yeast should be thawed at room temperature before using. Dried yeast is convenient to store and use, but it sometimes has a stronger flavour. The maker's specific instructions for using dried yeast should be followed carefully; note that only half as much dried as fresh yeast is needed in a recipe. Dried yeast needs about twenty minutes to start working well, before being added to flour.

Other ingredients   Fat and sugar are sometimes added to a basic bread mixture to give richer, longer-keeping bread. When yeast is creamed with sugar, the 'working' time is speeded up. Salt is an essential in bread, and is best dissolved first in a little liquid, as dry salt affects the growth of the yeast cells.

Procedure   In breadmaking, the yeast is set working by the addition of sugar and warm liquid, and is mixed and kneaded with flour and left to prove, or rise. The dough then has to be knocked back or lightly rekneaded, and shaped to fit the tins when these are used. Dough should be kneaded on a floured board, which means folding it over on itself and pushing with a firm rocking motion until the dough becomes smooth and shiny. A dough hook on an electric mixer is an inexpensive attachment which speeds up the work, and ensures that the yeast is worked right through the dough. If bread is to be baked as rolls or freehand shapes, a slightly firmer dough is needed than for bread baked in tins.

After a second rising, bread is baked in a really hot oven or on a piping hot griddle; the heat kills the yeast and prevents further rising. A container of water in the oven during baking gives a crisp crust. Bread is properly baked when it sounds hollow if tapped underneath with the knuckles. If it is not quite cooked, it should be returned without the tins and cooked for a further five to ten minutes.

If plain loaves are painted with rich milk or cream before baking, they will have a gleaming brown crust; beaten eggs give a dark crust, while melted butter or margarine gives a crisp, crunchy crust. A thick milk and sugar syrup painted on *after* baking gives loaves and buns a sweet sticky finish.

If a batch of bread is not successful, it may only be because one or two details have been overlooked. For instance, during bread-making, the implements and the ingredients should be *warm* to speed up the working of the yeast; but if the dough is made too hot during rising, the result is a very coarse, breakable crumb of irregular texture. The dough must be *worked thoroughly* to give an even distribution of the yeast, which enables the dough to rise properly. It should be on the *soft* side to achieve a light loaf; if it is too stiff, it cannot expand properly under the influence of the yeast. Again if the dough is not proved long enough, a heavy, soggy loaf will result, with a crust which breaks away from the top. If dough is left to rise for too long, however, there will be a loss of strength, colour, scent and flavour. It is also important to bake bread at a high temperature, or the result will be pale, moist and flavourless.

Using a griddle   Bread and scones used to be cooked on a griddle or heavy bakestone because few rural houses had ovens. Today, heavy iron griddles are still obtainable, but the hotplate of an electric or solid fuel cooker can be used equally well, or a heavy frying pan with a flat base.

The griddle should be put on to heat before the dough is mixed. To test the heat, a little flour should be sprinkled on. If it browns at once, the griddle is too hot. If the flour takes a few seconds to brown, the heat is right. For scones and bannocks, the griddle was traditionally floured; for crumpets and drop scones it was lightly greased to prevent sticking, using a piece of suet wrapped in a clean rag. The general rule was 'floured for dough, greased for batter'. A griddle should never be washed, but should be rubbed when hot with coarse salt and a piece of clean paper, and then dusted with a cloth.

WHITE BREAD

1·35 kg/3 lb plain white flour   15 g/½ oz salt
25 g/1 oz fresh yeast   750 ml/1½ pints warm water
50 g/2 oz fat (butter or lard)

Put flour in a large bowl, make a well in the centre, and sprinkle salt around the edge. Cream yeast with a little warm water and pour into the well. Add the rest of the water and the warmed fat and mix well to a soft putty-like consistency. Leave to prove until double in size. Put into tins and leave to prove again until bread reaches top of the tins. Bake at 450°F, 230°C, gas mark 8 for 45 minutes, turning bread once in the oven. Cool on a wire rack.

WHOLEMEAL BREAD

1·35 kg/3 lb wholemeal flour   40 g/1½ oz fresh yeast
25 g/1 oz salt   750 ml/1½ pints warm water
25 g/1 oz sugar

Take half the flour and make into a batter with all the water. Cream the yeast with two tablespoons of warm water and mix well into the batter. Cover the basin with a damp cloth and let the batter stand for 15 minutes. Add the rest of the flour, salt and sugar, and make the dough. Mix well and knead for 10 minutes. Warm and lightly grease four 450 g/1 lb loaf tins, and divide dough between them. Flatten each piece and roll up to fit lengthwise in the tin, pressing down to avoid cracks and folds. Leave for 1 hour in a warm place until the dough doubles in volume. Bake at 450°F, 230°C, gas mark 8 for 45 minutes, turning the loaves (move them through a right angle in the oven) half-way through cooking time. Turn out the loaves on to a wire tray and cool thoroughly before cutting.

MILK BREAD

1 teaspoon sugar
15 g/½ oz yeast
675 g/1½ lb plain white flour

½ teaspoon salt
50 g/2 oz butter
375 ml/¾ pint warm milk

Cream yeast and sugar together in a warm basin and cover with a little warm milk. Leave in a warm place for 15 minutes. Sift together the flour and salt and rub in the butter. Make a well in the centre and pour in the yeast mixture. Add the warm milk and knead the soft dough lightly. Cover and leave in a warm place until double in size. Grease two 450 g/1 lb loaf tins and divide the dough between them. Leave to rise for 15 minutes. Brush over with a little warm milk and bake at 400°F, 200°C, gas mark 6 for 30 minutes. This light dough is also excellent for forming into plaits, twists or buns or fruit loaves. For a fruit loaf, add 50 g/2 oz currants, 50 g/2 oz raisins and 25 g/1 oz chopped candied peel to the basic recipe. For plaits, twists and buns, allow a little less baking time, until the bread is pale golden-brown.

IRISH SODA BREAD

450 g/1 lb plain flour
1 level teaspoon salt
1 level teaspoon bicarbonate of
  soda

25 g/1 oz lard
250 ml/½ pint buttermilk or milk

Sift the dry ingredients into a basin and rub in the fat. Make a well in the centre and stir in enough buttermilk or milk to give a soft spongy dough. Knead lightly on a floured surface. Shape quickly into a round cake about 5 cm/2 inches thick. Put on a floured baking sheet and score the top lightly three times with a sharp knife. Bake at 400°F, 200°C, gas mark 6 for 35 minutes, or until well risen.

IRISH GRIDDLE BREAD

225 g/8 oz wholemeal flour
225 g/8 oz plain flour
2 teaspoons sugar
1 teaspoon bicarbonate of soda

1 teaspoon salt
2 teaspoons dripping
Milk

Mix together flours, and add sugar, soda and salt. Rub in dripping and mix to a batter with milk, to make a dough which is stiff but will roll easily. Roll out in a round 2·5 cm/1 inch thick, and cut into four sections. Cook on a hot griddle for 10 minutes on each side.

PLAITED HARVEST BREAD

450 g/1 lb plain flour
½ teaspoon salt
125 ml/¼ pint milk
50 g/2 oz butter
1 egg

25 g/1 oz fresh yeast
25 g/1 oz caster sugar
1 tablespoon currants
Pinch of grated nutmeg
2 teaspoons grated lemon rind

Put the flour and salt in a warm bowl. Warm the milk to blood heat, stir in the butter and continue stirring until it melts. Cool, then mix in the egg. Mix the yeast with a little of the sugar, and mix well. Add the remaining sugar to the flour and salt. When the yeast mixture froths, add it to the milk, mix in and stir both into the flour. Leave in a warm place to rise. When double the original size, cut into three pieces. Form each piece into three strips, and plait them. Damp the ends with milk to secure them. Place on a lightly-greased baking sheet, and allow to prove for 10–15 minutes. Bake at 425°F, 220°C, gas mark 7 for 15 minutes or until golden-brown.

THRESHING DAY BARLEY BREAD (NORTHUMBERLAND)

450 g/1 lb barley flour	1 teaspoon bicarbonate of soda
100 g/4 oz plain white flour	2 teaspoons cream of tartar
1 teaspoon salt	500 ml/1 pint buttermilk

Mix together the barley flour, white flour, salt, bicarbonate of soda and cream of tartar. Stir in the buttermilk to make a firm dough. Shape into a round cake 2·5 cm/1 inch thick, and cook on a very hot griddle, hotplate or heavy frying pan. When cooked on the underside, turn over and cook the second side. This may also be baked at 475°F, 240°C, gas mark 9 for 20 minutes without turning.

CURRANT BREAD

675 g/1½ lb white flour	100 g/4 oz warm butter
100 g/4 oz sugar	250 ml/½ pint warm milk
Pinch of salt	225 g/8 oz mixed dried fruit
25 g/1 oz fresh yeast	50 g/2 oz chopped mixed peel

Mix flour, sugar and salt, and add yeast creamed with a little sugar. Work in warm butter and milk. Knead and leave to prove for 1½ hours. Knead in fruit and peel, and shape into loaves or buns to prove for 45 minutes. Bake at 375°F, 190°C, gas mark 5 for 45 minutes, turning after 20 minutes. Small buns will need about 20 minutes' cooking time. Remove to a wire tray and glaze with a mixture of milk and sugar.

MALT BREAD

675 g/1½ lb white flour
  (or a mixture of plain white
  and wholemeal flour)
25 g/1 oz fresh yeast
¼ teaspoon salt

375 ml/¾ pint lukewarm water
2 tablespoons black treacle
2 tablespoons extract of malt
50 g/2 oz butter
50 g/2 oz sultanas

Sieve flour into a bowl. Cream yeast with a little water, and dissolve salt in rest of water. Add the yeast and water to the flour, then add treacle, malt, butter and sultanas. Knead to an even texture, prove till double in size, knead again and shape into tins. Prove until the mixture reaches the top of the tins, then bake at 425°F, 220°C, gas mark 7 for 45 minutes, turning the loaves halfway through cooking time. Remove to a wire tray and glaze with milk and sugar syrup.

BANNOCK WITH FRUIT

Batter ingredients:

50 g/2 oz plain flour
25 g/1 oz melted butter or lard

65 ml/2½ fl oz warm milk
8 g/¼ oz fresh yeast

Additional ingredients:

175 g/6 oz plain flour
25 g/1 oz caster sugar
65 ml/2½ fl oz warm milk

25 g/1 oz sultanas
25 g/1 oz currants
15 g/½ oz candied peel

Blend batter ingredients together in a mixing bowl and leave for 20–30 minutes until the batter is frothy. Add the additional ingredients and mix well. Knead the dough thoroughly for about 10 minutes on a lightly-floured board. Put the dough to rise in a warm place under a damp cloth and leave for 1 hour, until the dough springs back when pressed gently with a floured finger. Knead the dough again and shape into a ball. Flatten with the hands to approximately 20 cm/8 inches across and 1·25 cm/½ inch thick. Put on a greased and floured tray and slash half through with a sharp knife into eight equal sections. Brush top with milk, cover with a greased paper and leave to rise until the dough feels springy (about 45 minutes). Brush top again with milk, and bake towards the top of the oven set at 400°F, 200°C, gas mark 6 for 20 minutes. Cool on a wire tray.

GLOUCESTER BRAN BREAD

300 g/10 oz bran	75 g/3 oz butter
300 g/10 oz plain flour	1 tablespoon brown sugar or
¾ teaspoon salt	honey
¾ teaspoon bicarbonate of soda	500 ml/1 pint milk

Mix together the bran, flour, salt and bicarbonate of soda. Rub in the butter. Add the sugar or honey, and the milk to make a firm dough. Put into a greased 675 g/1½ lb loaf tin and bake at 350°F, 180°C, gas mark 4 for 1½ hours.

KENTISH HUFFKINS

675 g/1½ lb plain flour	375 ml/¾ pint warm milk and
1½ teaspoons salt	water
15 g/½ oz yeast	50 g/2 oz lard
1 teaspoon caster sugar	

Sift the flour and salt into a warm bowl. Cream the yeast and sugar and add the warm liquid. Make a well in the centre of the flour and work in the yeast mixture. Knead to a soft dough. Cover and leave in a warm place until double in size. Rub in the lard and leave to rise again. Divide into pieces weighing 50 g/2 oz and roll into balls with the hands. Roll out flat about 2·5 cm/ 1 inch thick and leave on a baking tin for 20 minutes to prove. Bake at 425°F, 220°C, gas mark 7 for 15 minutes. Turn over and continue baking for 10 minutes.

MUFFINS

1 egg
250 ml/½ pint milk
25 g/1 oz butter

450 g/1 lb flour
1 teaspoon salt
15 g/½ oz fresh yeast

Beat together egg, milk and warm butter. Put flour and salt into a bowl, and pour in yeast creamed with a little warm water. Add butter, milk and egg mixture, and knead thoroughly to a soft but not sticky dough. Cover and prove for 1½ hours. Roll out dough 1·25 cm/½ inch thick on a floured board, and cut out muffins with a large tumbler. Bake on a griddle, turning as soon as bottoms are browned, or on a baking sheet in a hot oven at 450°F, 230°C, gas mark 8 for 15 minutes, turning halfway through cooking.

ABERDEEN BUTTERY ROWIES

450 g/1 lb plain flour
1 teaspoon salt
25 g/1 oz yeast
1 tablespoon caster sugar

375 ml/¾ pint tepid water
175 g/6 oz lard
175 g/6 oz butter

Sieve the flour and the salt into a warm basin. Cream the yeast and the sugar in a smaller bowl, then add the flour along with the water. Set in a warm place to rise to twice its bulk. Beat the lard and butter together until thoroughly blended. Divide into three portions and divide each into small pieces. Roll out the dough on a floured board and dot the first portion of fat over it in small pats. Fold into three and roll out as for flaky pastry. Repeat the operation twice, so as to use up all the fat. Divide into pieces of equal size and form into oval shapes. Put on a greased and floured baking tray and prove in a warm place for 30 minutes. Bake at 400°F, 200°C, gas mark 6 for 20–25 minutes.

BAPS

450 g/1 lb plain flour
50 g/2 oz lard
2 level teaspoons salt
1 level teaspoon sugar

25 g/1 oz yeast
250 ml/½ pint lukewarm milk and
water

Sieve the flour, rub in the lard and sugar. Cream the yeast in half the liquid and dissolve the salt in the rest. Mix into the flour, knead and prove until double in size. Divide into pieces and make into small loaves about 10 cm/4 inches across. Brush with milk, put on to a greased baking sheet, prove again, and bake at 450°F, 230°C, gas mark 8 for 20 minutes.

SALLY LUNNS

350 g/12 oz plain flour
½ teaspoon salt
15 g/½ oz yeast
1 teaspoon sugar

375 ml/¾ pint milk
50 g/2 oz melted butter
1 egg

Warm the flour and salt. Cream the yeast with the sugar, add warm milk, and stir into the flour with melted butter and egg. Knead well and divide in half. Shape the pieces to fit two greased 15 cm/6 inch round cake tins or soufflé dishes. Leave in a warm place until risen to the top of the tins. Brush with egg and bake at 450°F, 230°C, gas mark 8 for 30 minutes. If the Sally Lunns are to be eaten hot, they should be split in four and spread thickly with butter, then the slices replaced and cut into wedges. They should be covered with a damp cloth and reheated in the oven until the butter has melted.

DEVONSHIRE SPLITS

450 g/1 lb plain flour
½ teaspoon salt
15 g/½ oz yeast
1 teaspoon caster sugar

25 g/1 oz butter
250 ml/½ pint skim milk
  (or 125 ml/¼ pint milk and
  125 ml/¼ pint water)

Sieve the flour and salt into a basin. Cream the yeast with the caster sugar and a little lukewarm milk. Melt the butter in the remaining milk. Pour all the liquid into a well in the centre of the flour and mix to a dough. Leave to prove in a warm place for 1 hour. Divide mixture into twelve pieces and knead each into a ball. Flatten into a round 1·25 cm/½ inch thick with the hands. Leave to prove for 20 minutes on a greased and floured baking tin in a warm place. Brush with milk and bake at 450°F, 230°C, gas mark 8 for 15 minutes. Cut through and serve hot with butter or Devonshire cream. (If serving the splits cold, sandwich them with jam and Devonshire cream.)

CORNISH SPLITS

450 g/1 lb plain flour
¼ teaspoon salt
15 g/½ oz yeast
15 g/½ oz caster sugar
250 ml/½ pint milk
25 g/1 oz butter

Sieve the flour and salt into a warm basin. Cream the yeast and sugar together and gradually add the milk. Add the milk mixture and the melted butter to the flour and mix to a smooth dough. Cover and leave in a warm place for 45 minutes. Shape into small round cakes and put on to a floured baking sheet. Bake at 475°F, 240°C, gas mark 9 for 15 minutes. Split and butter and serve very hot. Otherwise, leave them until cold, then split and butter; or split and eat with cream, jam or treacle. Splits eaten with cream and treacle are known as 'Thunder and Lightning'.

TEA CAKES

225 g/8 oz plain flour
Pinch of salt
15 g/½ oz butter
15 g/½ oz yeast
1 teaspoon sugar
1 egg
125 ml/¼ pint milk
50 g/2 oz sultanas

Warm the flour and salt and rub in the butter. Cream the yeast and sugar and add to the flour together with the egg, milk and sultanas. Knead well and leave in a warm place until double its size. Knead well again and divide into three, shaping into rather flat, round cakes. Put on greased tins, and prove for 10 minutes. Bake at 450°F, 230°C, gas mark 8 for 12 minutes. Brush over with milk and glaze with sugar immediately after removing from oven.

OVEN BOTTOM CAKE (YORKSHIRE)

100 g/4 oz bread dough   25 g/1 oz lard

Take the lump of dough and put on to a pastry board. Cut the lard into six pieces and push the pieces roughly into the dough. Fold over the dough and with the knuckles of one hand press the fat into the dough, giving it a lumpy appearance. Put on to a greased baking sheet and bake at 450°F, 230°C, gas mark 8 for about 15 minutes until golden-brown. Take out of the oven, wrap in a tea towel and place on a cushion. To serve, cut the cake in irregular pieces, split open and spread thickly with butter and jam. This cake was traditionally made at the end of baking day, having been put into the bottom of the oven when the loaves were taken out.

DERBYSHIRE PYCLETS

225 g/8 oz plain flour   1 teaspoon sugar
1 teaspoon salt   1 egg
8 g/¼ oz yeast   250 ml/½ pint milk

Put the flour and salt into a warm bowl. Cream the yeast and sugar, and add the beaten egg and warm milk. Add the liquid to the warm dry ingredients to make a thin batter, adding a little more warm milk if necessary. Cover the bowl and leave in a warm place for 30 minutes until double in size. Heat a griddle, hotplate or heavy frying pan and grease it lightly. Pour a small cupful of the yeast mixture on to the griddle. Cook one side, turn and cook the other side.

POTATO WHOLEMEAL BREAD

225 g/8 oz potatoes	25 g/1 oz butter
675 g/1½ lb 100% wholemeal flour	15 g/½ oz yeast
250 ml/½ pint hot potato water	3 level teaspoons salt
8 g/¼ oz sugar	

Use freshly boiled and sieved potatoes. Mix the potatoes, hot water, sugar and butter in a bowl, stirring until the mixture is well blended. Allow to cool to lukewarm. Crumble in the yeast, mix and leave in a warm place for 10 minutes. Add the flour and salt gradually to make a soft dough that does not stick to the bowl or hands. Knead until smooth and elastic. Put in a large bowl, cover with a clean cloth, and put in a warm place to rise until the dough is double in size. Knead again and shape into two loaves. Put into greased 450 g/1 lb loaf tins, cover and leave to rise until double in bulk. Bake at 450°F, 230°C, gas mark 8 for 15 minutes. Reduce heat to 375°F, 190°C, gas mark 5 and continue baking for 35–40 minutes until the bread gives a hollow sound when tapped on the bottom. Thorough cooking is essential. Turn out on a wire rack and cool. Potatoes give a pleasingly different flavour and texture to bread and cakes, and help keep them fresh and moist. Choose 'floury' potatoes and make sure they are well drained after cooking.

SAVOURY WILTSHIRE TEABREAD

100 g/4 oz rindless streaky bacon, finely chopped	50 g/2 oz dripping
4 sticks celery, chopped	2 level tablespoons chopped parsley
1 small onion, skinned and grated	250 ml/½ pint milk less 2 table-
450 g/1 lb self-raising flour	spoons
¼ level teaspoon salt	1 egg
Pepper	

Place finely-chopped bacon in a pan and fry gently for 2 minutes. Add chopped celery and grated onion and fry gently for 5 minutes. Cool. Sift together the flour, salt and pepper and rub in the dripping until the mixture resembles fine breadcrumbs. Stir bacon mixture into flour with the parsley. Beat together the milk and the egg and stir into the flour. Knead very lightly on a floured surface, shape into a rectangle and place in a greased 900 g/2 lb loaf tin. Bake at 375°F, 190°C, gas mark 5 for 1 hour. Remove from the tin and serve sliced, warm or cold, with butter.

CHEESE AND WALNUT LOAF

225 g/8 oz self-raising flour
1 level teaspoon dry mustard
  powder
1 level teaspoon salt
Pepper
75 g/3 oz butter

100 g/4 oz Cheddar cheese,
  grated
25 g/1 oz walnuts, chopped
2 eggs
125 ml/¼ pint milk

Sieve the flour, mustard and seasoning into a bowl and rub in the fat until the mixture resembles fine breadcrumbs. Stir in the grated cheese and chopped walnuts. Beat the eggs and milk together and add to the dry ingredients to give a soft dropping consistency. Place the mixture in a greased 450 g/1 lb loaf tin, smooth the top and bake in the centre of oven at 350°F, 180°C, gas mark 4 for ¾–1 hour until golden-brown and cooked through. Cool on a wire tray.

SCOTTISH BARLEY BANNOCKS

450 g/1 lb barley meal
100 g/4 oz plain white flour
2 teaspoons cream of tartar

½ teaspoon salt
300 ml/12 fl oz buttermilk
2 teaspoons bicarbonate of soda

Mix together barley meal, flour, cream of tartar and salt. Stir the bicarbonate of soda into the milk and stir quickly. When it fizzes up, pour into the flour mixture. Make into a soft dough and roll out very lightly 1·25 cm/½ inch thick. Cut into rounds the size of a meat plate and put on a hot griddle, hotplate or thick frying pan. Bake gently until the underside is brown. Turn and brown the other side.

Scones and such

BASIC DRY SCONE MIX

450 g/1 lb self-raising flour   75 g/3 oz butter
2 rounded teaspoons baking
  powder

Sift together flour and baking powder, and rub in butter until the mixture looks like fine breadcrumbs. Store in a plastic container in a cold place, keeping tightly covered. Half this mixture with the addition of 125 ml/¼ pint milk or water makes twelve scones.

For sweet scones, use milk, or an egg for 3 tablespoons of milk.

For cheese scones, add finely-grated dry cheese, and use water for a fluffy texture.

With plain flour, use 1 teaspoon bicarbonate of soda and 2 teaspoons cream of tartar as raising agents. If sour milk is used, for better texture, use only 1 teaspoon cream of tartar.

When the scones are mixed, roll out and cut in rounds. Place close together on greased baking sheet, and bake at 450°F, 230°C, gas mark 8 for 12 minutes.

SKYE SCONES

225 g/8 oz plain flour   1 heaped tablespoon caster sugar
Pinch of salt   50 g/2 oz butter
2 rounded teaspoons baking   1 egg
  powder   Milk

Sift the flour with the salt and baking powder. Stir in the caster sugar and rub in the butter. Break the egg into a measuring cup and make up to 125 ml/¼ pint with milk. Whisk the egg and milk together. Make a well in the centre of the flour mixture and pour in the liquid (saving a little for brushing the scones). Using a knife, cut and fold to moisten all the mixture until a spongy, non-sticky ball of dough is formed. Turn the dough on to a floured board, and knead for 30 seconds to smooth the underside. Turn the dough over and roll out gently to 1·25 cm/½ inch thickness. Form into one large round cake (for breakfast) or cut into 5 cm/ 2 inch rounds (for tea). Place on a buttered baking sheet, and brush with the reserved egg and milk. Sprinkle thickly with granulated sugar. Put into an oven set at 500°F, 250°C, gas mark 10, and then immediately turn the oven down to 425°F, 220°C, gas mark 7 for 10–12 minutes until the scones are puffy and a rich brown. Serve slightly warm, spread with cool butter.

WHEATMEAL SPOON SCONES

300 g/10 oz wholemeal flour
175 g/6 oz plain flour
1 level teaspoon salt
50 g/2 oz granulated sugar
1 level teaspoon bicarbonate of
  soda

2 level teaspoons cream of tartar
50 g/2 oz butter
1 tablespoon black treacle
250 ml/scant ½ pint milk

Sieve together dry ingredients and stir in sugar. Rub in butter, then mix with the treacle and milk to give a heavy dropping consistency. Drop spoonfuls of the mixture on to a baking sheet dusted with wholemeal flour. Brush lightly with milk and dredge with flour or rolled oats. Bake at 450°F, 230°C, gas mark 8 for 15 minutes.

SCOTCH PANCAKES OR DROP SCONES

225 g/8 oz plain flour
1 level teaspoon salt
2 level teaspoons cream of tartar
1 level teaspoon bicarbonate of
  soda

2 teaspoons caster sugar
2 eggs
2 teaspoons golden syrup
200 ml/8 fl oz milk

These are best cooked on a heavy iron griddle; but they can be cooked on the solid hotplate of an electric cooker, or in a frying pan with a cast iron base. Sieve together the flour, salt, cream of tartar and bicarbonate of soda. Add the sugar and mix to a very thick batter with the beaten eggs, syrup and milk, so that the mixture will only just fall from the spoon, yet will flow into a pancake on the hot griddle. Leave the batter to stand just long enough for bubbles of gas to rise to the surface. Lightly grease the pan or griddle and heat until you can feel the heat 2·5 cm/1 inch above the surface. Drop the mixture into small rounds from a dessertspoon, held point downwards. When bubbles start to burst, and the underside is a pale brown, turn each pancake over. Allow approximately 3 minutes for the first side and 2 minutes for the second. As the pancakes come off the pan, slip them into a folded tea towel to keep the steam in. Serve fresh and buttered. Any left over can later be toasted, or fried and served topped with eggs.

CREMPOG OR WELSH PANCAKES

175 g/6 oz plain flour
½ teaspoon bicarbonate of soda
½ teaspoon cream of tartar
50 g/2 oz sugar

25 g/1 oz butter
½ teaspoon vinegar
1 egg
Milk to mix

Sieve together the flour, bicarbonate of soda and cream of tartar. Stir in the sugar, and rub in the butter. Make a well in the centre and stir in the beaten egg and enough milk to make a thin batter. Add the vinegar last. Heat a griddle, hotplate or heavy frying pan, and grease it well. Put 2 tablespoons of the batter on to the hot surface and cook until brown on the underside. Turn and finish cooking the other side. Butter well and eat hot. These were traditionally made as large pancakes and spread with butter, then piled on a plate and cut into quarters.

WELSH OATMEAL PANCAKES (CREMPOG GEIRCH)

175 g/6 oz fine oatmeal   1 teaspoon sugar
450 g/1 lb plain white flour   A little warm milk
15 g/½ oz yeast

Mix the oatmeal and flour. Cream the yeast with the sugar and add a little warm milk. Add to the flour mixture, adding more warm milk as necessary to make a thin batter. Cook like pancakes in a thick frying pan, and eat hot with butter.

TYNESIDE SINGIN' HINNY

225 g/8 oz plain flour   50 g/2 oz lard
½ level teaspoon baking powder   75 g/3 oz currants
½ level teaspoon salt   Milk
50 g/2 oz butter

Sift flour, baking powder and salt together and rub in fats until mixture is like fine breadcrumbs. Stir in currants and mix with enough milk to make a stiff paste. Roll into a large cake 1·25 cm/½ inch thick (or cut into 7·5 cm/3 inch rounds), prick top and put on a greased griddle or frying pan. Cook both sides until golden, split and butter.

YORKSHIRE FAT CAKES

350 g/12 oz plain flour   100 g/4 oz lard
1 teaspoon baking powder   15 g/½ oz yeast
1 teaspoon salt   125 ml/¼ pint milk

Sift the flour, baking powder and salt into a basin. Rub in the lard. Make a well in the centre of the mixture. Cream the yeast with a little warm milk, and leave to stand for 5 minutes. Add to the flour mixture and then add the remaining warm milk. Mix to a soft dough. Divide into four pieces and roll these out in circles 1·25 cm/½ inch thick. Put on to a greased baking sheet and bake at

375°F, 190°C, gas mark 5 for 30 minutes. While still hot, split and butter thickly.

SHROPSHIRE FRIED CAKES

225 g/8 oz self-raising flour	Milk to mix
50 g/2 oz butter or lard	Bacon fat for frying
50 g/2 oz sugar	

Sieve the flour and rub in the fat. Add the sugar and mix with enough milk to make a firm dough. Turn the mixture on to a floured board and roll out 1·25 cm/½ inch thick, and cut into rounds. Put into a smoking hot frying pan with plenty of bacon fat. Cook until well risen and brown underneath. Turn over and cook the other side until brown. Eat while fresh.

SURREY LARDIES

225 g/8 oz bread dough	50 g/2 oz sugar
50 g/2 oz lard	25 g/1 oz currants

Roll the bread dough into a rectangle 0·5 cm/¼ inch thick. Divide the lard and sugar into three portions. Spread dough with one portion of lard and one portion of sugar. Fold into three and roll again. Repeat the process twice, adding currants the last time. Roll out and cut into rounds. Score with a knife and put on a greased baking sheet. Leave to rise for 20 minutes in a warm place. Bake at 450°F, 230°C, gas mark 8 for 25 minutes.

SUFFOLK BROTHERLY LOVE

450 g/1 lb bread dough	50 g/2 oz sugar
25 g/1 oz lard	

When making a batch of bread, take some of the dough and roll out in a rectangle 1·25 cm/½ inch thick. Cut lard in thin flakes, and spread over the dough. Scatter the surface with the sugar. Roll up like a Swiss roll, and cut in 2·5 cm/1 inch slices. Put on a greased baking sheet and bake at 425°F, 220°C, gas mark 7 for 30 minutes.

CORNISH HEAVY CAKE

2·25 kg/5 lb plain flour
850 g/1 lb 14 oz lard
850 g/1 lb 14 oz sugar
95 g/3¾ oz baking powder

625 ml/1¼ pints milk
2·25 kg/5 lb mixed dried fruit
  and chopped peel

Sift the flour, sugar and baking powder and lightly rub in the lard. Drop in the fruit and add the milk all at once, mixing lightly to a soft dough. Weigh out 550 g/1¼ lb of mixture for each 17·5 cm/7 inch sponge tin. Brush the top with beaten egg and bake at 425°F, 220°C, gas mark 7 for 30 minutes.

GLOUCESTER LARDY CAKE

450 g/1 lb basic bread dough
  which has risen once
100 g/4 oz lard

100 g/4 oz brown sugar
75 g/3 oz sultanas
50 g/2 oz currants

Roll out the dough into a rectangle as for puff pastry. Spread one-third of the lard, sugar and fruit over two-thirds of the surface and fold into three. Repeat this twice more and then set aside to rest. Roll the dough mixture out again, roll up like a Swiss roll and cut into two. Place each half cut-side down in greased 12·5 cm/5 inch diameter cake tins. Cover with a clean towel and leave in a warm place to prove. Bake at 400°F, 200°C, gas mark 6 for 45 minutes. Turn out of tins immediately when cooked.

WILTSHIRE SEED LARDY CAKE

450 g/1 lb bread dough
175 g/6 oz lard

175 g/6 oz sugar
15 g/½ oz caraway seeds

Roll out the dough into an oblong. Cut the lard into flakes. Put half the lard and half the sugar on to two-thirds of the dough.

Fold dough into three, bringing up the bottom third first and folding the top third over it. Seal the ends with a rolling pin. Give a half turn and roll into an oblong. Repeat the process, scattering on the caraway seeds with the sugar. Roll to fit a baking tin and score across in diamonds. Leave to rise for 30 minutes in a warm place and bake at 400°F, 200°C, gas mark 6 for 1 hour. Leave to stand for 5 minutes so that the fat soaks into the cake.

HARVEST BETSY CAKE

225 g/8 oz barley flour
225 g/8 oz plain flour
1½ teaspoons baking powder
½ teaspoons salt
100 g/4 oz butter

100 g/4 oz caster sugar
2 teaspoons golden syrup
250 ml/½ pint milk
225 g/8 oz sultanas

Sift the two kinds of flour together with baking powder and salt. Cream butter and sugar, and add syrup. Add the flour mixture and the milk alternately, then fold in the sultanas. Put into a buttered 17·5 cm/7 inch cake tin and bake at 350°F, 180°C, gas mark 4 for 1½ hours.

SUFFOLK HARVEST CAKE

450 g/1 lb white flour
100 g/4 oz cornflour
2 teaspoons baking powder
½ teaspoon bicarbonate of soda
Pinch of ground nutmeg
Pinch of ground cinnamon
25 g/1 oz finely crumbled yeast

450 g/1 lb sugar
225 g/8 oz lard
250 ml/½ pint milk
2 eggs
450 g/1 lb currants
100 g/4 oz chopped candied
  lemon peel

Sift together the flour, cornflour, baking powder, bicarbonate of soda, nutmeg and cinnamon. Rub in the crumbled yeast and stir in the sugar. Cut the lard into flakes and work into the dry ingredients. Beat together the eggs and milk and stir them into the other ingredients. Finally stir in currants and candied peel until the ingredients are well blended. Put into two greased and lined 25 cm/10 inch round tins and leave in a warm place for 30 minutes to rise. Bake at 350°F, 180°C, gas mark 4 for 2 hours.

SUFFOLK RUSKS

225 g/8 oz self-raising flour   1 egg
Pinch of salt   Milk or water to mix
75 g/3 oz butter

Sieve the flour and salt together. Rub in the butter lightly and mix with the beaten egg and just enough milk or water to make a smooth dough. Roll out lightly 2·5 cm/1 inch thick and cut in 6·25 cm/2½ inch rounds. Bake at 450°F, 230°C, gas mark 8 for 10 minutes. Remove from the oven and split in half. Put on baking sheets with the cut sides upwards. Bake at 375°F, 190°C, gas mark 5 for about 15 minutes until crisp and golden. Cool and serve with butter and cheese. These rusks store well in a tin.

WELSH OATCAKES (BARA CEIRCH)

225 g/8 oz medium oatmeal   250 ml/½ pint warm water
1 teaspoon bacon fat

Put the oatmeal into a basin. Melt the bacon fat in the water and stir into the oatmeal to make a fairly stiff dough. Put on a board dusted with oatmeal and divide into small pieces. Make each into a ball and press down, then roll out very thinly, pressing with the fingers where necessary to avoid cracks. Cook on a hot griddle, hotplate or frying pan. When the oatcakes start to curl at the sides, turn them and bake to a pale biscuit colour.

DERBYSHIRE OATCAKE

225 g/8 oz medium or fine   25 g/1 oz yeast
   oatmeal   1 teaspoon sugar
225 g/8 oz plain flour   250 ml/½ pint warm water
Pinch of salt

Sift the oatmeal and flour with the salt into a warm basin. Cream the yeast and sugar and gradually work in the warm water. Stir the yeast liquid into the flour mixture to form a thin batter, adding a little more warm water if necessary. Leave to stand in a warm place for 30 minutes until well risen. Heat a griddle, hotplate or heavy frying pan and grease it lightly. Pour a small cupful of batter on to the griddle and cook for 2 minutes. Turn and bake the other side. Eat hot. These oatcakes can later be fried with bacon, or toasted and served with butter or dripping.

POTATO BISCUITS

100 g/4 oz plain flour   75 g/3 oz butter
1 level teaspoon salt   100 g/4 oz cold mashed potatoes
100 g/4 oz rolled oats

Mix flour, salt and oats. Rub in the butter and then knead in the potatoes until a stiff dough is formed. Roll out thinly. Cut into 7·5 cm/3 inch rounds. Put on baking sheets and cook at 325°F, 170°C, gas mark 3 for 20–25 minutes until crisp and brown. Cool on a wire rack. These biscuits are excellent with cheese.

CHAPTER 7
TIME FOR TEA

TEA has always been a very important meal in a farmhouse, marking the end of the working day. It is therefore often served about 6 p.m., and combines supper dishes with cakes and a pot of tea, thus dispensing with a later, cooked evening meal. The farming family has instead a substantial bedtime snack of pies, sandwiches, cakes and hot drinks in the late evening.

A farmhouse tea or 'High Tea' can consist of cold meats or pies and salads, bread and butter, sandwiches, scones and teabreads, jams, cold sweets (such as stewed fruit, jellies or trifles), and a profusion of cakes and biscuits. Spice cakes, gingerbreads, fruit cakes and sponges are all popular, with iced sponges and cream-filled cakes on special occasions. Many of the plainer cakes appear again at the mid-morning break, or form part of next day's packed midday meal.

Use unsalted butter for sweet scones, cakes and biscuits if possible.

More scones, breads and plain cakes

GINGER SCONES

225 g/8 oz self-raising flour
1 teaspoon ground ginger
¼ teaspoon bicarbonate of soda
½ teaspoon cream of tartar
2 teaspoons caster sugar

40 g/1½ oz lard
1 egg
1 teaspoon golden syrup
65 ml/2½ fl oz milk

Sift the dry ingredients. Rub in the lard until fine. Add beaten egg, combined with the syrup and milk, to the dry ingredients. Mix to a soft dough. Turn dough on to a floured board and knead very lightly. Divide into two; shape each piece into a round and roll gently to about 15 cm/6 inches in diameter. Cut into half and each half into three, making six small triangular scones of each round. Bake near the top of the oven for 10 minutes at 400°F, 200°C, gas mark 6. If not quite done in 10 minutes, reduce the heat and move to a lower shelf in the oven for a further 5–10 minutes.

FAVOURITE SCONE RING

225 g/8 oz self-raising flour
Pinch of salt
50 g/2 oz butter
50 g/2 oz sugar

50 g/2 oz mixed dried fruit
1 egg
5 tablespoons milk

Sieve the flour and salt into a bowl and rub in butter. Add the sugar and dried fruit. Beat egg with the milk. Add most of the liquid to the mixture to make a fairly soft dough. Divide the dough into eight and lightly knead each piece into a round. Place scones overlapping to form a ring on a greased baking tray. Brush the tops only with the remaining milk and egg liquid. Bake at 425°F, 220°C, gas mark 7 for 20–25 minutes until golden-brown and cooked through. Cool on a wire tray.

NORTH COUNTRY OVERNIGHT SPICE CAKE

450 g/1 lb plain flour	2 teaspoons mixed spice
175 g/6 oz lard	2½ teaspoons bicarbonate of soda
50 g/2 oz unsalted butter	225 g/8 oz currants
225 g/8 oz caster sugar	225 g/8 oz raisins
100 g/4 oz ground almonds	250 ml/½ pint sour milk

Rub the fat into the flour until the mixture resembles fine crumbs. Sift in the sugar, almonds, spice and soda. Scatter the currants and raisins over the mixture. Mix to a soft dough with the milk. Place the mixture in a 20 cm/8 inch round cake tin, greased and lined with greaseproof paper. Leave overnight. Next day, bake at 325°F, 170°C, gas mark 3 for 1 hour, then reduce the heat to 300°F, 150°C, gas mark 2 for a further 1½ hours or until the cake is springy and brown. Cool well on a wire rack before cutting.

FARMHOUSE TEA LOAF

100 g/4 oz mixed dried fruit	2 tablespoons chunky marmalade
100 g/4 oz caster sugar	1 egg
125 ml/¼ pint hot tea	225 g/8 oz self-raising flour

Place the fruit, sugar and tea in a bowl. Leave to stand for at least 6 hours, but preferably overnight. Add the marmalade and egg, sieve in the flour and then mix well. Turn the mixture into a greased and base-lined 450 g/1 lb loaf tin and bake at 350°F, 180°C, gas mark 4 for 50–60 minutes, until cooked. Test with a skewer. Allow to cool, and serve thinly sliced and spread with butter.

SEED BREAD

225 g/8 oz plain flour	1 egg
¼ teaspoon salt	1 tablespoon caraway seeds
1 teaspoon bicarbonate of soda	50 g/2 oz chopped mixed peel
50 g/2 oz butter	125 ml/¼ pint hot water
50 g/2 oz sugar	

Sieve the flour, salt and bicarbonate of soda into a bowl. Put the butter, sugar, peel and caraway seeds into another bowl and pour over them the hot water. Stir well and leave to cool. Beat up the egg and fold this into the liquid mixture. Add the sieved dry ingredients and beat very hard. Pour into a greased 450 g/1 lb loaf tin, and bake at 375°F, 190°C, gas mark 5 for 50 minutes.

BARM BRACK

450 g/1 lb plain flour	250 ml/½ pint milk
¼ level teaspoon nutmeg	2 well-beaten eggs
Pinch of salt	225 g/8 oz sultanas
50 g/2 oz butter	225 g/8 oz currants
20 g/¾ oz fresh yeast	100 g/4 oz mixed chopped
50 g/2 oz sugar	candied peel

Sieve the flour, nutmeg and salt together. Rub in the butter. Cream the yeast with a little of the sugar. Add remaining sugar to flour mixture. Warm the milk gently, and add to the liquid yeast and eggs (reserve a little egg for glazing the bread). Beat liquid into dry ingredients until batter is stiff but elastic. Fold in the dried fruit and peel, and turn into a buttered 20 cm/8 inch cake tin. Cover with a cloth and put into a warm place for 1 hour. Brush with beaten egg and bake in a fairly hot oven, 400°F, 200°C, gas mark 6 for 1 hour. Brush over with 1 tablespoon sugar dissolved in 2 tablespoons boiling water, and return to the oven for 3 minutes. Turn out and cool on a wire rack. Serve in slices with butter. When stale, the bread can be toasted and buttered.

BARA BRIETH

125 ml/¼ pint milk	½ teaspoon mixed spice
25 g/1 oz yeast	350 g/12 oz mixed currants,
900 g/2 lb plain flour	sultanas, raisins
225 g/8 oz butter	100 g/4 oz chopped mixed
225 g/8 oz brown sugar	candied peel
Pinch of salt	

Mix yeast with the warmed milk. Put the flour into a bowl and rub in butter. Add sugar, fruit, salt and spice and mix in the warm liquid. Cover and leave to rise in a warm place for 1½ hours until double its size. Knead into a loaf shape and put into two 450 g/1 lb loaf tins. Leave to rise for 10 minutes. Bake at 400°F, 200°C, gas mark 6 for 1 hour. Cool, slice thinly and spread with butter.

BREAD PUDDING (CAKE)

8 slices bread (toast thickness)	2 tablespoons marmalade
250 ml/½ pint milk	3 tablespoons self-raising flour
350 g/12 oz mixed dried fruit	2 eggs
50 g/2 oz mixed chopped candied peel	Squeeze of lemon juice
1 apple	1 teaspoon ground cinnamon
3 tablespoons brown sugar	100 g/4 oz butter

Soak the bread in the milk until it is really soft. Add dried fruit and peel, grated peeled apple, sugar, marmalade, flour, eggs, lemon juice and cinnamon. Beat very thoroughly together. Melt the butter and pour half into the mixture. Beat and put into a greased meat tin. Pour on remaining butter. Bake at 300°F, 150°C, gas mark 2 for 1½ hours; then at 350°F, 180°C, gas mark 4 for 30 minutes. Leave until cold, sprinkle with icing sugar, and cut in slices like a cake.

COUNTRY TEA BREAD

200 g/7 oz mixed currants, sultanas and seedless raisins	1 egg
	225 g/8 oz self-raising flour
25 g/1 oz chopped peel	Salt
125 ml/¼ pint tea	25 g/1 oz melted butter
100 g/4 oz clear honey	

Topping:

Clear honey to taste	8 g/¼ oz Demerara sugar
25 g/1 oz chopped walnuts	

Put the fruit, peel, tea and 100 g/4 oz honey into a bowl, cover and leave overnight to allow the fruit to swell and absorb the tea flavour. Stir in the beaten egg, sifted flour and salt and melted butter, in that order. Transfer to a greased 450 g/1 lb loaf tin and bake for about 1 hour 10 minutes at 350°F, 180°C, gas mark 4. After 50 minutes remove the bread from the oven, brush with honey and sprinkle nuts and sugar on top. Trickle more honey over and return to the oven to finish cooking.

APPLE LOAF

450 g/1 lb plain flour, sifted
Pinch of salt
1 teaspoon baking powder
100 g/4 oz butter
100 g/4 oz lard
2 eggs, beaten
50 g/2 oz currants
50 g/2 oz raisins, seeded

1 cooking apple, peeled, cored and sliced
Milk to mix
100 g/4 oz icing sugar, sifted
A little water
1 tart eating apple (red), cored and sliced

Dip the fruit in a little lemon juice as soon as prepared, to prevent discoloration.

Sift together the flour, salt and baking powder. Rub in the fat, mix in the beaten eggs, currants, raisins, cooking apple and milk. Mix well. Turn into a 450 g/1 lb lined loaf tin, and bake in a moderate oven at 375°F, 190°C, gas mark 5 for 40–45 minutes, or until springy and browned. When cool, spread the loaf with a thin icing made with icing sugar and water, and decorate with sliced eating apple. Serve for high tea, especially when salads are scarce.

CUMBERLAND BUTTERMILK CAKE

450 g/1 lb plain flour
75 g/3 oz lard
75 g/3 oz unsalted butter
100 g/4 oz caster sugar
225 g/8 oz chopped candied lemon peel

100 g/4 oz seedless raisins
2 tablespoons marmalade
1 teaspoon bicarbonate of soda
175 ml/7 fl oz buttermilk or sour milk

Sift the flour, and rub in the fats till the mixture resembles fine crumbs. Add the sugar. Scatter the peel and raisins over the surface. Mix the marmalade into the milk, warm to dissolve, then cool. Mix the soda into the milk mixture, and use it to mix the dry ingredients to a soft dough. Place in a lined and greased 20 cm/ 8 inch cake tin, and bake at 325°F, 170°C, gas mark 3 for 1 hour. Lower the heat to 300°F, 150°C, gas mark 2, and bake for a further 45 minutes or until the cake is springy and browned. Cool well before cutting.

DRIPPING CAKE

225 g/8 oz mixed dried fruit and candied peel
75 g/3 oz clarified beef dripping
150 g/5 oz brown sugar
175 ml/7 fl oz water
225 g/8 oz wholemeal flour

1 teaspoon baking powder
Pinch of nutmeg
Pinch of cinnamon
Pinch of mixed spice
½ teaspoon bicarbonate of soda

Put the fruit in a heavy pan with dripping, sugar and water, bring to the boil and simmer for 10 minutes. Leave to cool, then pour into the rest of the ingredients which have been sifted together. Blend well but do not beat. Put into a greased 15 cm/6 inch cake tin and bake at 350°F, 180°C, gas mark 4 for 1¼–1½ hours.

VICTORIAN LUNCHEON CAKE

225 g/8 oz self-raising flour
100 g/4 oz beef dripping
100 g/4 oz soft brown sugar
1 egg

3 tablespoons milk
1 rounded teaspoon baking powder
225 g/8 oz currants

Butter and flour the sides and base of a 15 cm/6 inch loose-bottomed cake tin. Cream the dripping thoroughly, add sugar, and cream again. Sift the flour and baking powder together. Add 2 tablespoons flour to dripping mixture, then the egg and whip again. Continue adding flour gradually with single spoonfuls of milk until both ingredients are absorbed. Turn into the prepared tin. Flour the currants and shake off the surplus flour in a sieve. Turn on to top of cake mixture and work in with a fork, being careful not to let the fork touch the base of the tin. Bake on middle shelf of oven at 325°F, 170°C, gas mark 3 for 1 hour plus 10–15 minutes.

DUNDEE CAKE

225 g/8 oz butter
225 g/8 oz sugar
5 eggs
225 g/8 oz self-raising flour
½ teaspoon nutmeg
350 g/12 oz mixed currants and sultanas

75 g/3 oz ground almonds
75 g/3 oz chopped glacé cherries
50 g/2 oz chopped candied peel
50 g/2 oz split blanched almonds

Cream butter and sugar and add eggs one at a time, each with a sprinkling of flour to avoid curdling. Beat well after each addition. Stir in most of the flour, the nutmeg, the ground almonds and lastly the fruit lightly coated with the rest of the flour. Turn into a 22·5 cm/9 inch cake tin lined with greased paper, smooth the top and arrange almonds on surface. Bake at 325°F, 170°C, gas mark 3 for 2–2½ hours.

LEMON CAKE

100 g/4 oz butter

175 g/6 oz caster sugar

175 g/6 oz self-raising flour

2 eggs

Pinch of salt

125 ml/¼ pint milk

Grated rind and juice of 1 lemon

1 heaped tablespoon caster sugar

Mix butter, sugar, flour, eggs, salt, milk and lemon rind together and bake in a 450 g/1 lb loaf tin for 1 hour at 350°F, 180°C, gas mark 4. Combine the lemon juice and sugar and pour over the cake while still hot.

IRISH WHISKEY CAKE

2 tablespoons Irish whiskey

1 orange

175 g/6 oz sultanas

175 g/6 oz butter

175 g/6 oz sugar

3 eggs

225 g/8 oz plain flour

Pinch of salt

1 teaspoon baking powder

Put the whiskey into a small bowl. Peel the orange thinly and soak the rind in the whiskey for a few hours. Discard the peel. Leave the sultanas to soak in the whiskey while preparing the rest of the cake. Cream the butter and sugar. Add the eggs, one at a time, with a teaspoon of flour for each one, beating well between each addition. Sift flour, salt and baking powder together and fold into the egg mixture. Fold in the whiskey and sultanas. Line a greased 17·5 cm/7 inch round cake tin with greased paper. Put in the mixture and bake in a moderate oven, 350°F, 180°C, gas mark 4. Cool on a wire rack.

GRANNY'S GINGERBREAD

450 g/1 lb black treacle

175 g/6 oz butter

100 g/4 oz dark soft brown sugar

450 g/1 lb wholemeal flour

1 teaspoon baking powder

4 teaspoons ground ginger

A good pinch of salt

2 eggs

125 ml/¼ pint milk

Melt butter in a saucepan with the sugar and treacle, but do not allow the mixture to get too hot. Mix the flour, baking powder, ginger and salt together in a basin. Beat the eggs and milk lightly together. Beat in all the other ingredients. Pour into two greased 450 g/1 lb loaf tins. Bake for 1 hour at 350°F, 180°C, gas mark 4. This gingerbread keeps for weeks in an airtight tin.

LANCASHIRE GINGERBREAD

1 tablespoon bitter marmalade
450 g/1 lb butter
½ level teaspoon bicarbonate of soda
225 g/8 oz wholemeal flour
225 g/8 oz self-raising flour
2 teaspoons ground ginger

2 teaspoons mixed spice
Handful of sultanas
450 g/1 lb black treacle
175 g/6 oz dark soft brown sugar
3 eggs
250 ml/½ pint milk

Melt butter in a saucepan. Add treacle, sugar, milk and marmalade, and stir over a low heat until sugar has dissolved. While this mixture cools, measure into a large bowl the wholemeal and self-raising flours, spice, ginger, bicarbonate of soda and sultanas. Beat eggs and stir with flour mixture, gradually adding warm butter mixture from the saucepan. Pour the cake into a deep baking tin lined with buttered paper, and bake at 350°F, 180°C, gas mark 4 for about 1½ hours. Cool on a sieve and leave the cake until quite cold before cutting.

OLD-FASHIONED GINGERBREAD

225 g/8 oz plain flour
1 level teaspoon bicarbonate of soda
1 heaped teaspoon ground ginger
1 level teaspoon ground cinnamon
75 g/3 oz dark soft brown sugar

Pinch of salt
100 g/4 oz black treacle
75 g/3 oz lard
100 g/4 oz mixed cake fruit
1 egg
4–5 tablespoons milk

Line a 15 cm/6 inch square tin with greaseproof paper. Heat the
oven to 375°F, 190°C, gas mark 5. Put the treacle and the lard in
a small saucepan and melt. Sieve all the dry ingredients together
and add the sugar to them with the fruit. Beat up the egg in a
separate basin and add the milk to it. Pour into the centre of the
flour and stir all together with the melted lard mixture. Mix
thoroughly and turn into the prepared tin. Bake in the centre of
the oven for 30–40 minutes, reducing heat slightly after the first
15 minutes.

GRANNY'S HIGH TEA CAKE

225 g/8 oz self-raising flour
1 rounded teaspoon mixed spice
1 level teaspoon grated nutmeg
Pinch of salt
150 g/5 oz butter
6 level tablespoons golden syrup
100 g/4 oz chopped stoned dates
225 g/8 oz stoned raisins

225 g/8 oz currants
100 g/4 oz sultanas
100 g/4 oz chopped mixed peel
125 ml/¼ pint and 2 tablespoons
  milk
2 eggs
½ level teaspoon bicarbonate of
  soda

Put the butter, syrup, fruit, peel and milk into a saucepan. Heat
slowly until butter is melted, then simmer gently 5 minutes,
stirring once or twice. Remove and cool. Beat eggs lightly. Make a
well in the centre of the dry ingredients. Add the eggs but do not
stir. Stir bicarbonate of soda quickly into cooled mixture, add to
dry ingredients and mix thoroughly, beating well. Put into a
17·5 cm/7 inch cake tin lined with greaseproof paper and brushed
inside with melted butter. Bake for 1¾ hours on the middle shelf
at 325°F, 170°C, gas mark 3. Cool on wire tray.

OVERNIGHT CAKE

450 g/1 lb plain flour
225 g/8 oz currants
225 g/8 oz sultanas
225 g/8 oz sugar

50 g/2 oz mixed peel
175 g/6 oz lard
1 tablespoon golden syrup
2 teaspoons bicarbonate of soda

Mix all dry ingredients and mix in the melted lard and syrup, together with the bicarbonate of soda dissolved in a little milk and 250 ml/½ pint water. Put into a greased tin and leave overnight. Bake at 325°F, 170°C, gas mark 3 for 1¾ hours.

DEVONSHIRE SAFFRON CAKE

¼ teaspoon saffron strands
25 g/1 oz yeast
900 g/2 lb plain flour
225 g/8 oz sugar
¼ teaspoon mixed spice
Pinch of salt

100 g/4 oz lard
100 g/4 oz butter
250 ml/½ pint milk
350 g/12 oz mixed dried fruit
50 g/2 oz chopped mixed peel

Prepare the saffron by cutting up the stamens finely and putting them into 50 ml/2 fl oz warm water. Leave this mixture overnight. Mix the yeast with 2 tablespoons of the flour. Mix with 75 ml/ 3 fl oz warm water and 1 teaspoon sugar. Put in a warm place and leave for 30 minutes. Put the flour into a bowl and mix with the sugar, spice and salt. Rub in the lard and butter until the mixture is like fine breadcrumbs. Add the risen yeast mixture. Warm the milk to lukewarm and stir in the saffron liquid and pieces of saffron. Pour this into the flour mixture, and add the dried fruit and peel. Mix well and leave in a warm place covered with a cloth for 4 hours. Put into two loaf tins and bake at 425°F, 220°C, gas mark 7 for 40 minutes.

DORSET APPLE CAKE

100 g/4 oz lard or butter
225 g/8 oz plain flour
Pinch of salt
1½ teaspoons baking powder

225 g/8 oz peeled, cored and
chopped apples
100 g/4 oz sugar
1 egg

Rub the lard or butter into the flour and salt. Stir in the baking powder. Mix the apples with the sugar and stir into the flour mixture. Mix to a dough with the beaten egg. Put into a greased

20 cm/8 inch cake tin, spreading the mixture about 2·5 cm/1 inch thick. Bake at 350°F, 180°C, gas mark 4 for 50 minutes. Cut open while still hot and spread with butter. A few currants or raisins can be added to the mixture.

PLUM LOAF

225 g/8 oz self-raising flour
50 g/2 oz lard
50 g/2 oz butter
50 g/2 oz sugar
2 tablespoons treacle

100 g/4 oz currants
50 g/2 oz sultanas
50 g/2 oz raisins
Milk

Put flour into bowl and rub in the butter and lard. Add sugar, treacle and fruit. Mix with milk to a stiff mixture. Put into a greaseproof-paper lined 450 g/1 lb loaf tin, and place on low oven shelf at 300°F, 150°C, gas mark 2 for 2 hours.

SEED CAKE

225 g/8 oz plain flour
Pinch of salt
1 teaspoon baking powder
150 g/5 oz butter
150 g/5 oz caster sugar

2 eggs
2 tablespoons milk
3 teaspoons caraway seeds
50 g/2 oz chopped mixed peel

Sieve together the flour, salt and baking powder. Cream the butter and sugar together. Separate the eggs. Beat the yolks and stir them into the creamed butter mixture, then fold in the flour mixture, and stir in the milk. Add the caraway seeds and the peel. Whisk the egg whites very stiffly, and fold them into the cake mixture. Put into a greased 17·5 cm/7 inch tin, and bake on the middle shelf of the oven at 350°F, 180°C, gas mark 4 for 1 hour. Leave in the tin for 5 minutes before turning out on a wire cake tray to cool.

POUND CAKE

300 g/10 oz plain flour
¼ teaspoon salt
1 teaspoon baking powder
225 g/8 oz butter
225 g/8 oz sugar
4 eggs

100 g/4 oz sultanas
100 g/4 oz currants
Grated rind of 1 lemon
50 g/2 oz chopped mixed peel
75 ml/3 fl oz brandy

Sieve together the flour, salt and baking powder. Cream the butter and sugar. Add the eggs to the creamed mixture alternately with some of the flour mixture. When the eggs and flour have been incorporated, add the sultanas, currants, lemon rind and mixed peel, stirring but not beating. Stir in the brandy. Put into a greased 20 cm/8 inch tin and bake at 350°F, 180°C, gas mark 4 for 1¾ hours.

Sweeter cakes

LIGHT CREAM CHOCOLATE CAKE

4 eggs
115 g/4½ oz caster sugar
65 g/2½ oz plain flour

25 g/1 oz drinking chocolate
    powder
125 ml/¼ pint double cream

Whip the eggs and sugar together until light and fluffy. Carefully fold in the flour and drinking chocolate powder sifted together. Bake in two 17·5 cm/7 inch greased sponge tins at 400°F, 200°C, gas mark 6 for 15 minutes. Cool on a wire cake tray. Whip the cream with about 1 tablespoon sugar, and use to sandwich the cakes together when they are quite cold.

MOIST CHOCOLATE CAKE

225 g/8 oz butter	4 eggs
175 g/6 oz light soft brown sugar	175 g/6 oz self-raising flour
175 g/6 oz black treacle	50 g/2 oz cocoa

Cream together the butter, sugar and treacle. Gradually beat in the eggs, adding a tablespoon of sieved flour with the last amount of egg. Sieve together flour and cocoa and fold into the creamed mixture. Turn into two greased and bottom-lined 20 cm/8 inch sponge sandwich tins and bake at 350°F, 180°C, gas mark 4 for 50 minutes. Turn out. When cold sandwich together with fresh cream or buttercream and top with chocolate glacé icing.

SPECIAL DAY COCOA CAKE

5 large eggs	1 level tablespoon cocoa
150 g/5 oz caster sugar	175 g/6 oz butter
150 g/5 oz plain flour	300 g/10 oz sifted icing sugar
1 level teaspoon baking powder	3 tablespoons cocoa
A few drops of vanilla essence	50 g/2 oz grated plain chocolate

Grease a tin measuring 35 × 25 cm (14 × 10 inches) and a 20 cm/ 8 inch round tin, and line with greaseproof paper. Whisk the eggs and sugar together in a bowl placed over a pan of hot water, until really thick. The whisk should leave a good trail. Sieve the flour with a pinch of salt and the baking powder, and fold carefully into the mixture with the vanilla essence, leaving no pockets of dry flour. Place a good half of the mixture into the prepared rectangular tin. Gently shake the tin to level off the surface. Sieve the 1 tablespoon cocoa and fold into remaining mixture. Place in the round cake tin, levelling off the surface again. Bake the cakes one above the other at 400°F, 200°C, gas mark 6 for 10–15 minutes, until cooked and springy to the touch. The bottom cake may take a little longer to cook. Turn out on to a wire tray to cool.

To assemble the cake: Cream together the icing sugar and butter to make a buttercream. Keep out 1 tablespoon of the plain butter-cream for the top. Blend the three tablespoons cocoa with a little boiling water and beat into remaining buttercream. Cut the rectangular cake lengthways into five 35 cm/14 inch even-sized strips. Split the chocolate cake in half, spread the cut surfaces with chocolate buttercream. Spread the strips of cake with butter-cream and form into a circle, placing it on a round of chocolate cake as you do so. Use all the plain sponge to make a complete spiral. Place the remaining chocolate cake on top. Cover with chocolate buttercream, coat the sides with grated chocolate, then lift on to a plate. Soften the plain buttercream with a little hot water; pipe straight lines about an inch apart on the top of the cake. Make a 'feather' pattern by drawing a skewer in alternate directions across the lines.

ICED MARMALADE CAKE

175 g/6 oz butter
175 g/6 oz caster sugar
3 eggs
300 g/10 oz self-raising flour
3 level tablespoons chunky
  marmalade

50 g/2 oz chopped mixed peel
Grated rind of 1 orange
5 tablespoons water

Icing:

100 g/4 oz icing sugar
Juice of 1 orange

2–3 slices of crystallized orange

Line and grease a 17·5 cm/7 inch round cake tin. Beat butter and sugar together until light and creamy. Beat in the egg yolks, one at a time, then 1 tablespoon of the flour. Stir in marmalade, peel, orange, rind and water. Fold in the remaining flour. Whisk the egg whites until just stiff and fold into the cake mixture. Turn into the prepared tin and bake at 350°F, 180°C, gas mark 4 for 1¼ hours until risen and firm to the touch. Cool.

Icing: Blend icing sugar with sufficient orange juice to give a stiff coating consistency. Pour over cake and allow icing to trickle down sides. Leave to set. Cut slices of crystallized orange in half and use to decorate the top.

LEMON SLICES

175 g/6 oz butter
175 g/6 oz caster sugar
3 eggs
175 g/6 oz self-raising flour
Grated rind of 1 lemon

Grated rind of 1 orange
3 drops vanilla essence
Juice of ½ lemon
Juice of ½ orange
Icing sugar

Cream together the butter and sugar. Gradually work in the beaten eggs, alternately with the flour. Add the grated fruit rinds and the essence, and pour into a greased rectangular tin. Bake at 375°F, 190°C, gas mark 5 for 30 minutes. Cool and ice with the fruit juices mixed with enough icing sugar to make a spreading consistency. Cut in squares to serve.

OLD-FASHIONED SPONGE CAKE

3 eggs
75 g/3 oz caster sugar
3 teaspoons hot water

75 g/3 oz plain flour
3 drops vanilla essence

Put the eggs, sugar, water and essence into a bowl and put them over a saucepan which has been half-filled with boiling water. Whisk the mixture well over this heat for 5 minutes. Put the saucepan over the heat, and continue whisking for 5 minutes. Take the bowl from the saucepan and whisk until the mixture is cold and thick. Fold in the sifted flour very carefully. Pour into a 20 cm/8 inch greased and lined cake tin, and bake at 400°F, 200°C, gas mark 6 for 25 minutes. Cool on a wire cake tray. When the cake is cold, split with a sharp knife and fill with jam or lemon curd. Dust the top with icing sugar.

Tarts and biscuits

BLACKBERRY BAKESTONE TART

350 g/12 oz blackberries   25 g/1 oz butter
225 g/8 oz shortcrust pastry   50 g/2 oz brown sugar

Clean the fruit. Rhubarb, gooseberries or apples can be used instead of blackberries. Roll out the pastry into a circle and put the fruit in half of it. Fold over the pastry and seal the edges. Bake at 375°F, 190°C, gas mark 5 for 40 minutes. Take from the oven and, just before serving, gently lift the top and insert small pieces of butter and sprinkle in the brown sugar.

This is a Welsh dish which used to be cooked on a warm greased bakestone, and turned half-way through cooking. It is easier, now, to bake the tart, but it can be cooked in a thick frying pan instead.

RASPBERRY TART

225 g/8 oz puff pastry   175 g/6 oz caster sugar
450 g/1 lb raspberries   3 large eggs

Line a 20 cm/8 inch pie plate with the pastry. Mix the raspberries with half the sugar and put them in the pastry case. Beat the eggs roughly with the remaining sugar and pour over the fruit. Bake at 375°F, 190°C, gas mark 5 for 30 minutes.

WELSH BUTTER TARTS

225 g/8 oz shortcrust pastry   100 g/4 oz raisins
65 g/2½ oz butter   1 egg
175 g/6 oz light soft brown sugar 1 teaspoon vanilla essence
2 tablespoons milk or cream

Line small tartlet tins with the pastry. Melt the butter and mix all the other ingredients together. Fill the pastry cases and bake at 50°F, 180°C, gas mark 4 for 25 minutes. Makes 12–15 tarts.

BERWICK MAY DAY TARTS

150 g/5 oz plain flour
25 g/1 oz lard
40 g/1½ oz salted butter
50 g/2 oz unsalted butter,
  softened
50 g/2 oz caster sugar
1 egg

25 g/1 oz ground almonds
25 g/1 oz chopped candied peel
50 g/2 oz currants
Almond essence or rose-water to
  taste
Lemon glacé icing

Rub the lard and salted butter into the flour, and mix to a stiff
pastry dough with cold water. Roll out, and line twelve 6·25 cm/
2½ inch tartlet pans, well greased. Cream together the unsalted
butter and sugar, and beat in the egg. Sift in the almonds, add the
peel, currants and flavouring, and mix thoroughly. Fill the pastry
shells with the mixture. Trim the pastry edges and use any scraps
to make a decorative design on each tartlet. Bake the tartlets at
400°F, 200°C, gas mark 6 for 7 minutes, then reduce the heat to
350°F, 180°C, gas mark 4, for a further 15 minutes. While still
slightly warm, trickle the icing over the tartlets.

STRAWBERRY TARTLETS

350 g/12 oz shortcrust pastry
450 g/1 lb ripe strawberries

65 g/2½ oz icing sugar
4 eggs

Roll out the pastry and line sixteen tartlet tins with it. Crush the
strawberries and mix them with the sugar. Whisk the eggs and
gradually add them to the strawberry mixture. Beat the mixture
until well blended and pour into the pastry cases. Bake at 375°F,
190°C, gas mark 5 for 12 minutes.

BISCUITS FOR THE DIGESTION

100 g/4 oz porridge oats
150 g/5 oz self-raising flour
50 g/2 oz lard
½ teaspoon bicarbonate of soda

25 g/1 oz sugar
1 tablespoon syrup
Pinch salt

Mix together the dry ingredients. Melt lard, sugar, syrup and bicarbonate of soda in a pan and add to dry ingredients. Roll out very thin, cut out and place on a greased tray. Bake at 350°F, 180°C, gas mark 4 for 10 minutes.

NORFOLK SHORTCAKES

225 g/8 oz plain flour
½ teaspoon baking powder
100 g/4 oz butter or lard

40 g/1½ oz granulated sugar
40 g/1½ oz currants
65 ml/2½ fl oz water

Sieve the flour with the baking powder and rub in half the fat. Divide the rest of the fat into three portions; also the currants and sugar. Mix the flour into a pliable paste with the cold water and roll it out into a long strip. Spread this with dabs of fat and sprinkle with sugar and currants. Fold into three layers, give the paste a half turn and repeat this process twice more. Roll out thinly, cut into twenty-four 6·25 cm/2½ inch rounds or squares and bake at 400°F, 200°C, gas mark 6 for 15 minutes until golden-brown. Dredge with caster sugar when cooked.

ALMOND HONEY BISCUITS

175 g/6 oz butter
2 tablespoons honey
A few drops of vanilla essence

200 g/7 oz plain flour
25 g/1 oz icing sugar
50 g/2 oz blanched almonds

Filling:

40 g/1½ oz softened butter
1 tablespoon honey

75 g/3 oz icing sugar

Beat together the butter and honey until well blended. Add the vanilla essence and carefully stir in flour and icing sugar. Beat until the mixture is smooth. Leave to chill for 30 minutes. Roll into 20–24 equal-sized balls. Place on a floured baking sheet, spacing out well. Press lightly to flatten. Sprinkle chopped almonds on half the biscuits. Bake at 325°F, 170°C, gas mark 3 for

18–20 minutes until lightly browned. Leave to cool for 5 minutes before removing from the tray. Beat filling ingredients together until creamy. Spread a little of the filling on the biscuits without the nuts and sandwich the the nut-topped biscuits.

NORFOLK GINGERS

100 g/4 oz brown sugar	225 g/8 oz plain flour
100 g/4 oz butter	About 2 tablespoons milk
2 teaspoons ground ginger	1 egg
½ teaspoon mixed spice	
1 small teaspoon bicarbonate of soda	

Sift the flour, spices and sugar into a basin and rub in butter. Dissolve the bicarbonate of soda in warm milk. Add the egg and beat until blended. Stir into the dry ingredients, and knead until smooth. Flour the hands lightly, and roll equal-sized small portions of dough into balls. Place well apart on a greased baking sheet. Press each ball lightly on top. Bake in a moderate oven, 350°F, 180°C, gas mark 4 for 25 minutes. Leave on the baking sheet until they cool.

HUNTER NUTS

225 g/8 oz plain flour	175 g/6 oz sugar
1 level teaspoon ground ginger	1 small egg
75 g/3 oz butter	75 g/3 oz black treacle

Sift the flour and ginger. Rub in the butter. Stir in the sugar and bind with beaten egg and treacle. Form into small balls about the size of marbles and place on a greased baking sheet, 2·5–5 cm/ 1–2 inches apart. Bake in a slow oven, 325°F, 170°C, gas mark 3 for 30 minutes.

OLD SPICE BISCUITS

175 g/6 oz plain flour
½ level teaspoon bicarbonate of
   soda
½ level teaspoon ginger
1 level teaspoon mixed spice

1 level teaspoon cinnamon
75 g/3 oz butter
50 g/2 oz caster sugar
2 tablespoons black treacle

Sift together the dry ingredients. Put butter, sugar and treacle into a pan and melt slowly over a low heat. Remove from the heat and stir in the sifted dry ingredients. Work with fingertips until well blended. Roll the mixture into small balls and transfer to greased baking trays, allowing plenty of room between each for spreading. Press flat with a knife or the prongs of a fork. Bake in the centre of the oven, at 350°F, 180°C, gas mark 4 for 10–15 minutes. Cool on a wire tray, then store in an airtight container.

CORNISH FAIRINGS

100 g/4 oz plain flour
Pinch of salt
¼ teaspoon ground ginger
¼ teaspoon mixed spice
¼ teaspoon cinnamon

1½ teaspoons bicarbonate of soda
50 g/2 oz butter
50 g/2 oz caster sugar
2½ level tablespoons golden syrup

Sift the flour, salt, ground ginger, cinnamon, spice and bicarbonate of soda into a basin. Rub the butter into the dry ingredients. Mix in the sugar. Melt the syrup and stir it into the mixture, to make a soft dough. Roll the mixture between the hands into balls about the size of marbles and place them on greased baking trays with a space between them to allow them to spread. Bake the fairings at 350°F, 180°C, gas mark 4 for 10 minutes. Take the tray out of the oven and hit it on a solid surface to make the fairings crack and spread. Then put them back into the oven for another 5 minutes to finish baking.

GINGER SHORTIES

175 g/6 oz self-raising flour	1 egg
4 level teaspoons ground ginger	2 tablespoons ginger marmalade
100 g/4 oz butter	100 g/4 oz sifted icing sugar
75 g/3 oz caster sugar	Crystallized ginger

Sieve the flour with the ginger and rub in the butter. Add the sugar and enough beaten egg to bind the mixture together. Turn on to a lightly floured surface, divide mixture in half and knead lightly. Roll into two 17·5 cm/7 inch circles to fit a shallow cake tin. Place one circle in the tin, spread over the ginger marmalade and then place the other circle on top. Bake at 350°F, 180°C, gas mark 4 for 50 minutes until golden-brown. Turn the shortcake on to a wire tray to cool. Stir a little water into the icing sugar, to make a soft icing. Pour on to the shortcake and decorate with pieces of ginger. Cut in wedges to serve.

Savoury high-tea dishes

COLD PRESSED BEEF

3·25 kg/7 lb salt beef brisket	1 turnip
2 carrots	20 peppercorns
1 onion	6 cloves

Peel or scrape the carrots, peel the onion and turnip, and cut up all the vegetables so that they are in even-sized pieces. Place them, with the salt brisket, peppercorns and cloves, in a thick-based saucepan of warm water and cook very slowly for 6 or 7 hours, until the meat will come away from the bone and a fork pierces it easily. When the meat is tender, remove from the pan. Take out the bone carefully, put the meat into a cloth and pat it into a good shape. Press between two plates and tie together with string. Put very heavy weights on top of the plates and leave until next day.

CIDER-BAKED HAM

1·8–2 kg/4–5 lb ham in a piece	12 cloves
2 onions	Demerara sugar
3 carrots	250 ml/½ pint cider
3 sticks celery	

Soak the ham in cold water overnight. Drain, and put into a pan with enough water to cover, and the vegetables cut into pieces. Simmer gently, allowing 25 minutes per 450 g/1 lb but subtracting 40 minutes from the total. At the end of the time, remove the pan from the heat and leave for 30 minutes. Lift the ham from the liquid, place in a baking tin, remove the skin and stud the fat with the cloves. Spread thickly with Demerara sugar and pour the cider over the ham. Bake at 350°F, 180°C, gas mark 4 for 40 minutes, basting three times with the cider during this period. Lift on to a rack to cool. Stand the rack on a dish and baste a further two or three times as the ham cools.

BUBBLE AND SQUEAK

450 g/1 lb cold boiled beef	50 g/2 oz butter
1 cabbage	Salt and pepper
1 onion	A little beef stock
1 carrot	

The beef is best if slightly underdone. It should be cut in thin pieces. Boil the cabbage, onion and carrot until just tender. Drain very well, and mince finely. Melt the butter and put in the beef to warm, taking care it does not dry up. Remove the meat and put in the vegetables and cook them until very hot, moistening with a little stock. Add salt and pepper and dish the vegetables with the meat in a shallow dish, moistening with a little more stock.

Bubble and squeak is usually thought of as fried left-over vegetables, most often potatoes and cabbage or sprouts. The original dish always included boiled beef, either fresh or salt. This version comes from a handwritten family cookery book dated 1847.

RAISED PORK PIE

150 g/5 oz lard	450 g/1 lb pork
250 ml/½ pint water	Salt and pepper
450 g/1 lb plain flour	2 pig's feet
½ teaspoon salt	500 ml/1 pint water

Bring lard and water to the boil in a pan, stirring all the time. Add salt and flour to make a smooth, stiff paste, working with the hands until there are no cracks in the dough. Cover with a cloth and leave for 30 minutes in a warm place. Dice the meat, keeping the fat and lean separate. Cook the pig's feet in water for 1½ hours to make a stock which will jelly when cold. When the paste is just warm, mould it into a pie casing with a mould, or over a jam jar or cake tin, retaining enough to make a lid. Put the meat inside, in layers of lean and fat alternately, season well and moisten with a little stock. Cover with the remaining pastry, sealing the edges, and making a small hole in the top. Tie a piece of greaseproof paper or foil all round the pie to keep it a good shape. Bake at 350°F, 180°C, gas mark 4 for 2–2½ hours, and leave until cool. Pour more stock through the hole at the top and leave until cold.

EGG AND APPLE BREAD

8 apples	3 eggs
50 g/2 oz butter	3 tablespoons milk
65 g/2½ oz granulated sugar	8 slices bread
4–5 tablespoons water	Bacon as required

Core the apples and cut them into 1·25 cm/½ inch slices without peeling them. Heat 25 g/1 oz butter and fry the apple rings golden-brown on one side. Sprinkle with sugar, turn, and fry. Sprinkle with water and simmer 3 minutes.

Heat the remaining butter in another frying pan. Combine the eggs and milk and dip the bread slices in it. Fry the bread until light brown on both sides, turning once. To serve, place a slice of this fried French toast on each plate, top with equal portions of fried apples, and surround with hot, crisp bacon.

RABBIT BRAWN

1 large rabbit	Blade of mace
2 pig's trotters	2 cloves
12 peppercorns	2 hard-boiled eggs, sliced

Cut up the rabbit and leave it to soak in cold salted water. Simmer the trotters in water for $2\frac{1}{2}$ hours. Add the rabbit and spices and continue simmering for about 2 hours until the meat leaves the bones. Cut the meat in pieces. Put the slices of hard-boiled eggs in the bottom of a bowl, put in the meat, and pour over the strained stock. Leave to set.

CRUMBLED BACON AND LETTUCE SALAD

2–3 round lettuces	3 tablespoons lemon juice
A few small dandelion leaves (optional)	3 teaspoons granulated sugar
	$\frac{1}{2}$ teaspoon salt
6 rashers lean rindless bacon, minced	$\frac{1}{4}$ teaspoon dry mustard

Separate and wash the leaves. Drain, dry thoroughly, and tear into shreds. Toss the minced bacon in a hot pan until crisp, then drain on soft kitchen paper.

Add the lemon juice, sugar, salt and mustard to the bacon fat remaining in the frying pan. Heat for 2–3 minutes, or until the sugar is dissolved. Arrange the lettuce leaves in a salad bowl, pour the hot dressing over, and toss gently.

Serve immediately, topped with the crumbled bacon.

YORKSHIRE PLOUGHMAN'S SALAD

1 lettuce	1 saltspoon pepper
Small bunch of chives	2 tablespoons vinegar
1 saltspoon salt	1 tablespoon black treacle

Wash the lettuce and drain and dry it well. Shred the lettuce and add it to the chives chopped very finely. Mix the salt, pepper, vinegar and treacle, and toss the lettuce and chives in this dressing.

SAGE BRAWN

½ pig's head, unsalted	10 sage leaves
2 pig's trotters	Salt and pepper

Clean the head and trotters carefully. Cover them with water and add the chopped sage leaves and seasoning. Boil gently for 4 hours, until the meat leaves the bones. When cool enough to handle, take out all the bones, and chop up the meat. Mix the meat and the cooking liquid and pour into pudding basins to set. Seasoning should be adjusted before the mixture is poured into basins, and a pinch of nutmeg added is delicious.

CHAPTER 8

MEALS IN THE FIELD

SOLID packed meals are always needed in the country since workers are out in the fields at midday, and children often have a long, cold walk to school. Sportsmen, too, need easily-eaten, concentrated food; and picnic meals are popular for race meetings, agricultural shows and the like.

All such meals must be easy to carry, tasty and nourishing. Pies and pasties are always popular, and so are sandwiches filled with pressed or potted meats or herb-flavoured brawn (these meats are also liked for high tea when everyone comes home). Often, the packed meal is completed with a hard-boiled egg, an apple, or a chunk of cheese with a wedge of gingerbread or rich fruit cake.

Spiced and jellied meats

MEAT LOAF

225 g/8 oz ham
225 g/8 oz rump steak
100 g/4 oz soft white breadcrumbs
1 egg

Salt and pepper
$\frac{1}{4}$ teaspoon mace
$\frac{1}{4}$ teaspoon allspice
$\frac{1}{4}$ teaspoon thyme

Mince the ham and beef, add the breadcrumbs and bind with the egg. Add salt and pepper, spices and thyme. Put into a greased basin covered with foil, and steam for 3 hours. This is very good to eat with cold poultry.

MIXED MEAT SAUSAGE SHAPE

450 g/1 lb beef sausage meat
450 g/1 lb pork sausage meat
450 g/1 lb cooked ham or tongue
2 teaspoons chopped pickles
1 teaspoon mixed spice
Pinch of freshly-ground black pepper
1 tablespoon sweet stout
1 tablespoon Worcestershire sauce
Pinch of rosemary
Salt
Stock

Mix together the sausage meats and finely-chopped ham or tongue. Add pickles, spice, pepper, stout, Worcestershire sauce, rosemary and salt to taste. Tie in a cloth, and cook very slowly in stock for 2 hours. Lift out and press between two dishes under heavy weights until cold. This loaf can be used for sandwiches, or may be glazed when cold to serve with salad.

DORSET SAUSAGE

450 g/1 lb lean beef
450 g/1 lb bacon
175 g/6 oz soft white bread-crumbs
$\frac{1}{2}$ teaspoon ground nutmeg
$\frac{1}{2}$ teaspoon ground mace
2 eggs
Salt and pepper

Mince the beef and bacon together coarsely. Mix with all the other ingredients. Put into a piece of foil and form into a sausage shape. Bake the sausage in a tin at 350°F, 180°C, gas mark 4 for $1\frac{1}{2}$ hours. Remove from the oven and leave until cold under weights. The sausage may be finished with a light aspic glaze, or it may be scattered with crisp brown breadcrumbs.

LIVER LOAF

225 g/8 oz liver
50 g/2 oz rindless streaky bacon
100 g/4 oz pork sausage meat
1 onion
50 g/2 oz soft white breadcrumbs

1 teaspoon Worcestershire sauce
1 egg
125 ml/¼ pint water
Salt and pepper

Fry the liver lightly in a little butter or bacon fat. Put the liver through a coarse mincer with the bacon and onion. Mix with the sausage meat, breadcrumbs, sauce, egg and seasoning. Add enough of the water to make a soft mixture. Put into a greased loaf tin or terrine and cover with a lid or foil. Bake at 400°F, 200°C, gas mark 6 for 45 minutes. Cool and serve in slices. A little sage is nice added to this mixture if the sausage meat is not highly seasoned.

LINCOLNSHIRE HASLET

900 g/2 lb lean pork
1 small onion
225 g/8 oz stale bread

15 g/½ oz salt
1 teaspoon white pepper
1 teaspoon sage, chopped

Mince the meat coarsely with the onion. Cut the bread into cubes and soak in a little water. Squeeze out the moisture, and mix the bread with the meat. Season with the salt and pepper and the finely chopped sage. Put into a loaf tin or casserole, and bake at 350°F, 180°C, gas mark 4 for 1 hour. Cool in the tin or casserole before turning out. Cut in slices to serve with salad, or use in sandwiches.

NORFOLK PORK CHEESE

1 salt pork hock with trotter
Pepper

Powdered sage

Simmer in water to cover for about 1½ hours, until the meat falls off the bones. Cut the meat into pieces and toss them lightly in pepper and sage. Put the bones back in the liquid and boil them until the stock is reduced to 250 ml/½ pint. Strain over the meat, mix well, and pour into bowls. When cold and beginning to set like a jelly, mix again and pack into portable containers. Cover and place light weights on top until fully set.

CHICKEN BRAWN

1 boiling chicken and giblets	Strip of lemon peel
½ salted pig's head	1 onion
12 peppercorns	2 bay leaves
1 teaspoon salt	Pinch of nutmeg
Parsley	

Put the chicken and giblets into a pan with water, peppercorns, salt, parsley, lemon peel, and *unpeeled* onion (this colours the liquid). Simmer for 2 hours. Put the pig's head into another pan and cover with water. Bring it to the boil, and drain. Cover with fresh water and add bay leaves and nutmeg. Simmer for 2 hours. Slice the chicken meat in neat pieces and put round the bowl or moulds. Put in some chopped pork from the head, and then alternate layers of chicken and pork. Season with pepper as you pack in the layers. Mix the two cooking liquids, strain and pour over the meat. Leave in a cool place to set.

KENTISH BRAWN

1 calf's foot	1 sprig parsley
225 g/8 oz shin beef	1 sprig thyme
8 peppercorns	1 medium-sized onion
Pinch of ground allspice	1 clove
1 bay leaf	Salt

Put the calf's foot into a saucepan and cover with water. Bring to the boil quickly and strain off the water immediately. Wash the calf's foot and put into a clean pan with the beef and cold water to cover. Bring to the boil and skim. Add the peppercorns, allspice, herbs, the onion with the clove stuck in it and a little salt. Simmer very gently for 4 hours. Cut up the beef into small dice with the flesh from the calf's foot. Put the meat into a wetted basin. Strain over the liquid and leave to set.

SUFFOLK OXTAIL BRAWN

1 oxtail	Bunch of mixed herbs
25 g/1 oz butter	Salt and pepper
1 onion	2 tablespoons vinegar
3 cloves	1 hard-boiled egg, sliced

Wash the oxtail and cut it into joints. Dry it well and dust it lightly with a little flour. Melt the butter and fry the oxtail, turning it so that it is brown all over. Add the onion stuck with the cloves, the bunch of herbs, salt and pepper and the vinegar, and cover with cold water. Bring to the boil and simmer for 4 hours until the meat leaves the bones. Cool slightly and then chop the meat. Grease a mould lightly with butter and decorate it with slices of hard-boiled egg. Put the meat into this mould. Return the oxtail bones to the saucepan and boil rapidly until the liquid is reduced to 250 ml/½ pint. Cool slightly and then fill the mould. Turn out when cold.

Meat pies and pasties

SAUSAGE AND EGG ROLL

450 g/1 lb pork sausage meat	3 shallots
225 g/8 oz shortcrust pastry	Sage, salt and pepper
2 hard-boiled eggs, chopped	Grated Double Gloucester cheese

Press sausage meat flat on a floured board or table. Cover with chopped hard-boiled egg and finely-chopped shallot. Sprinkle with some dried or fresh sage and season to taste. Roll up as for a Swiss roll. Roll out the pastry and put the sausage in the middle.

Bring up the sides and seal well. Brush with milk and pat on some grated cheese. Bake at 400°F, 200°C, gas mark 6 for about 45 minutes.

HAND-RAISED PORK PIE

350 g/12 oz self-raising flour	125 ml/¼ pint water
½ teaspoon salt	1 egg
100 g/4 oz lard	

Filling:

550 g/1¼ lb shoulder pork	Salt and pepper
½ teaspoon powdered sage	

Jelly:

450 g/1 lb pork bones or a trotter	Seasoning
1 litre/2 pints water	1 teaspoon gelatine
1 onion	

Sieve the flour and salt into a bowl. Boil the lard and the water in a pan. When dissolved, pour into the centre of the flour while hot. Work all together until a smooth dough is obtained. Cut off a third of the dough and reserve for the lid. Work the remainder on a floured board, gradually moulding to form a bowl shape. A cake tin can be used as a guide. Put on a greased baking sheet and fill the centre with the diced pork, sage and seasoning. Roll out the reserved third for the lid, brush edges of the pie with beaten egg and seal on the lid. Use trimmings to form leaves for decoration. Make a hole in the top and brush the pie all over with the egg. Bake at 400°F, 200°C, gas mark 6 for 30 minutes, then reduce heat to 350°F, 180°C, gas mark 4 for a further 1½ hours. Make a jelly from the bones, water, onion and seasoning by boiling for about 2 hours. Strain, and add the dissolved gelatine. Allow to cool but not set. Pour enough into the hole in the lid when the pie is cool to fill it; leave to set before cutting.

CORNISH PASTIES

450 g/1 lb plain flour
1 teaspoon salt
175 g/6 oz lard
4 tablespoons finely-grated suet
Water to mix
2 large potatoes

1 small turnip
1 onion
350 g/12 oz lean chopped chuck
  steak
Salt and pepper

Mix the flour and salt, rub in the lard and add the suet. Mix to a stiff paste with water, and roll out to 0·5 cm/¼ inch thickness. Cut into six rounds, using a 16·5 cm/6½ inch plate to cut the size. Slice the potatoes, turnip and onion finely, and place the mixture down the centre of each round, seasoning well. On top put the chopped meat. Damp the edges of each round, and close each pasty across the top, sealing the edges firmly. Pinch the edges between finger and thumb to give a fluted top. Put on a baking sheet and bake in a very hot oven, 450°F, 230°C, gas mark 8, for 10 minutes. Reduce heat to moderate, 350°F, 180°C, gas mark 4, and continue cooking until the meat is tender (about 45 minutes).

CORNISH PASTY

Shortcrust pastry:

100 g/4 oz plain flour
50 g/2 oz fat

Pinch of salt
Water to mix to a firm dough

Filling:

Potato, finely sliced (not diced)
Onion and/or turnip, finely cut

100 g/4 oz chuck or skirt steak
Seasoning

Roll pastry into rounds. Pile up sliced potato on about half the pastry. Put onion and/or turnip on potato. Cut meat in small pieces and spread over. Season with salt and pepper. Place a few thin pieces of potato on top to save the meat drying. Damp edges of pastry. Fold over to semi-circle and crimp edges. (Crimp by pinching the pastry with the left hand and folding over with

right hand, forming a rope-like effect on the side of the pastry.)
Place on an unfloured baking sheet and bake at 425°F, 220°C, gas
mark 7 for 10–15 minutes; reduce the heat to 350°F, 180°C, gas
mark 4 for a further 30 minutes.

BACON PASTIES

350 g/12 oz shortcrust pastry	1 large onion
225 g/8 oz minced raw steak	Salt and pepper
175 g/6 oz rindless streaky bacon	½ teaspoon Worcestershire sauce
100 g/4 oz lamb's kidneys	Egg for glazing

Roll out the pastry and cut out six 17·5 cm/7 inch rounds. Chop
the bacon, kidney and onion, and mix with the steak, seasoning
and sauce. Put mixture on half of each round and fold over pastry.
Pinch edges together and brush with beaten egg. Put on to a wet
baking sheet. Bake at 425°F, 220°C, gas mark 7 for 15 minutes;
then at 350°F, 180°C, gas mark 4 for 45 minutes. Serve hot or
cold.

SAUSAGE AND ONION PIE

225 g/8 oz shortcrust pastry	1 egg
225 g/8 oz sausage meat	Mixed herbs
1 onion	

Roll out the pasty and cut into two circles to fit a 17·5 cm/7 inch
pie plate. Line the plate with one round of pastry. Mix the
sausage meat, chopped onion, beaten egg and plenty of chopped
fresh herbs. Cover with the pastry lid. Bake at 425°F, 220°C, gas
mark 7 for 30 minutes.

BACON AND EGG PIE

175 g/6 oz shortcrust pastry	4 eggs
4 thick lean rindless bacon	Salt and pepper
rashers	Beaten egg

Line a 17·5 cm/7 inch sponge tin with pastry, leaving enough for a lid. Cut the bacon into small pieces and arrange them in the tin. Break the four eggs on top of the bacon, leaving them whole. Season with salt and pepper and cover with the remaining pastry. Brush the pastry well with milk or a little beaten egg. Bake at 400°F, 200°C, gas mark 6 for 10 minutes. Lower heat to 350°F, 180°C, gas mark 4 for 30 minutes. A little chopped parsley is a pleasant addition to this pie.

CHICKEN AND EGG PIE

1·35–1·5 kg/3–3½ lb roasting or boiling chicken
250 ml/½ pint water
1 bay leaf
Salt and pepper

25 g/1 oz butter
1 onion
175 g/6 oz button mushrooms
1 teaspoon mixed herbs
4 hard-boiled eggs

For the pastry:

300 g/10 oz plain flour
¼ teaspoon salt
65 g/2½ oz butter

65 g/2½ oz lard
3–4 tablespoons water
Beaten egg for glazing

Place the chicken in a pan with water, bay leaf and seasoning. Bring slowly to the boil, cover tightly and simmer very gently until the meat is tender; it will take 50 minutes if using a roasting chicken, or 2½ hours if using a boiling chicken. Remove the chicken meat from the carcass and chop it roughly. Skim the fat from the pan, remove the bay leaf and reserve the stock. Melt the butter in a pan and fry the chopped onion gently for 5 minutes. Add the chopped mushrooms and cook for a further 2 minutes. Add the chicken meat and herbs, and season to taste. Cool.

For the pastry, sift together the flour and the salt and rub in the fats until the mixture resembles fine breadcrumbs. Add the water and mix to a firm dough. Turn on to a floured surface, and knead lightly until smooth. Roll out into a circle approximately 32·5 cm/ 13 inches in diameter. Cut out a section representing a quarter of the circle and reserve for the lid. Line a round cake tin 17·5 cm/ 7 inches in diameter and 7·5 cm/3 inches deep with the larger piece of pastry, joining cut edges. Spoon half of the chicken mixture into the tin and press down.

Arrange the hard-boiled eggs on top and cover with the remaining chicken mixture, pressing it down between the eggs to fill the spaces. Spoon over 4 tablespoons of the chicken stock. Damp the edges of the pastry. Roll out the remaining pastry for the lid and cover the pie. Trim off excess pastry, press edges together and flute. Roll out trimmings and cut leaves to decorate centre of pie. Brush with glaze and make a hole in the centre of the pie. Bake at 400°F, 200°C, gas mark 6 for 30 minutes. Reduce heat to 350°F, 180°C, gas mark 4 for a further 30 minutes. Leave to cool in the tin. Remove from the tin and pour stock through the hole in the centre until the pie is full. Leave to set.

Pasties with fruit

APPLE TURNOVERS

350 g/12 oz shortcrust or flaky   25 g/1 oz raisins
  pastry   50 g/2 oz butter
675 g/1½ lb cooking apples
4 tablespoons light soft brown
  sugar

Roll out the pastry and cut into 10 cm/4 inch circles (cut round a saucer for the shape). Peel and slice the apples and cook gently with the sugar, raisins and butter until soft. If you like a pinch of cloves or cinnamon, add them during the cooking. Put a spoonful of mixture on to half of each circle, fold over and press edges together, damping them a little first. Bake at 425°F, 220°C, gas mark 7 for 25 minutes.

BUCKINGHAMSHIRE CHERRY BUMPERS

450 g/1 lb black cherries   225 g/8 oz shortcrust pastry
75 g/3 oz sugar

Stone the cherries and sprinkle them with sugar. Roll out the
pastry about 0·5 cm/¼ inch thick. Cut into 10 cm/4 inch rounds.
Heap the centre of each with cherries. Damp the edges of the
pastry, fold them over and seal them by pinching together with
the fingers. Bake at 400°F, 200°C, gas mark 6 for 25 minutes.
Dredge with sugar.

BEDFORDSHIRE CLANGER

For the savoury filling:

1 small onion, finely-chopped   1 cooking apple, peeled, cored
1 tablespoon lard   and chopped
225 g/8 oz minced pork   50 g/2 oz cooked peas
1 teaspoon dried sage   Seasoning

For the sweet filling:

2 dessert apples, cored and   2 tablespoons caster sugar
  chopped   50 g/2 oz stoned dates, chopped
Grated rind and juice of 1 orange   50 g/2 oz sultanas

For the covering:

450 g/1 lb shortcrust pastry   Granulated or crushed lump
1 egg   sugar

This is an old 'packed meal' containing both a savoury and a
sweet filling; it was taken by the men to the fields when the work
was too heavy or too far from home for them to return at midday.

First make the savoury filling. Fry the chopped onion in the
lard until soft. Add the pork and sage and cook gently for 10
minutes, stirring often. Add the chopped apple after 5 minutes.
Stir in the peas after 10 minutes and remove from the heat. Leave
aside. Make the sweet filling by mixing all the ingredients
together thoroughly.

Roll out the pastry and cut into two 25 cm/10 inch circles. Using trimmings, cut a 25 cm/10 inch strip or roll of pastry and lay it across the centre of one circle. Make it hold with a little beaten egg. Brush the edge of the circle with beaten egg likewise. Hold the pastry circle with both hands grasping the ends of the dividing roll. Lift the two edges and pinch together, pinching the dividing roll too, to make a wall of pastry across the centre of the pastry. Fill one side with half the savoury filling, the other side with half the sweet filling. Pinch the pastry edges firmly over them, forming a conventional pasty shape. Glaze with beaten egg, and sprinkle with sugar. Make a second pasty in the same way, and bake at 425°F, 220°C, gas mark 7 for 15–20 minutes or until crisp and golden.

CHAPTER 9
OLD-FASHIONED PUDDINGS

COUNTRY families have always been fond of sweet puddings to follow their main meat, poultry or fish dish. These puddings serve a double purpose, providing sweetness which gives energy for heavy outdoor work, and also adding bulk to an often frugal main course. The ingredients most commonly used are those which are always to hand in the country – flour, bread, suet, milk and cream, soft fruit in season, or easily-stored apples and pears. Spices, dried fruits and home-made jams from the store cupboard provide a little extra sparkle for the simple recipes.

Steamed puddings, batters and pastry tarts and pies are the popular hot sweets; cool creams, fools and flummeries provide a delicious ending to lighter summer meals.

APPLE-SAUCE PUDDING

100 g/4 oz butter
75 g/3 oz light soft brown sugar
3 tablespoons thick unsweetened
    apple sauce or purée
1 egg

150 g/5 oz self-raising flour
1 teaspoon bicarbonate of soda
1 teaspoon ground cinnamon
75 g/3 oz sultanas
75 g/3 oz chopped dates

Cream together the butter and brown sugar until light and fluffy. Beat in the egg and apple sauce. Stir in the dry ingredients and the dried fruit to make a thick batter. Turn into a greased pudding dish and bake at 350°F, 180°C, gas mark 4 for 1 hour. Serve with custard or cream.

COWSLIP PUDDING

450 g/1 lb cowslip petals
250 ml/½ pint milk
2 teaspoons lemon juice
3 egg yolks

50 g/2 oz breadcrumbs
50 g/2 oz sugar
25 g/1 oz butter

Sauce :

3 egg whites
125 ml/¼ pint sweet white wine

25 g/1 oz sugar

Simmer the cowslip petals in milk until they are soft. Take off the heat and stir in the remaining ingredients. Put into a buttered 1 litre/2 pint pudding basin, cover and steam for 1½ hours. Make the sauce by beating the egg whites, adding the wine and sugar and beating them in a basin over a pan of hot water until thick and frothy. The original early Victorian version of this dish used cowslip wine for the sauce.

BAKEWELL PUDDING

225 g/8 oz puff pastry
Strawberry jam
100 g/4 oz butter
175 g/6 oz caster sugar

Yolks of 5 eggs
White of 3 eggs
Almond essence

Line a flan ring or baking tin with the pastry, and spread with jam. Melt together the butter and sugar, and mix in the egg yolks and whites and the essence. Bake at 375°F, 190°C, gas mark 5 for about 25 minutes.

BROWN BREAD PUDDING

175 g/6 oz brown breadcrumbs
250 ml/½ pint milk
50 g/2 oz raisins (or chopped candied peel)
Grating of nutmeg

1 teaspoon cinnamon
Pinch of salt
75 g/3 oz butter
100 g/4 oz sugar
3 eggs

Put the breadcrumbs in a bowl and pour on the hot milk. Add the spices, raisins, and salt. Cream the butter and sugar, and add the eggs one at a time. Gradually work in the breadcrumb mixture. Put into a well-buttered mould, cover with foil or buttered paper and steam for 2 hours. Serve with jam, fruit syrup or custard.

FULBOURN APPLE PUDDING

225 g/8 oz self-raising flour
Pinch of salt
100 g/4 oz shredded suet
6 large eating apples

50 g/2 oz butter
Grated rind of 1 lemon
175 g/6 oz sugar
225 g/8 oz apricot jam

Sift the flour and salt together. Stir in the suet and mix with enough cold water to make a firm dough. Roll out this dough and line a pudding basin, leaving enough for a lid. Peel and core the apples and cut them into slices. Put them into a saucepan with the butter, lemon rind, sugar and jam and heat gently until the apples soften but do not break up. Cool, then put the apple mixture into the pudding basin. Cover with a lid of the suet pastry and cover with greased paper and foil. Steam for 2 hours. (This recipe is about 150 years old, but has been slightly adapted to suit modern ingredients. In the original recipe, the method of cooking apples was also recommended when making Apple Charlotte, or serving apples with rice or whipped cream.)

COTTAGE PUDDING

65 g/2½ oz shredded suet
225 g/8 oz plain flour
100 g/4 oz seeded raisins
100 g/4 oz sugar
½ tablespoon cream of tartar

Pinch of salt
4 tablespoons milk
¼ teaspoon bicarbonate of soda
1 egg

Mix the suet, flour, raisins, sugar, cream of tartar and salt together. Dissolve the soda in the milk, add it to the well-beaten egg, mix well, and stir into the dry ingredients. The mixture must be rather stiff. Turn into a greased roasting tin, and bake at 350°F, 180°C, gas mark 4 for 40 minutes. Cut the pudding into squares, and serve, after dusting it over with white sugar.

DRIPPING PUDDING

150 g/5 oz plain flour
2 teaspoons baking powder
75 g/3 oz caster sugar
75 g/3 oz dripping

1 egg
125 ml/¼ pint milk
Jam or stiffly-whipped egg white

Sift together the flour and baking powder, and stir in the sugar. Mix in the dripping with your fingers until it is well blended with the flour and sugar. Stir in the beaten egg and milk and pour into a greased pie dish. Bake at 350°F, 180°C, gas mark 4 for 45 minutes. To serve, cover with jam, or with stiffly-whipped egg white quickly browned in the oven.

DORSET STIR-IN PUDDING

450 g/1 lb self-raising flour
200 g/7 oz lard
½ teaspoon salt

225 g/8 oz sugar
350 g/12 oz fresh fruit
Milk

Rub together the flour, salt and lard to make fine crumbs. Stir in the sugar. Stir in prepared gooseberries, chopped apple, halved plums or chopped rhubarb. Mix with sufficient milk and water to make a soft dough which will drop easily into a greased basin. Cover with greased paper, then foil. Steam for 2 hours. Serve with fresh cream or smooth, creamy custard.

HAMPSHIRE SIX-CUP PUDDING

100 g/4 oz self-raising flour
100 g/4 oz soft white breadcrumbs
100 g/4 oz suet
175 g/6 oz brown sugar

200 ml/8 fl oz milk
100 g/4 oz mixed raisins,
   sultanas and currants
1 teaspoon bicarbonate of soda

Mix all the dry ingredients together except the bicarbonate of soda. Warm the milk and dissolve the bicarbonate of soda in it. Leave to cool. Add the milk to the other ingredients. Place in a greased bowl and steam for 4 hours.

GOOSEBERRY PUDDING

225 g/8 oz self-raising flour
Pinch of salt
100 g/4 oz shredded suet

25 g/1 oz butter
450 g/1 lb gooseberries
100 g/4 oz sugar

Rub the suet and butter into the flour and salt and add enough cold water to make a firm dough. Roll out the dough and line a small greased pudding basin, leaving enough for the lid. Top and tail the gooseberries and fill the basin, adding the sugar. Cover with the suet pastry lid and seal the edges. Cover with greased paper and foil, and steam for 2½ hours. Turn out and serve with cream or custard. This pudding is particularly good served with hot apricot jam and cream.

WHOLE LEMON PUDDING

450 g/1 lb plain flour
225 g/8 oz shredded suet
½–1 teaspoon salt
1 egg, mixed with milk
  (or plain cold water)

1 lemon
100 g/4 oz Demerara sugar
Pinch each grated nutmeg and
  ground allspice
½ tablespoon firm, chilled butter

Sift the flour into a basin, add the suet, salt, a little grated lemon rind and 2–3 teaspoons of the sugar. Make a well in the centre of the mixture, trickle in the egg and milk or water, and work with the hand into a soft dough. Place the dough in a big, greased pudding basin, and make a hole in the centre with your fist. Work the dough up the sides, so that there is plenty of room in the hole; then place in it the lemon cut in quarters, the sugar and spice and the butter cut in flakes. Close up the hole, make sure that the dough seals it over completely without cracks. Have ready a large saucepan two-thirds full of boiling water. Cover and seal the basin, and boil for 2–2½ hours. Serve with a lemon-flavoured custard, or a sauce of hot golden syrup flavoured with lemon juice.

OLD-FASHIONED RHUBARB PUDDING

25 g/1 oz butter
Light soft brown sugar
225 g/8 oz self-raising flour
1 teaspoon salt
75 g/3 oz suet
125 ml/¼ pint water
675 g/1½ lb young rhubarb

25 g/1 oz chopped candied peel
50 g/2 oz currants
Rind and juice of ½ lemon
100 g/4 oz sugar
Pinch of ground cinnamon
75 ml/3 fl oz water

Butter a 1 litre/2 pint pudding basin thickly and sprinkle plenti-fully with brown sugar. Make a suet crust by sieving together the flour and salt and working in the suet and water. Knead the pastry until smooth and cut off one third of the pastry for lid. Line the basin with the larger portion of suet crust pastry. Cut the rhubarb into 2·5 cm/1 inch pieces and put half into the basin. Sprinkle over the peel, currants, lemon rind and juice, half the sugar, and the cinnamon. Add the rest of the rhubarb and sugar, and pour in the water. Cover with suet crust lid, and a greased paper on top. Bake at 350°F, 180°C, gas mark 4 for 1¼ hours. Turn out to serve, and hand round cream or egg custard.

SUSSEX POND PUDDING

225 g/8 oz plain flour	Milk or water to mix
1 teaspoon baking powder	100 g/4 oz dried fruit
Pinch of salt	75 g/3 oz butter
100 g/4 oz suet	100 g/4 oz light soft brown sugar

Mix all the dry ingredients and mix to an elastic dough with milk or water. Turn on to a floured board and roll into a neat round about 22·5 cm/9 inches wide. Take the dried fruit, butter and brown sugar and place in the middle of the pastry. Gather the edges together at the top and make secure. Tie in a cloth or place in a greased basin and boil for 2 hours. Serve on a large dish deep enough to catch the filling which comes out once the pudding has been cut.

CLOOTIE DUMPLING

300 g/10 oz flour	225 g/8 oz sugar
1½ teaspoons baking powder	100 g/4 oz raisins
2 teaspoons ground cinnamon	225 g/8 oz sultanas
1 teaspoon mixed spice	¼ teaspoon salt
100 g/4 oz shredded suet	Milk

Mix the dry ingredients, add the fruit and enough milk to mix to a fairly stiff consistency. Have a saucepan of boiling water ready, with a plate on the bottom. Dip a cloth into the boiling water. Sprinkle the cloth with some flour; shape the dough into a ball on the cloth and tie up securely. Put into boiling water and make sure the water does *not* cover the whole dumpling. Keep at boiling point for 4 hours, topping up the saucepan frequently with boiling water. Eat as a pudding, or slice when cold and fry to eat with bacon.

PANCAKES

100 g/4 oz plain flour	2 eggs
Pinch of salt	Sugar
250 ml/½ pint milk	Lemon wedges

Sift flour and salt, and beat in milk and eggs lightly. Beat with a fork till the mixture bubbles. Heat a frying pan well greased with lard and pour in a little batter. Tilt the frying pan at various angles quickly, to spread the batter all over the pan's bottom. Cook till light brown underneath, then turn and cook briefly on the other side. Lift on to a plate and fold in three like an envelope or lay flat with a circle of greaseproof paper on top. Keep warm while you cook the rest of the pancakes. If folded, serve at once with lemon wedges and sugar. If flat, the pancakes can wait in a warm (not hot) oven if an extra one is stacked on top and discarded before serving. Pancakes also freeze perfectly if packed flat between paper circles.

BAKED CHERRY BATTER

450 g/1 lb black cherries	125 ml/¼ pint double or clotted
100 g/4 oz sugar	cream
50 g/2 oz plain flour	Pinch of mace
3 tablespoons milk	Grated rind of 1 lemon
50 g/2 oz caster sugar	3 eggs

Simmer the cherries with the sugar and a little water until tender. Cool and take out the cherry stones. Mix the flour, milk, sugar, cream and mace and heat to lukewarm. Add the beaten egg yolks and lemon rind. Whisk the egg whites stiffly and fold into the mixture. Butter an ovenproof dish and put in a layer of cherries. Add a layer of batter and then more cherries. Continue the layers until the dish is full. Cover with a piece of greased paper or foil and bake at 350°F, 180°C, gas mark 4 for 45 minutes. Sprinkle with caster sugar and serve hot with cream or egg custard.

CHERRY BATTER PUDDING (BOILED)

3 tablespoons plain flour	2 eggs
500 ml/1 pint milk	Pinch of salt
25 g/1 oz butter	450 g/1 lb black cherries

Put the flour into a bowl and mix to a smooth paste with a little of the milk. Gradually work in the remaining milk, melted butter, lightly-beaten eggs and salt. When the mixture is smooth, stir in the stoned cherries. Put into a buttered 1 litre/2 pint basin and cover with foil, greaseproof paper or a cloth. Put into a pan of boiling water, and boil for 2 hours. Serve quickly, sprinkled with caster sugar.

YORKSHIRE SUMMER BATTER

150 g/5 oz plain flour	225 g/8 oz summer fruit (black-
500 ml/1 pint milk	currants, redcurrants, goose-
2 eggs	berries or raspberries)
100 g/4 oz sugar	

Mix the flour smoothly with 125 ml/¼ pint milk. Boil the remaining milk and add this gradually to the flour mixture. Return to the pan, and boil the mixture for 5 minutes, stirring all the time. Leave until lukewarm, then beat in the eggs and sugar. Beat thoroughly and stir in the fresh fruit. Put into a buttered pudding basin. Cover with greaseproof paper, and foil or a pudding cloth. Put into a saucepan of boiling water, and boil for 1½ hours. Turn out and sprinkle with sugar. Serve with cream or custard.

NORTHALLERTON BATTER PUDDING

100 g/4 oz plain flour
1 egg
1 tablespoon caster sugar

250 ml/½ pint milk
2 drops vanilla essence
25 g/1 oz lard

Sieve the flour into a mixing bowl. Make a well in the centre, add the egg and sugar and gradually beat the egg into the flour, adding a little milk to make a smooth paste. Add the vanilla essence and beat in the remaining milk until small bubbles rise to the surface. Leave to stand for 30 minutes. Heat the lard in a baking dish until smoking, add batter and bake at 425°F, 220°C, gas mark 7 for 30 minutes. Serve with golden syrup and cream.

NORFOLK APPLE PIE

350 g/12 oz shortcrust pastry
900 g/2 lb cooking apples
25 g/1 oz butter

1 tablespoon granulated sugar
2 tablespoons orange marmalade
1 tablespoon currants

Line a deep 20 cm/8 inch pie plate with half the pastry. Peel, core and slice the apples and cook them without any water, adding the small knob of butter to prevent burning. When they are soft, stir in the sugar and beat them to a pulp. Pour half of this into the pastry case, spread the marmalade over, and sprinkle on the currants. Spread the remaining apple pulp on the top. Make a lid from the other piece of pastry and put on top. Trim and decorate the edges. Bake at 400°F, 200°C, gas mark 6 for 15 minutes, then reduce heat to 350°F, 180°C, gas mark 4 for 25 minutes more.

COUNTRY GRAPE PIE

225 g/8 oz shortcrust pastry
450 g/1 lb small, tart green grapes
150 g/5 oz caster sugar

3 tablespoons flour
1 tablespoon lemon juice
1 tablespoon unsalted butter

Use half the pastry or a little more to line a 20 cm/8 inch greased pie plate. Halve the grapes and take out the pips with a knife-point. Mix half the flour and sugar together; sprinkle the bottom of the pastry shell with the remaining flour, then scatter over it the flour and sugar mixed. Mix the grapes and lemon juice and fill the shell. Mound them high since they shrink in cooking. Cover with the remaining sugar and flakes of butter. Cover with the remaining pastry. If you like, reserve a little sugar to sprinkle on the outside crust. Bake at 350°F, 180°C, gas mark 4 for 20–30 minutes until the pastry is 'set' and golden. Serve hot with single cream or custard.

If this seems a curious recipe for a farmhouse, remember that in the past many great houses had their own vines. Small tart fruit were picked off to give the remainder room and strength, and, if not wanted for making a flavouring or pickles, were thrown away or given to the farm hands for sweet dishes. Many a cottage garden had its own vine too, and used the fruit for the same purposes.

RAISED GOOSEBERRY PIE

Make this unusual pie exactly like a raised pork pie, using the same pastry but slightly sweetened instead of with salt and pepper seasoning. Fill it with well-drained green gooseberries. When baked and cooled, fill with warmed melted apple jelly and allow to cool again completely before serving. It can then be cut like a pork pie.

OATMEAL RAISIN PIE

350 g/12 oz shortcrust pastry	2 tablespoons black treacle
2 tablespoons oatmeal	75 g/3 oz raisins

Roll out the pastry thinly and use half to line a pie plate. Cover with the oatmeal and pour on the treacle. Sprinkle the raisins evenly over the tart. Moisten the edges of the tart with water and cover with the rest of the pastry. Press the edges together to seal, and trim off any surplus pastry. Flute the edges. Bake at 425°F, 220°C, gas mark 7 for 25 minutes. Serve hot or cold.

TREACLE CUSTARD PIE

175 g/6 oz shortcrust pastry
2 teaspoons coarse semolina or
  rolled oats
1 tablespoon black treacle

250 ml/½ pint milk
2 eggs
25 g/1 oz caster sugar

Roll out the pastry and with it line a 17·5 cm/7 inch heatproof pie plate. Sprinkle the base with semolina or oats, then pour in the treacle. Combine the milk and eggs and beat until well blended. Stir in the sugar, then pour the custard into the lined pie plate. Bake in the centre of the oven at 425°F, 220°C, gas mark 7 for 10 minutes; then at 325°F, 170°C, gas mark 3 for 30 minutes.

MARMALADE TART

225 g/8 oz puff pastry
50 g/2 oz butter
50 g/2 oz sugar

1 egg
2 tablespoons marmalade

Line a dish with the pastry. Cream together the butter, sugar, well beaten egg and marmalade, and fill the pastry case. Bake at 375°F, 190°C, gas mark 5 for 35 minutes.

NORFOLK MARROW TART

225 g/8 oz shortcrust pastry
50 g/2 oz jam
450 g/1 lb vegetable marrow

1 egg
Pinch of ground nutmeg
1½ tablespoons sugar

Line a flan tin with the pastry, keeping the trimmings to decorate the top of the tart. Spread with a thin layer of jam. Boil the marrow until soft, and place in a colander to remove all the liquid. When cold, add a well-beaten egg, and the nutmeg and sugar. Beat together with a fork and put in the bottom of the flan.

Sprinkle a little more nutmeg over the top. Decorate with strips of pastry. Bake at 400°F, 200°C, gas mark 6 for 10–15 minutes until turning brown. Continue at 350°F, 180°C, gas mark 4 for 10 minutes until the pastry is golden. Serve hot or cold.

NORFOLK TREACLE TART

175 g/6 oz shortcrust pastry
1 egg

2 tablespoons golden syrup
Rind and juice of ½ lemon

Line a pie plate with the pastry. Beat the egg lightly until mixed. Warm the syrup and beat the egg into it, and add the lemon rind and juice. Pour this mixture into the pastry case and bake at 375°F, 190°C, gas mark 5 for 35 minutes. Eat cold.

KENTISH APPLE TART

175 g/6 oz shortcrust pastry
2 large cooking apples
75 g/3 oz sugar

1 egg
50 g/2 oz softened butter
Rind and juice of 1 lemon

Line a pie plate with the pastry. Peel the apples, and grate the flesh into a basin. Add the sugar, beaten egg, butter, lemon rind and juice and mix well. Put this mixture into the pastry case and bake at 375°F, 190°C, gas mark 5 for 35 minutes.

MATRIMONY CAKE

225 g/8 oz shortcrust pastry
4 tablespoons brown breadcrumbs
4 large apples
50 g/2 oz mixed raisins and
  currants

½ teaspoon mixed ginger and
  nutmeg
Juice of 1 lemon
2 tablespoons sugar
2 tablespoons golden syrup
1 large slice lemon

Line a greased 20 cm/8 inch flan ring with half the pastry. Put the breadcrumbs on the bottom of the pastry case. Peel and core the apples and cut them in rings. Put the apple rings into the pastry case and cover with the remaining ingredients, putting the lemon slice on top. Cover with the remaining pastry. Brush with milk and bake at 350°F, 180°C, gas mark 4 for 45 minutes until golden-brown. Eat hot with thick cream.

BAKED APPLE DUMPLINGS

225 g/8 oz shortcrust pastry
4 small cooking apples
25 g/1 oz raisins

25 g/1 oz light soft brown sugar
25 g/1 oz butter
¼ teaspoon ground cinnamon

Roll out the pastry and cut four circles round a saucer. Peel and core the apples and put one in the centre of each piece of pastry. Fill the centre of the apples with a mixture of raisins, sugar, butter and cinnamon. Enclose the apples completely in pastry and invert on to a baking sheet. Brush the pastry with egg or milk and bake at 425°F, 220°C, gas mark 7 for 25 minutes. Sprinkle with caster sugar as they come out of the oven, and serve hot or cold with cream.

FEN COUNTRY APPLE CAKE

675 g/1½ lb cooking apples
Juice of ½ lemon
25 g/1 oz butter
50 g/2 oz caster sugar
2 rounded tablespoons semolina

225 g/8 oz shortcrust or puff
  pastry
25 g/1 oz currants
3 tablespoons black treacle

Peel, core and slice the apples. Put apples, lemon juice and butter into a pan, cover, and simmer slowly until pulpy. Add sugar and semolina, and bring slowly to the boil. Cook gently for 5 minutes or until the mixture has thickened. Remove from the heat and leave until completely cold. Divide the pastry into two pieces. Roll out one portion and with it line a 17·5 cm/7 inch heatproof plate. Spread with half the apple-filling to within 1·25 cm/½ inch of edges. Sprinkle with currants and add treacle, and then top with the remaining filling. Roll out the rest of pastry into a 20 cm/

8 inch round, moisten edges with water and cover the pie. Press the edges well together to seal, and knock up with the back of a knife. Brush the top with beaten egg or milk and then bake towards the top of the oven set at 425°F, 220°C, gas mark 7 for 25–30 minutes or until pale gold.

RHUBARB TANSY

450 g/1 lb rhubarb
100 g/4 oz butter
50 g/2 oz sugar
2 egg yolks, beaten

125 ml/¼ pint double cream
2 tablespoons lemon juice
Caster sugar to taste

Prepare and chop the rhubarb into 2·5 cm/1 inch pieces. Simmer gently in the butter until cooked. Add the beaten egg yolks and the lightly-whipped cream; sweeten to taste. Boil the mixture gently until it is barely firm. Turn out immediately into a serving dish. Sprinkle with caster sugar and lemon juice. Serve hot or cold.

CIDER-BAKED PEARS OR QUINCES

900 g/2 lb hard pears or quinces
100 g/4 oz caster sugar or honey
250 ml/½ pint cider

250 ml/½ pint water
Shredded blanched almonds
A piece of lemon peel

Peel the pears or quinces leaving the stems on, and arrange them upright in a deep casserole. Add sugar or honey, pour over the cider and water and add the lemon peel. Cook at 300°F, 150°C, gas mark 2 until the pears or quinces are tender and can be pierced with a fork. Leave to cool in the juice, then remove the fruit and reduce the juice by heating until thick and syrupy. Spike the fruit with almonds, and serve with thick cream. The quinces are best flavoured with honey.

SOMERSET APPLE CAKE

4 apples	2 eggs
75 g/3 oz butter	50 g/2 oz plain flour
125 ml/¼ pint milk	3 tablespoons sugar

Peel and slice apples and fry them in hot butter. Mix the milk, eggs and flour. Stir in the apples and butter. Put in a greased 17·5 cm/7 inch sponge sandwich tin and bake at 375°F, 190°C, gas mark 5 for 20 minutes. Turn out, sprinkle with sugar, and brown in the oven or under the grill.

SOMERSET BLACKBERRY AND APPLE CHARLOTTE

225 g/8 oz blackberries	100 g/4 oz soft white bread-
3 large cooking apples	crumbs
50 g/2 oz butter	100 g/4 oz Demerara sugar
¼ teaspoon cinnamon	

Peel, core and slice the apples thinly. Wash the blackberries. Melt the butter in a pan. Mix the breadcrumbs with cinnamon and sugar and throw into the hot butter. Sprinkle a thin layer of well-stirred crumbs on to the bottom of a lightly greased 750 ml/1½ pint pie dish. Cover with a layer of apple, then a layer of crumbs. Repeat this twice. Then cover with blackberries, then crumbs, apple and lastly crumbs. Bake at 325°F, 170°C, gas mark 3 for about 1 hour until the top is golden-brown. Serve with cream or creamy custard.

FRIAR'S OMELET (HOT OR COLD)

450 g/1 lb apples	2 egg yolks, beaten
100 g/4 oz light soft brown sugar	100 g/4 oz soft white bread-
3 cloves	crumbs
100 g/4 oz butter	A little extra butter
2 tablespoons lemon juice	A little water

Peel, core and slice the apples. Simmer the slices with the sugar and cloves in just enough water to prevent them from sticking to the pan. When thoroughly pulped, remove from the heat and beat well with a wooden spoon. Add the butter and lemon juice and set aside until cold. Take out the cloves. When ready to cook, stir in the beaten egg yolks. Butter a deep fireproof dish and cover the bottom and the sides with a generous layer of breadcrumbs. Put in the apple mixture and cover the top with the rest of the breadcrumbs. Bake at 375°F, 190°C, gas mark 5 for 25 minutes. Serve hot or cold. If to be served cold, turn out when cool and sprinkle the top with caster sugar.

APPLE TANSY

2 medium-sized tart cooking
  apples
1 tablespoon unsalted butter
3 eggs, separated

1 tablespoon triple-strength
  rose-water
$\frac{1}{4}$ teaspoon grated nutmeg
1 tablespoon caster sugar

Peel, core and slice the apples. Heat the butter in a frying pan, and fry the apple slices very gently until just softening. Beat the egg yolks in a basin with two dessertspoons water and the rose-water, nutmeg and sugar. Beat the egg whites separately until stiff (but not dry), then fold the whites into the yolk mixture. Tip this mixture very gently over the apples, and fry until the underside is set. While it cooks, heat the grill, and as soon as the omelet is set underneath, slide the pan under the grill flame to brown the top.

The difficult part of making this light tansy is to fold it with the cooked apple inside. The best way is to have a sheet of warmed foil or greased greaseproof paper ready, and to invert the whole pan on to it. Then tip up one side of the sheet, to fold the omelet. Dredge the omelet with caster sugar before serving it.

WHIPPED SYLLABUB

250 ml/½ pint double cream
250 ml/½ pint white wine
2 tablespoons brandy or cream
  sherry

100 g/4 oz caster sugar
Grated rind of 1 lemon

Put the cream into a deep bowl and pour in the wine from a height. Traditionally, cider or raisin wine was used, but a white wine came to be used most often, with 2 tablespoons brandy or sherry included. Add the sugar and the lemon rind, and whip the mixture briskly. As the cream rises, remove the top with a slotted spoon or fish slice. Place the light and fluffy cream in small glasses or custard cups, and set aside in a cool larder or a refrigerator. Sometimes, this kind of syllabub is served with crisp almond or shortbread biscuit, dipped in brandy, placed in each glass.

Originally the syllabub was made by milking the cow into the wine mixture, and skimming off the froth which arose into serving glasses.

NORFOLK SYLLABUB

Scant 125 ml/¼ pint white wine
1 tablespoon sherry
2 tablespoons brandy
1 lemon or 1 bitter (Seville)
  orange

50 g/2 oz caster sugar
250 ml/½ pint double cream

Put the wine, sherry and brandy into a basin. Peel the lemon or orange very thinly and squeeze out the juice. Put the peel and the juice into the wine mixture. Leave overnight, and remove the peel. Stir in the sugar until it dissolves. Add the cream and whip until the mixture forms soft peaks. Put into four tall glasses. This syllabub will hold its shape for 12 hours.

APPLE BARLEY FLUMMERY

4 tablespoons pearl barley
1 litre/2 pints water
675 g/1½ lb eating apples

40 g/1½ oz caster sugar
Juice of 1 lemon
3 tablespoons double cream

Put the barley into the water, and bring to the boil. When boiling, add peeled and sliced apples, and cook until the barley and apples are soft. Put the mixture through a sieve, and return to the saucepan. Stir in the sugar and lemon juice and bring to the boil. Cool and stir in the cream and pour into a serving dish. Serve very cold.

BLACKCURRANT FLUMMERY

450 g/1 lb blackcurrants
500 ml/1 pint water
2 teaspoons cornflour

100 g/4 oz caster sugar
2 teaspoons lemon juice
2 eggs

Remove the stalks and wash the currants. Stew gently in the water until tender, and then sieve them. Mix the cornflour to a smooth paste with a tablespoonful of the blackcurrant purée. Put the rest of the purée on to boil with the sugar. When boiling, add the blended cornflour and the lemon juice, and cook for 2 minutes, stirring all the time to prevent the mixture sticking. Leave to cool. Separate the eggs, beat the yolks, and add to the cooled blackcurrant mixture, mixing well. Whip the egg whites to a stiff foam and fold into the mixture when cold. Pour into a serving bowl. Serve with cream.

GLOUCESTER GOOSEBERRY MOULD

675 g/1½ lb gooseberries
15 g/½ oz gelatine

Sugar to taste
250 ml/½ pint water

Soak the gelatine for 1 hour in half the water. Cook the fruit in the rest of the water until tender. Add the sugar and dissolve. Bring fruit again to the boil, stirring all the time. Beat in the softened gelatine and, when quite dissolved, turn the mixture into a wetted mould or basin and leave to set. Turn on to a plate and serve with cream.

GOOSEBERRY FLUMMERY

450 g/1 lb gooseberries
225 g/8 oz sugar
1 teaspoon lemon juice

250 ml/½ pint milk
4 tablespoons fine semolina

Simmer the gooseberries with the sugar and very little water in a covered pan until the skins burst and the fruit is pulpy. Remove from the heat and add the lemon juice. Warm the milk, and sprinkle on the semolina. Bring just to the boil, then simmer for 3 minutes. Take off the heat and stir in the gooseberries. Tint with a little green vegetable colouring if liked. Pour into a bowl and serve chilled, with thick cream.

RICE FLUMMERY

500 ml/1 pint milk
Strip of lemon peel
2·5 cm/1 inch cinnamon stick
50 g/2 oz caster sugar

75 g/3 oz ground rice
25 g/1 oz butter
4 drops almond essence

Heat the milk just to boiling point with the lemon peel and cinnamon. Remove the peel and cinnamon stick, and stir sugar into the milk. Mix the ground rice with a little cold milk and then stir in the hot milk with the butter and essence. Cook gently, stirring all the time, until the mixture thickens and leaves the sides of the saucepan. Pour into a wetted mould and leave until cold. Turn out and serve with fresh fruit, jam or cream.

MRS NUPERY'S CALF'S FOOT JELLY

2 calf's feet
Juice of 3 lemons
Grated rind of 1 lemon
175 ml/7 fl oz white wine

225 g/8 oz sugar
1 egg yolk
4 egg whites

Put the calf's feet into cold water and leave to soak all night. Simmer them for 12 hours, then remove the feet, and reduce the liquid to 1 litre/1 quart by rapid boiling. The next day, take off any fat on the surface. Add the lemon juice and rind, wine, sugar, and egg yolk. Whip the egg whites to a stiff froth and add to the mixture, breaking up the jelly. Add all the shells from the eggs, and break up all the shells in the jelly. Place over gentle heat until the mixture boils, but do not stir. Leave the jelly to stand in a warm place for 3 minutes, and then pour it into a jelly bag or cloth. Rinse a mould in cold water but do not dry it. Let the jelly drip directly into the mould. Leave until cold and set.

Not many people would make this dish these days, but this early Victorian version is nourishing and delicious.

RICH GOOSEBERRY FOOL

450 g/1 lb gooseberries
225 g/8 oz sugar
2 teaspoons orange-flower water
375 ml/$\frac{3}{4}$ pint single cream

Simmer the gooseberries with the sugar in 125 ml/$\frac{1}{4}$ pint water until pulpy. Put through a sieve and cool. Mix with the orange-flower water and cream. Chill before serving in a stemmed glass bowl; decorate with candied orange peel or angelica strips.

LEMON SOLID

750 ml/1$\frac{1}{2}$ pints milk
250 ml/$\frac{1}{2}$ pint single cream
25 g/1 oz gelatine
2 lemons
150 g/5 oz granulated sugar

Put gelatine to stand in 500 ml/1 pint of milk. Put remaining milk and cream in a pan with the sugar. Warm until the sugar has melted and bring to near boiling point. Add the rind of the lemons. Pour in the other milk and slowly stir in the juice of the lemons. It should slightly curdle. Pour into a mould, set and turn out.

STONE CREAM

225 g/8 oz apricot, plum or
  strawberry jam
500 ml/1 pint single cream

50 g/2 oz icing sugar
8 g/¼ oz gelatine

Cover the bottom of a glass dish about 2·5 cm/1 inch thick with the jam. Put the cream into a thick pan with the sugar and bring only just to the boil. Mix the gelatine with a tablespoon of water and stand it in a bowl of hot water until the gelatine is syrupy. Stir this into the cream. Strain the mixture and when it is nearly cold, stir it well and pour it gently over the jam.

This dish was first mentioned in the seventeenth century. It should be made the day before it is needed. Isinglass gives the best result, but is little used now, so gelatine will suffice. Sometimes the juice and grated rind of a lemon, and a wineglass of white wine were poured over the jam before the cream was added and the cream used to be prettily decorated. Apricot jam is recommended, but other kinds will do. The cream should not be stiff.

CHAPTER 10

SWEETMEATS

THE sweetmeats best known and loved by country children were until lately those made from homely ingredients in their mothers' kitchens. They were mostly simple boiled mixtures of butter, sugar and milk, made into toffees and fudges both wholesome and delicious. Sugar thermometers were not known, but the cooking time could be tested by dropping a little of the mixture into cold water. This is still the method used most. The varying degrees of hardness show whether the mixture will remain soft or become brittle when it cools.

HONEYCOMB

175 g/6 oz sugar
2 tablespoons golden syrup
25 g/1 oz butter

2 tablespoons water
½ teaspoon vinegar
1 teaspoon bicarbonate of soda

Put the sugar, syrup, butter and water into a heavy pan, and stir over a low heat until the sugar has melted. Boil steadily until a little of the mixture forms a firm ball when dropped into cold water. Take off the heat and stir in the vinegar and then the bicarbonate of soda. The mixture will froth up in the pan. Pour into an oiled tin and break into pieces when cold. This toffee does not store well and is best eaten quickly.

BUTTERSCOTCH

450 g/1 lb soft brown sugar   225 g/8 oz butter
75 ml/3 fl oz water

Dissolve the sugar over a low heat in the water. Stir in the butter and boil until the mixture is thick. When it is thick, stir very well so that it does not 'catch' on the bottom of the pan, and cook until a little dropped into cold water is brittle. Pour into a buttered shallow tin and mark into small squares before it sets.

BARLEY SUGAR

450 g/1 lb cube sugar   Rind of 1 lemon
125 ml/¼ pint water   A little yellow food colouring
2 teaspoons strained lemon juice

Put the sugar, water and lemon juice into a heavy pan, together with the thinly peeled lemon rind. Stir over a gentle heat until the sugar has dissolved. Bring to the boil, and boil quickly. Take out the lemon rind just after the mixture begins to boil. Continue boiling until a little of the mixture is very brittle when dropped into cold water. Remove from the heat, stir in a little yellow colouring, and leave to cool slightly. When the mixture is cool enough to handle, roll on an oiled surface into long thin strips. Twist up, and leave to set.

HUMBUGS

450 g/1 lb Demerara sugar   3 drops oil of peppermint
125 ml/¼ pint water   Pinch of cream of tartar
50 g/2 oz butter

Put all the ingredients into a heavy pan and boil until a little of the mixture will form a fine thread when dropped into cold water. Remove from the heat, cool for 1 minute and pour on to an oiled surface. When it is cool enough to handle, pull the mixture into long strips. Pull half the mixture until it becomes much paler than the other pieces. Twist the two colours together, and cut into short pieces.

SIMPLE TOFFEE

100 g/4 oz butter	2 tablespoons vinegar
225 g/8 oz granulated sugar	2 tablespoons golden syrup

Put the butter into a heavy pan and let it start melting over a low heat. Add the remaining ingredients and stir until the sugar has melted. Bring to the boil; boil quickly, only stirring occasionally, until the mixture is golden-brown and a little dropped into cold water is brittle. Pour into a greased shallow tin and mark into squares just before it sets.

BONFIRE TOFFEE

450 g/1 lb granulated sugar	1 tablespoon golden syrup
50 g/2 oz butter	1 teaspoon lemon juice
200 ml/8 fl oz tin sweetened condensed milk	

Put sugar, butter and syrup into a large heavy pan and stir over a low heat until they have melted together. Bring to the boil, add the milk and lemon juice, and boil until a little dropped in cold water forms a firm ball. Take the pan off the fire and leave to stand until the toffee stops bubbling, then pour into a well-greased tin. Mark into squares when nearly set.

TREACLE TOFFEE

300 g/10 oz black treacle or
  golden syrup
100 g/4 oz brown sugar
15 g/½ oz butter

2 teaspoons vinegar
½ teaspoon bicarbonate of soda
1 teaspoon lemon juice

Mix the treacle, sugar, butter and vinegar in a saucepan, and boil without stirring until a few drops in cold water are brittle. Add the bicarbonate of soda to the mixture. Boil again for about 8 minutes, pour out on to a greased tin, and sprinkle the lemon juice on top. When it is cool enough to handle, smear a scrap of butter on the hands and roll the toffee into small balls. Leave to harden.

ALMOND TOFFEE

150 g/5 oz whole almonds
450 g/1 lb sugar
250 ml/½ pint water

Pinch of cream of tartar
3 drops almond essence

Blanch the almonds, skin them and cut them in half crosswise. Put them on a baking tray and dry them in the oven without browning. Dissolve the sugar in the water, add the cream of tartar, and boil until the syrup becomes dark amber in colour. A little dropped in cold water will be brittle. Stir in the almonds and essence and pour into a greased tin to set. Mark in squares or irregular shapes just before setting.

TOFFEE APPLES

Apples
450 g/1 lb Demerara sugar

100 g/4 oz butter
65 ml/2½ fl oz vinegar

Use small crisp apples for these; spear them on wooden sticks about 10 cm/4 inches long. Do not peel them, but wash them well and wipe them very dry. Put the butter and sugar into a heavy pan and stir over a low heat until the sugar has melted. Add the vinegar and boil the mixture quickly until it becomes dark brown and is brittle when a little is dropped into cold water. Put the apples ready with their sticks, and as soon as the toffee is ready, dip quickly into the toffee so they are completely coated. Twirl them in the air, and put them on a tin to set.

PULLED TOFFEE

675 g/1½ lb granulated sugar   1 teaspoon vanilla essence
65 ml/2½ fl oz vinegar   125 ml/¼ pint water
15 g/½ oz butter

Pour the vinegar and water into a clean pan, add the sugar and boil for 15 minutes. Add the butter in little bits, and boil for another 15 minutes. Have ready a plate greased with butter, turn out the toffee on it and sprinkle on the vanilla essence. Turn the edges inward (as if folding them) when cool enough to handle, smear the fingers with butter and hang the mixture over a hook. Pull the toffee lengthways, then hang it up again and again for 8–10 minutes until it is all white, or streaked with white. Then twist in sticks about 1·75 cm/¾ inch thick, and before it can set, cut into 2·5 cm/1 inch lengths with a pair of scissors. Place on greased paper to harden.

PULLED TREACLE CANDY

450 g/1 lb black treacle   50 g/2 oz butter
350 g/12 oz dark soft brown   1 tablespoon vinegar
  sugar   1 teaspoon bicarbonate of soda

Put the treacle, sugar, butter and vinegar into a pan and boil until a few drops harden at once when dropped into cold water. Dissolve the bicarbonate of soda in a very little boiling water, and stir into the candy. Pour into a greased tin. As the edges begin to cool, turn them in with a knife. As soon as the candy is cool enough to be handled, put it on to a marble slab and pull it out until it hardens. Twist it into sticks and cut it into short lengths.

RUSSIAN TOFFEE

225 g/8 oz cube sugar
100 g/4 oz butter

125 ml/¼ pint single cream
1 tablespoon redcurrant jelly

Put the sugar, butter and cream into a thick pan, and stir on a very low heat until the mixture thickens and leaves the side of the pan. Add the redcurrant jelly, stir and pour into a greased tin. Cut into squares when cold.

CREAM TOFFEE

450 g/1 lb sugar
125 ml/¼ pint water
225 g/8 oz golden syrup

40 g/1½ oz butter
200 ml/8 fl oz tin condensed milk

Heat the water and sugar gently until the sugar has dissolved. Stir in the syrup, butter and condensed milk. Boil until a little of the mixture forms a hard ball when dropped in cold water. Pour into a greased tray and mark in squares when it is cooling.

NUT BRITTLE

225 g/8 oz nuts (almonds,
   hazelnuts or peanuts)
450 g/1 lb sugar

125 ml/¼ pint water
Few drops almond essence

Skin the nuts by pouring hot water over them and leaving them for a few minutes until the skins can be rubbed off. Dry carefully, and spread the nuts on a baking sheet. Brown, but do not overbrown, in a moderate oven 350°F, 180°C, gas mark 4. Put the sugar and water into a thick pan and put over a low heat. When it begins to boil, add the nuts. Boil hard until the syrup becomes pale brown, stirring well. Take off the heat. Add a few drops of almond essence and stir well. Put tablespoons of the mixture on to an oiled tin to set.

EASY FUDGE

450 g/1 lb sugar
250 ml/½ pint milk
25 g/1 oz cocoa

⅛ teaspoon cream of tartar
50 g/2 oz butter
½ teaspoon vanilla essence

Dissolve the sugar in the milk over a gentle heat. Add the cocoa and cream of tartar and boil until a little of the mixture forms a soft ball in cold water. Remove from the heat and add the butter and the vanilla essence. Beat until creamy and smooth and pour into a greased tin. Cut into squares when cold.

CHOCOLATE FUDGE

450 g/1 lb sugar
65 ml/2½ fl oz milk

25 g/1 oz butter
225 g/8 oz plain chocolate

Mix the sugar and milk and cook in a double saucepan until it is a thick paste. Add the butter and chocolate broken into small pieces. Now put the saucepan directly on the heat and cook very gently until the sugar and chocolate are completely melted. The reason for using the double boiler is that, if the fudge is boiled before this stage, it will crystallize. Boil for 5 minutes, stirring all the time. Take off the heat, and beat hard until the fudge is thick. Pour into a greased tray, and cut into squares before it is completely cold.

NUT FUDGE

125 ml/¼ pint milk
550 g/1¼ lb granulated sugar
50 g/2 oz butter

225 g/8 oz nuts (hazelnuts or walnuts)

Put the milk and sugar into a saucepan and leave to soak for 45 minutes. Add the butter and heat gently, stirring very occasionally until the sugar has dissolved. When the sugar has dissolved, bring the mixture to the boil and boil quickly, sometimes stirring so the mixture does not stick on the bottom of the pan, for about 15 minutes, until a little of the mixture forms a soft ball when dropped into a cup of cold water. Add the chopped nuts and beat until the fudge is thick and creamy. Pour into a greased tin. Just before it sets, mark into squares.

SCOTS TABLET

900 g/2 lb granulated sugar   Flavouring
350 ml/14 fl oz single cream

Put the sugar and cream into a heavy pan. Bring gradually to boiling point, stirring all the time. Boil for a few minutes, but do not boil hard. Test for setting, until the mixture forms a soft ball when a little is dropped into cold water. Add the chosen flavouring. Put the pan into a basin of cold water and stir quickly with a spoon, scraping down the edges of the pan as the mixture begins to solidify round the edge. When the mixture is looking a little grained, pour it into a buttered tin. This is a little tricky and practice will make perfect. If the mixture is too highly grained, it will not pour out flat, and if it is too thin, the tablet will be sticky. When firm, mark into bars with a knife or cut into circles with a pastry cutter.

Favourite *tablet flavourings* are: cinnamon; desiccated coconut; chopped dried figs; ground and chopped ginger; lemon essence; orange juice and rind; peppermint oil; vanilla essence; chopped walnuts.

BLACKBERRY PASTE CANDIES

900 g/2 lb blackberries   Water
Sugar

Heat the fruit in just enough water to cover until it is soft. Drain through a jelly bag and weigh the juice, and use an equal quantity of sugar. Stir together over gentle heat until the mixture is thick and dry. Pour this thick mixture into a baking tin and sprinkle it with caster sugar. When the paste is cold and hard, cut it into pieces, dip them in caster sugar, and store in a wooden box lined with waxed paper. These candies are also good made with red-currants, as Redcurrant Paste Candies.

PEPPERMINT CREAMS

1 egg white
450 g/1 lb icing sugar

Oil of peppermint

Beat the egg white until it is frothy but not stiff. Sieve the icing sugar and mix it gradually into the egg white until the mixture is a firm paste. Add peppermint to taste (oil of peppermint gives the best flavour, although peppermint essence can be used). Knead the mixture until it is smooth, and then roll it out on a board dusted with icing sugar. Cut into small circles. If preferred, the mixture can be rolled into small balls with the hands and then flattened with a fork. Leave overnight to become firm. When firm, these peppermint creams can be dipped into melted plain chocolate if liked.

COCONUT ICE

900 g/2 lb cube sugar
250 ml/½ pint water

300 g/10 oz desiccated coconut

Put the sugar and water in a strong saucepan and stand it over a gentle heat until the sugar is dissolved. Bring to the boil, and continue boiling rapidly for 10 minutes, stirring all the time. Remove from the heat, stir in the coconut and mix well. Pour half the mixture into an oiled rectangular tin. Colour the remainder lightly with cochineal and press on top of the white ice. Mark into twelve bars when partly cool and finish cutting when cold.

CHAPTER 11
THE STILLROOM

IN the days before refrigeration, every country housewife had her store cupboard full of preserved foods to see her through the winter. In the larger houses and more prosperous farmhouses, there was a special stillroom for storing jams, jellies and syrups, dried fruits and vegetables, pickles, chutneys and sauces, smoked and salted meat and fish, and potted meats or fish for short-term storage. In the cottages, there was little room for more than a jam cupboard, but there were hooks for ham and bacon, and vegetables could be 'clamped' in the garden plot or stored in an out-house. With these varied preserving methods, the housewife kept her surplus produce, and provided some stimulating flavours, at least to vary an otherwise boring winter diet.

Jams and jellies

JAM-MAKING

Use a strong preserving pan or large saucepan for jam-making. Make sure it is large enough for the jam to boil rapidly without boiling over, and wide enough to allow rapid evaporation of liquid to aid setting. An aluminium pan is best; copper may be used and will keep green fruits green, but can spoil the colour of red fruit. Have a long-handled wooden spoon for stirring so that hot splashes of jam do not reach the hands. Use clean glass jars and screwtops or buy packets of wax discs, transparent covers and labels.

Fruit must be fresh and sound, and not mushy, and is best if slightly under-ripe as very ripe fruit has reduced sugar content, and will affect the setting and keeping quality of the jam. Acid in the form of lemon juice, citric or tartaric acid, or redcurrant or gooseberry juice is added to some fruits before cooking to extract pectin, improve colour and prevent crystallization. The setting property of jam depends on its pectin content. Cooking apples, blackcurrants, damsons, gooseberries, plums, quinces and redcurrants have good pectin content. Fresh apricots, early blackberries, greengages and loganberries have medium pectin content. Fruit which is low in pectin includes late blackberries, cherries, elderberries, marrows, medlars, pears, rhubarb, strawberries and tomatoes, so that these fruits are commonly mixed with those which have a high pectin content, or acid is added to the recipes.

Special preserving sugar can be bought for jam, which dissolves quickly, but this is expensive, and granulated sugar is commonly used. Sugar must be stirred carefully into the fruit until dissolved, as if crystals remain, they may burn on the bottom of the pan. If sugar is warmed slightly before adding to the fruit, it will dissolve more quickly.

Fruit must be cooked slowly, with the addition of water, to extract pectin, soften skins and keep a good colour. Once the sugar has been stirred in and dissolved, it must be boiled rapidly without stirring, and this gives a high yield, better flavour and colour. A little jam dropped on a cold plate will start to set in a few seconds and wrinkle when pushed with the finger when setting point has been reached. The jars should be filled to the brim, and covered at once with a wax disc. Covers should be put on while the jam is boiling hot, or else completely cold. Jars should be completely cleaned and dried, and then stored in a cool, dark, dry place.

APPLE, PEAR AND PLUM JAM

675 g/1½ lb cooking apples
675 g/1½ lb ripe pears
675 g/1½ lb plums

1·75 kg/3¾ lb sugar
15 g/½ oz root ginger

Peel and core the apples and pears. Skin and stone the plums. Put the fruit into a pan, and add the bruised root ginger tied into a muslin bag. Simmer until the fruit is soft but not broken, adding a little water if necessary to prevent burning. Stir in the sugar until dissolved, then boil quickly to setting point. Remove the ginger, and pour into hot jars. This is sometimes called Mock Apricot Jam.

BLACKBERRY AND APPLE JAM

675 g/1½ lb blackberries
675 g/1½ lb apples

125–250 ml/¼–½ pint water
1·35 kg/3 lb sugar

Prepare the fruit, and simmer gently with water until soft. Add sugar, and cook rapidly until setting point is reached. Pour into warm jars and cover.

BLACKCURRANT AND CHERRY JAM

900 g/2 lb blackcurrants
900 g/2 lb black cherries

500 ml/1 pint water
1·35 kg/3 lb sugar

Simmer the blackcurrants in the water for 1 hour, and put through a jelly bag. Simmer stoned cherries in the blackcurrant juice for 20 minutes. Stir in the sugar until dissolved, then boil quickly to setting point. Pour into hot jars, cover and seal when cold.

CHERRY AND GOOSEBERRY JAM

1·35 kg/3 lb Morello cherries
675 g/1½ lb red gooseberries

8 g/¼ oz tartaric acid
1·8 kg/4 lb sugar

Stone the cherries, and top and tail the gooseberries. Put into a pan and heat until the juice flows. Add the acid and simmer until the fruit is soft. Stir in the sugar until dissolved, then boil quickly to setting point. Pour into hot jars, cover and seal when cold.

MARROW JAM

1·8 kg/4 lb diced marrow
2·25 kg/5 lb sugar
Ground ginger (optional)

500 ml/1 pint apple juice (made from windfalls, cores, skin and all, and as little water as possible)

Overnight, in a big bowl, stand the diced marrow covered with 1·8 kg/4 lb sugar. Next morning add the apple juice, the ground ginger (if used) and the remaining sugar. Boil until the marrow is cooked and slightly transparent (about 45 minutes). Pour into jars and cover as usual.

PEAR MARMALADE

2·7 kg/6 lb pears
500 ml/1 pint sweet cider
1·8 kg/4 lb sugar

Juice of 1 lemon
Pink colouring

Do not peel or core the pears, but cut into small pieces. Heat the cider and then add the pears and simmer gently until tender. Put through a sieve. Return to the pan with the sugar and lemon and stir until the sugar is dissolved. Boil moderately fast, stirring constantly, until setting point is reached. Tint lightly with pink colouring and pour into hot jars. Cover as usual.

RASPBERRY AND RHUBARB JAM

1·35 kg/3 lb raspberries	500 ml/1 pint water
1·35 kg/3 lb rhubarb	2·75 kg/6 lb sugar

Cut the rhubarb into pieces and simmer in the water until soft. Add the raspberries and cook until soft. Stir in the sugar until dissolved, then boil rapidly to setting point. Pour into hot jars, cover and seal when cold.

RHUBARB AND FIG JAM

900 g/2 lb rhubarb	1·35 kg/3 lb sugar
225 g/8 oz dried figs	Juice of 1 lemon

Cut rhubarb and figs finely, combine with sugar and lemon juice, and leave to stand for 24 hours. Bring to boil, and boil rapidly until a little sets when tested on a cool plate. Leave to stand for 30 minutes before filling jars. Cover, then secure and seal when cold.

ROSE-PETAL AND RHUBARB JAM

100 g/4 oz dark-red rose petals	Juice of 1 lemon
450 g/1 lb rhubarb	450 g/1 lb sugar

Clean and cut up the rhubarb and leave it to stand overnight with the lemon juice and sugar. Cut the white tips off the rose petals, then cut the petals in pieces and add to the mixture. Bring to the boil, and then boil to setting point. Pour into small hot jars and cover. This is delicious with scones or rusks.

WHOLE STRAWBERRY JAM

1·8 kg/4 lb strawberries   1·8 kg/4 lb sugar

Put the strawberries into a bowl with the sugar in layers and leave overnight. Put into a pan and bring to the boil. Boil for 5 minutes and return to the bowl. Leave overnight, then boil to setting point. Cool for 15 minutes, stir well, and pour into hot jars. Cover and seal in the usual way.

TOMATO JAM

2·7 kg/6 lb ripe tomatoes   1 teaspoon salt
6 lemons   1 tablespoon ground ginger
2·7 kg/6 lb granulated sugar

Skin the tomatoes. Grate the lemon rind and put the rind and juice into a pan with the chopped tomatoes. Cook gently until the mixture is reduced to a pulp. Remove from the heat and carefully stir in the sugar, salt and ground ginger. Return to the heat and boil until setting point is reached. Pour into warmed jam jars, allow to cool, seal, and store in a cool, dark place.

RHUBARB PRESERVE

1·5 kg/3½ lb rhubarb   1 lemon
1·5 kg/3½ lb sugar   50 g/2 oz blanched split almonds

Peel the rhubarb and cut it into neat pieces. Put over a low heat until the juice runs. Add warm sugar, grated rind and juice of the lemon, and split almonds. Stir until sugar is dissolved, and boil for 45 minutes until thick and brown. Pour into hot jars and cover. This is a good way of using autumn rhubarb.

RASPBERRY PRESERVE

1·35 kg/3 lb raspberries   25 g/1 oz butter
1·35 kg/3 lb sugar

Warm a pan and rub it with the butter. Put in the raspberries and
heat very slowly until the juice runs. Warm the sugar in the oven.
Add warm sugar to the raspberries and beat with a wooden spoon
over a low heat for 30 minutes. Pour into hot jars and cover.

PEAR CONSERVE

1·35 kg/3 lb firm eating pears   125 ml/¼ pint water
1½ lemons   550 g/1¼ lb sugar

Peel and core the pears and cut the flesh into neat pieces. Peel
the lemons thinly and squeeze out the juice. Boil the pear peel
and cores and the lemon peel in 125 ml/¼ pint water for
10 minutes, and strain. Put the liquid into a pan with the pears
and lemon juice, and simmer until tender. Add the sugar and stir
until dissolved. Bring to the boil, and boil to setting point. Pour
into hot jars and cover.

QUINCE CONSERVE

1 kg/2½ lb quinces   1·25 kg/2¾ lb sugar
1·4 litres/2¾ pints water

Peel and core the quinces and cut the flesh into small cubes. Put
the cubes into 1 litre/2 pints of water and bring to the boil. Add
the sugar, remove from the heat and stir until the sugar dissolves.
Return to the heat and cook gently until the fruit is soft but not
broken. Meanwhile put the cores and peel into the remaining
water and cook until the pulp is reduced by half. Strain the liquid
into the quinces. Boil hard to setting point. Cool a little and stir
before putting into warm pots. This gives a clear red jelly with
small cubes of quince.

CONSERVE OF FLOWERS

1·8 kg/4 lb cooking apples
1 litre/2 pints water
225 g/8 oz flower petals

(carnations, jasmine,
primroses, violets, roses)
Sugar

Choose the flowers according to the season of the year. Cut the fruit in pieces and put into preserving pan with water and flower petals. Simmer until the fruit is pulpy, and strain through a jelly bag. Measure the juice and allow 450 g/1 lb sugar to each 500 ml/ 1 pint of juice. Stir in the sugar until dissolved, and boil rapidly to setting point.

MARIGOLD CONSERVE

150 g/5 oz marigold petals
450 g/1 lb sugar

Lemon juice

Pound the petals (using a pestle and mortar, or a blender on slow speed). Make them very small, adding a little lemon juice to aid the process if necessary. Gradually work in the sugar until it is thoroughly absorbed. Put into small jars and cover. This conserve was originally valued as a cure for melancholy.

APPLE AND ELDERBERRY JELLY

1·35 kg/3 lb cooking apples
1·8 kg/4 lb elderberries (weighed
  off stalks)
Rind of 1 orange

½ cinnamon stick
1 litre/2 pints water
Sugar

Wash the apples, cut into pieces and put into a pan with the elderberries. Add water, cover the pan, and simmer to a pulp. Leave to drip through a jelly bag. Measure the juice and allow 450 g/1 lb sugar to 500 ml/1 pint juice. Put into a pan, stir well and put in orange rind and cinnamon tied in muslin. Boil rapidly to setting point, remove the orange peel and cinnamon, put into warm jars and cover. This jelly is nice if soft and not too firm, and is an excellent way of using elderberries.

BRAMBLE JELLY

1·8 kg/4 lb blackberries   Sugar
375 ml/¾ pint water   Juice of 1 lemon

Wash the blackberries and put them into a pan with the water. Bring to the boil and simmer gently until the juice runs from the fruit. Strain and leave the juice to drip through a jelly bag. Allow 450 g/1 lb sugar to each 500 ml/1 pint of juice. Heat gently together until the sugar dissolves, and then bring to the boil and add the lemon juice. Boil rapidly for 20 minutes until setting point is reached. Put into warm pots and cover.

BLACKBERRY AND SLOE JELLY

1·8 kg/4 lb blackberries   Sugar
450 g/1 lb sloes

Put the blackberries into a pan with the sloes which have been pricked with a needle. Cover with water and simmer until tender. Strain through a jelly bag and measure the juice. Allow 450 g/1 lb sugar to each 500 ml/1 pint of juice. Heat the juice gently, stirring in the sugar until dissolved. Boil hard to setting point and pour into hot jars. Cover.

BLACKCURRANT JELLY

1·8 kg/4 lb ripe blackcurrants   Sugar
1·25 litres/2½ pints water

Simmer the fruit in 750 ml/1½ pints water, mash well. Strain through a clean, scalded jelly bag, or closely woven linen tea towel for 10 minutes. Put pulp from the cloth back into the pan, add 500 ml/1 pint of water and simmer for 30 minutes. Strain the pulp again and mix together the two extracts. Add 350 g/12 oz sugar to each 500 ml/1 pint of juice and cook for 5 minutes. Pour into jars and seal as usual.

CRAB-APPLE JELLY

1·8 kg/4 lb crab-apples	6 cloves
1 litre/2 pints water	Sugar

Do not peel or core the fruit. Cut into quarters and put into a pan with the water and the cloves. Bring to the boil, and then simmer until the apples are very soft. Add a little more water if the fruit is boiling dry. Strain through a jelly bag and measure the juice. Allow 450 g/1 lb sugar to each 500 ml/1 pint of juice. Heat the juice gently and stir in the sugar until dissolved. Boil hard to setting point and pour into hot jars. Seal as usual.

CRAB-APPLE AND GERANIUM JELLY

2 good pressed-down handfuls of scented rose geranium leaves	1·35 kg/3 lb crab-apples

Shred the leaves and cut up the apples. Cover with water and boil until the fruit is soft. Strain through a jelly bag. To each 500 ml/1 pint of juice, add 450 g/1 lb sugar. Stir to dissolve, then bring to the boil, and boil to setting point. Seal as usual.

FIVE FRUIT JELLY

225 g/8 oz each strawberries, raspberries, cherries, redcurrants, gooseberries	375 ml/¾ pint water Sugar

Wash the fruit, cover with the water and simmer gently until soft (probably about 30–40 minutes). Turn into a jelly bag or cloth and leave to drip until thoroughly drained. Measure the juice, making up to an even 500 ml/1 pint or 250 ml/½ pint if necessary. Bring to the boil, take off the heat and stir in and thoroughly dissolve 450 g/1 lb sugar to each 500 ml/1 pint of juice. Bring to a good rolling boil and boil until setting point is reached (about 10–15 minutes). Seal as usual.

MEDLAR JELLY

900 g/2 lb medlars   1 lemon
Sugar

Peel very ripe medlars, remove the pips, and slice the flesh into a pan with enough water to cover the fruit. Simmer with the cut-up lemon until soft. Strain the juice through a jelly bag. Allow 350 g/ 12 oz sugar to each 500 ml/1 pint of juice and stir until dissolved. Boil fast for 10 minutes until transparent. Skim well and cool slightly before pouring into jars and sealing. This can be eaten with bread and butter, or served with game.

MINT JELLY

2·7 kg/6 lb apples   1·8 kg/4 lb sugar
900 g/2 lb mint leaves

Quarter the apples, leaving the skins on and the cores in. Chop mint leaves roughly. Put apples and mint into a large saucepan. Cover with cold water and bring to the boil. Simmer until thoroughly cooked. Put the mixture into a jelly bag over a large basin and drain overnight. Measure the liquid and add 450 g/1 lb sugar for every 500 ml/1 pint. Turn into a large saucepan, add sugar and bring to the boil. When sugar is dissolved, boil rapidly until the jelly reaches setting point when tested on a cold saucer. To improve colour, a few drops of green colouring may be stirred well in at this stage. Pour the jelly into clean, hot jars. Leave until cold then cover and seal.

RASPBERRY AND REDCURRANT JELLY

900 g/2 lb raspberries	500 ml/1 pint water
900 g/2 lb redcurrants	Sugar

Put the fruit into the water and simmer gently until the fruit is very soft. Strain through a jelly bag and measure the juice. Allow 450 g/1 lb sugar to each 500 ml/1 pint of juice. Heat the juice gently, stirring in the sugar until dissolved. Boil quickly to setting point, and pour into small jars. Cover and seal. This makes an excellent glaze for cakes and flans.

ROSEHIP JELLY

Rosehips	Sugar

The rosehips should be left until they are ripe and soft. Take off the tops, cut up the hips and put them into a pan with just enough water to cover. Bring to the boil and then reduce the heat and simmer to a pulp. Squeeze through a coarse jelly bag or cheese cloth, and then pass through an ordinary jelly bag. Allow 450 g/1 lb sugar to each 500 ml/1 pint of juice. Put together in a preserving pan and stir until the sugar is dissolved. Boil for 20 minutes to setting point. Put into small jars. This jelly is very good with hare or turkey.

ROWANBERRY JELLY

1·8 kg/4 lb rowanberries	750 ml/1½ pints water
5 tablespoons lemon juice	Sugar

Use ripe rowanberries. Remove them from their stems and put into a pan with the lemon juice and water. Simmer for 45 minutes until the fruit is soft. Strain through a jelly bag and measure the juice. Allow 450 g/1 lb sugar to each 500 ml/1 pint of juice. Heat the juice gently, stirring in the sugar until dissolved. Boil rapidly to setting point and pour into hot jars. Cover and seal as usual. This jelly is good with venison, game and roast lamb or mutton.

SPICED REDCURRANT JELLY

1·35 kg/3 lb redcurrants
500 ml/1 pint water
125 ml/¼ pint white vinegar

3 cloves
½ stick cinnamon
Sugar

Simmer the redcurrants with the water and vinegar. Put the spices in a muslin bag and suspend in the pan. When the fruit is soft, remove the spice bag. Strain through a jelly bag and measure the juice. Allow 450 g/1 lb sugar to each 500 ml/1 pint of juice. Heat the juice gently, stirring in the sugar until dissolved. Boil rapidly to setting point and pour into hot jars. Cover and seal. This is excellent with roast lamb or with game.

Other fruit preserves

BLACKBERRY AND APPLE CURD

450 g/1 lb apples
900 g/2 lb blackberries
Juice of 2 lemons

225 g/8 oz butter
1 kg/2½ lb caster sugar
4 eggs

Peel and core the apples, and cook with the blackberries in very little water until soft. Put through a sieve. Cook in a double saucepan with lemon juice, butter and sugar. When the butter and sugar have melted, add the well-beaten eggs and cook until the mixture thickens, stirring well. Pour into hot jars and cover. This will keep for about 2 months.

LEMON CURD

450 g/1 lb caster sugar	4 lemons
225 g/8 oz butter	4 eggs

Put the sugar and butter into a double saucepan over hot water. Grate the lemon rind, and squeeze out the juice. Add rind and juice to the sugar, together with lightly beaten eggs. Cook gently, stirring often, until the mixture is smooth, thick and creamy. Put into small pots and cover. Keep in a cool place, and use within 4 weeks.

Variation

4 lemons	450 g/1 lb clear honey
100 g/4 oz butter	4 eggs and 2 egg yolks

To make Lemon Curd with Honey: Grate the lemon rinds, and squeeze and strain the juice. Put into a double saucepan with the butter and honey. Beat the eggs and the egg yolks and strain them into the mixture. Cook and stir over a gentle heat until thick and creamy. Pour into hot jars and cover. This will keep 2 months.

SPICY APPLE BUTTER

2·7 kg/6 lb apples	1 teaspoon ground cinnamon
1 litre/2 pints water	1 teaspoon nutmeg
1 litre/2 pints cider	Granulated or soft brown sugar
1 teaspoon ground cloves	

Do not peel the apples, but cut them into large pieces. Simmer in water and cider until soft and put through a sieve. Weigh the pulp and simmer until thick. Add 350 g/12 oz sugar to each 450 g/1 lb of weighed apples. Stir sugar and spices into apples, and cook gently, stirring frequently, until no surplus liquid remains. Pour into hot jars and cover. This is particularly good made with equal quantities of differently flavoured apples; six different kinds could be used for this recipe. The best apple butter is slightly sharp-flavoured. The same recipe can be used with crab-apples, to make Crab-Apple Butter.

APPLE AND PLUM BUTTER

1·35 kg/3 lb apples	350 g/12 oz sugar to each
450 g/1 lb plums	500 ml/1 pint of pulp

Peel and core the apples and cut them in slices, and cook in very little water until soft. Add stoned plums and cook until soft. Put through a sieve, measure and add sugar. Boil to setting point and put into warm jars. This is a stiff 'butter'. It may be used with bread and butter, or, if put into straight-sided jars, it can be turned out, sliced and eaten with cream.

CHERRY BUTTER

1·8 kg/4 lb cherries	900 g/2 lb sugar
1 lemon	

Take the stones from the cherries. Remove the kernels from a few of them, blanch and skin. Put the cherries in layers in a bowl with the sugar and the grated rind and juice of the lemon. Leave overnight.

Simmer for 20 minutes, add the kernels and then boil quickly until very thick, stirring well. Pour into small hot jars and cover. Use within 6 weeks.

FRUIT BLACK BUTTER

Redcurrants	Strawberries
Blackcurrants	Sugar
Gooseberries	

A mixture of some or all of the fruits can be used. For each 900 g/ 2 lb fruit, allow 450 g/1 lb sugar. Prepare and mix the fruits and heat gently in a pan until the juices start to run. Stir in sugar until dissolved, and boil until very thick. Pour into small hot jars and cover. Use within 4 weeks.

DAMSON CHEESE

Damsons   Sugar

Wash the damsons and just cover them with water. Simmer until the fruit is soft. Put through a sieve and weigh the pulp. Add 350 g/12 oz sugar to each 500 ml/1 pint of damson pulp. Stir the sugar into the pulp until it is dissolved and then cook and stir for about 45 minutes until the mixture is thick enough to hold the impression of a spoon. Pour into hot jars and cover. Keep for several weeks before use. It should be firm enough to slice and eat on bread like cheese.

GOOSEBERRY CHEESE

1·35 kg/3 lb green gooseberries   Sugar
250 ml/½ pint water

Top and tail the gooseberries and simmer them in water until soft. Put through a sieve and weigh the pulp. Allow 350 g/12 oz sugar to each 450 g/1 lb pulp. Stir in the sugar until dissolved and bring to the boil. Cook gently, stirring all the time, until the mixture is very thick. Pour into hot jars and cover. Keep for some months before use if possible. This is then very good as a spread; or it can be sliced and eaten with cold meat, particularly lamb.

APPLE HONEY

2·2 kg/5 lb apples   1 tablespoon lemon juice
900 g/2 lb sugar   25 g/1 oz butter
Grated rind of 1 lemon

The best apples are those which 'fluff' quickly while cooking.

Peel and core the apples and cut into small pieces. Put into a pan with a tight-fitting lid and very little water, and cook gently to a fine pulp. Stir the apples occasionally to prevent burning. Add the sugar, lemon rind and juice, and butter. Bring to the boil, and then simmer for 15 minutes. Pour into hot jars and seal. This will keep for 2–3 months.

PARSLEY HONEY

100 g/4 oz fresh parsley   450 g/1 lb sugar
625 ml/1¼ pints water   2 teaspoons vinegar

Wash the parsley well and chop it up roughly, including the stalks. Put it into a pan with the water and bring to the boil. Boil gently until the liquid has been reduced to 500 ml/1 pint. Strain the liquid and put it into a clean saucepan with warm sugar. Stir well and when the sugar has dissolved, bring to the boil. Add the vinegar and boil slowly for about 30 minutes until the mixture is like clear honey. Pour into pots and cover. Keeps well, like jam.

TOMATO HONEY

450 g/1 lb red tomatoes   1 lemon
450 g/1 lb sugar

Chop the tomatoes and put them into a pan with the grated rind of the lemon. Simmer until soft, and put the mixture through a sieve. Put the pulp into the pan with the sugar and juice of the lemon, and stir until the sugar has dissolved. Boil rapidly until thick. This is a delicious and unusual filling for tarts.

MINCEMEAT

1·8 kg/4 lb apples
1 kg/2½ lb shredded suet
1·5 kg/3½ lb dark soft brown sugar
1·35 kg/3 lb currants
1 kg/2¼ lb raisins

675 g/1½ lb finely-chopped peel
2 teaspoons salt
1 tablespoon mixed spice
2 teaspoons ground nutmeg
2 teaspoons ground cloves

Peel and core the apples, and simmer them in very little water until soft. Leave overnight. Mix with all the other ingredients and put in jars.

WELSH MINCEMEAT

225 g/8 oz butter
450 g/1 lb currants
450 g/1 lb sultanas
450 g/1 lb raisins
100 g/4 oz peel
225 g/8 oz skinned, chopped, almonds

675 g/1½ lb dark soft brown sugar
900 g/2 lb apples
300 ml/12 fl oz rum or brandy

Put all the ingredients except sugar and currants through a mincer. Mix well, stand overnight, re-mix and put into jars.

COOKED MINCEMEAT

375 ml/¾ pint apple juice (see method)
450 g/1 lb seedless raisins
450 g/1 lb currants
450 g/1 lb shredded suet
675 g/1½ lb light soft brown sugar

2·7 kg/6 lb cooking apples
450 g/1 lb chopped mixed peel
½ teaspoon ground mace
1½ teaspoons ground cinnamon
75 ml/3 fl oz brandy

Make the apple juice by mincing a large quantity of apples, and squeezing them in muslin to get a clear juice. Put the juice in a large pan, and bring it rapidly to the boil. Add the dried fruit, suet, brown sugar, chopped apples, peel and spices. Simmer slowly for 1 hour. Stir in the brandy and put into screw-topped jars. This mincemeat will keep for 1 year.

GINGERED PEARS

3·5 kg/8 lb pears   100 g/4 oz stem ginger
1·8 kg/4 lb sugar   4 lemons

Peel, quarter and core the pears. Cut the quarters into small slices, add sugar, chopped ginger and the strained juice of the lemons. Cut the lemon rind into long thin strips, and add to the fruit and mix. Cover and allow to stand in a cool place overnight. Stir over moderate heat until the sugar has dissolved, and then bring quickly to boil. Cook very slowly for 3 hours until clear and thick. Pour into jars and cover.

BRANDIED PEARS

2·7 kg/6 lb hard pears   2 kg/4½ lb sugar
3 lemons   10 cm/4 inch cinnamon stick
8 cloves   6 tablespoons brandy

Peel the pears, quarter them and take out the cores. Grate the rind off the lemons and squeeze out the juice. Layer the pears, sugar and lemon rind in a large bowl and sprinkle the lemon juice over the top. Cover the bowl and leave overnight. Transfer the pears to a large casserole, covering them with the juice which has formed during the night. Add cinnamon and cloves. Cover with a lid and bake at 275°F, 140°C, gas mark 1 for 6 hours until the pears are tender and golden. Leave to cool, and then stir in the brandy. Remove the cinnamon stick and cloves, and transfer the pears to jars, screwing them down for storage.

PRESERVED QUINCES

2·2 kg/5 lb quinces   1·35 kg/3 lb sugar
750 ml/1½ pints cold water

Peel, quarter and core the quinces, dropping them into cold water to prevent discoloration. Cook the peelings and cores in boiling water to cover for 15 minutes, then strain off the liquid. Add the quinces to the liquid and cook slowly until tender. Remove the quinces to a basin with a perforated spoon so that the liquid runs back into the pan. Add the sugar. Stir until dissolved, and then bring quickly to the boil. Add the quinces and cook until clear. Turn into heated jars and cover.

EVERLASTING RUM-POT

1 bottle light or dark rum   Strawberries, cherries, apricots,
Granulated sugar   raspberries, plums, redcurrants
                                                   peaches, grapes, melon

The fruit should be sound, whole and ripe. The rum-pot should not be over-loaded with fruit and it is best to preserve a little at a time, using only the choicest fruits. Citrus fruits, apples, bananas and pears should not be used. Gently wipe the fruit, and do not peel or stone (except for melon which should be peeled, seeded and cut into large chunks). Put fruit into a large stone crock with its own weight of sugar, and cover with rum. Cover the crock tightly with waxed paper and a lid and keep in a cool place. You can then continue adding fruit to the rum-pot throughout the season, and replacing any you use.

The fruit and syrup can be used by serving small quantities with cream or yoghurt. It can also be used with a fresh fruit salad of oranges, apples and nuts, or put into a pastry case.

APPLE GINGER

1·8 kg/4 lb apples	1·5 litres/3 pints water
1·8 kg/4 lb sugar	50 g/2 oz ground ginger

Peel and core apples and cut them into thin slices. Dissolve the sugar in the water and boil syrup until thick. Add the apple slices and boil until transparent. Stir in ginger, boil for 5 minutes, pour into jars and cover. This is very good for filling tarts.

FRUIT SYRUP

Syrups are best stored in lever-stoppered bottles with a china cap and rubber washer, or in screw-topped bottles; ordinary bottles tend to burst. The full bottles should be sterilized by putting them in a deep pan filled with cold water to cover them. The water should be heated slowly so that it reaches simmering point within an hour, and it should then remain at this temperature for 30 minutes. When the bottles have been cooled, they should be stored in a cool dark place. To avoid the problems of sterilization and storage, the syrups can be poured into freezer containers, leaving room for expansion, and frozen solid. Colour and flavour remain perfect by this method.

Use single fruits or a mixture for syrups. They can be made from raspberries, strawberries, elderberries, blackberries and blackcurrants. Fruit should be clean and ripe, and should not be washed if possible. A little water should be added to the fruit (about 125 ml/¼ pint to 1·35 kg/3 lb raspberries or strawberries, but 250 ml/½ pint to the same weight of blackcurrants). Simmer the fruit gently for an hour, crushing the fruit at intervals. Strain through a jellybag and allow 100 g/4 oz sugar to each 500 ml/1 pint of juice. Stir until dissolved, and then strain and bottle or freeze. In the past, syrups were often used as soothing medicine for coughs and colds. Syrups are good, diluted, as winter drinks; or they can be used as sauces for puddings.

Candied fruit and crystallized flowers

Few farmers' wives in time past had the leisure or inclination
for the elaborate processes of candying and crystallizing for
decoration; but they knew the value of saving the delicate flavour
of flowers, herbs and the rare and treasured citrus fruit for special
occasions in simple preserves. Sometimes they reduced the thick
fruit pulp left from jelly-making and cooked it with sugar to make
chewy sweetmeats, or candied the homely marrow too.

PRESERVED ORANGE PEEL

Peel from oranges   Sugar

Wipe orange skins and remove as much white pith as possible.
Cut the peel into pieces a little thinner than a matchstick. Put a
layer of peel about 1·25 cm/½ inch thick in a jar and sprinkle
lightly with sugar. Continue with these layers until the jar is full,
put on a lid, and shake well. During the first week, shake the jar
daily, and occasionally stand the jar upside down. Store in a cool
dark place.

This orange peel lasts for years and is good for flavouring cakes
and puddings. The longer it is kept, the richer the flavour. The
jar can be topped up from time to time with fresh layers of peel
and sugar.

FRUIT PASTES

Apple, pear, quince, plum and apricot pastes are made with
pulped cooked fruit, cooked again with an equal quantity of sugar
to make a thick paste; they are rather like the fruit butters or
cheeses.

CRYSTALLIZED ANGELICA

Young angelica stems	100 g/4 oz salt
500 ml/1 pint water	675 g/1½ lb sugar

Use young stems, which are best cut in April. Cut them into 10 cm/4 inch lengths and put them into a glass or china bowl. Pour on a solution of boiling water and salt, and leave under cover for 24 hours. Lift out the pieces, drain them, peel them and wash them in cold water. Make a syrup with the sugar and 750 ml/1½ pints fresh water and boil for 10 minutes. Put the angelica stems into the boiling syrup for 20 minutes. Lift them out and drain them on a rack for 4 days. Re-boil again for 20 minutes in the same syrup. Leave to cool in the syrup, lift out and drain for 4 days. Toss in sugar and store in airtight jars. Angelica is delicious cooked with rhubarb, and used in rhubarb jam, as well as for cake decoration.

CRYSTALLIZED FLOWERS

Spring or summer flowers	Rose or orange-flower water
Gum arabic crystals	Caster sugar

The most suitable flowers are primroses, violets, polyanthus, roses, carnation petals, forget-me-nots, mimosa, cowslips, sweet peas and fruit blossom. Flowers from bulbs should not be eaten. Use 3 teaspoons gum arabic crystals to 3 tablespoons rose or orange-flower water. Mix them in a screw-topped jar and leave them for 3 days, shaking occasionally until the mixture is like sticky glue. Use a small paint brush to paint the flowers (or petals of large flowers) with this solution. Coat the petals completely, as bare spots will shrivel and will not keep. Dredge lightly and put on a rack covered with sugared, greaseproof paper. Dry in an airing cupboard or very cool oven for 24 hours. Store in tins layered with waxed paper.

Pickles, chutneys and sauces

NOTE: Use malt vinegar for the recipes in this section.

PICKLED BEETROOT WITH MUSTARD

1·8 kg/4 lb beetroot
500 ml/1 pint vinegar
6 teaspoons sugar

2 teaspoons dry mustard powder
2 teaspoons salt

Boil the beetroot until tender. Peel and slice into a jar. Put the vinegar and dry ingredients into a saucepan and bring slowly to the boil. Boil for 5 minutes, then pour over the beetroot. Cover when cool.

PICKLED BEETROOT WITH HORSERADISH

8 medium-sized beetroot
8 g/¼ oz whole black peppercorns
1 small root horseradish (grated)

1 litre/2 pints malt vinegar
8 g/¼ oz whole allspice berries
1 teaspoon rock or sea salt

Bake the beetroot in the oven for 1½–2 hours. When cool, skin and slice, and place in jars. Boil the vinegar, horseradish, salt, pepper and spice together. When cool, pour over the beetroot. Store in a dry place.

PICKLED EGGS

16 hard-boiled eggs
15 g/½ oz black peppercorns
15 g/½ oz whole allspice berries

15 g/½ oz root ginger
1 litre/2 pints white vinegar

The eggs are best if boiled for 10 minutes. Simmer the vinegar with the peppercorns, allspice and bruised ginger for 5 minutes. Peel the eggs and put them into a jar. Pour the boiling vinegar over the eggs and cover. Store in a cool dry place. These eggs can be eaten within 2 weeks, but they will keep indefinitely.

PICKLED GREEN TOMATOES

1 kg/2½ lb green tomatoes	225 g/8 oz sugar
225 g/8 oz onions	500 ml/1 pint white vinegar

Slice the tomatoes and the onions. Sprinkle generously with salt. Leave for 24 hours, then drain off the salt liquid completely. Make a syrup with the sugar and vinegar and put in the tomatoes and onions. Simmer until tender, pour into preserving jars and cover while hot.

PICKLED ONIONS

Small button onions	To each litre/2 pints vinegar
Vinegar to cover	allow 2 teaspoons allspice
	and 2 teaspoons whole
	black peppercorns

Peel onions into clean dry jars, boil vinegar with spices, and immediately or when cold pour it over to fill jars completely; cover with parchment paper and store in a dry place. They will be ready in 2 weeks if the vinegar is used cold, but much earlier if it is used while hot.

PICCALILLI WITH CAULIFLOWER

2·2 kg/5 lb cauliflower	25 g/1 oz turmeric powder
450 g/1 lb onions	25 g/1 oz ground ginger
Salt	8 chillies
75 g/3 oz dry mustard powder	8 cloves
300 g/10 oz sugar	2·25 litres/4 pints vinegar

Cut the vegetables into small pieces and put into a pan. Sprinkle with salt and allow to stand overnight. Mix the remaining ingredients. Put the vegetables into a saucepan, pour on the mixture, and boil until tender. When cold, the pickle is ready for use. The vegetables can be varied; make Marrow Piccalilli or Green Tomato Piccalilli instead of cauliflower.

MILITARY PICKLE

1 marrow	7 chillies
1 cauliflower	25 g/1 oz turmeric powder
450 g/1 lb beans	25 g/1 oz ground ginger
450 g/1 lb onions	100 g/4 oz plain flour
450 g/1 lb Demerara sugar	2·25 litres/4 pints vinegar

Cut the vegetables into small pieces and cover with salt. Allow to stand overnight, and then drain. Put into a saucepan, add the vinegar and boil for 5 minutes. Add the sugar and chillies. Mix the remaining ingredients to a smooth paste with a little vinegar and add while boiling. Boil for 30 minutes. Stir well to prevent burning. Bottle when cold.

BEAN PICKLE (CUMBERLAND)

2·7 kg/6 lb runner beans	50 g/2 oz dry mustard powder
6 large onions	450 g/1 lb sugar
1 litre/2 pints white vinegar	1 teaspoon black pepper
100 g/4 oz plain flour	1 teaspoon turmeric powder

Slice the beans and onions thinly and cook in a little water until tender. Drain thoroughly. Moisten the flour with a little vinegar, then mix together in a saucepan the vinegar, flour, mustard, sugar, pepper and turmeric. Bring to the boil and continue stirring all the time until the mixture is thick. Add beans and onions and continue stirring until the mixture boils again. Put into jars, and cover while hot.

PICKLED CABBAGE

1 large firm red cabbage	Cayenne pepper
Salt	Vinegar

Cut the cabbage into quarters and remove the stalk. Cut the leaves into very thin slices and put them on a large flat dish. Sprinkle with plenty of salt and leave overnight. Next morning, stir well to mix in the salt, and then drain the cabbage. Fill clean bottles with the cabbage, and sprinkle $\frac{1}{4}$ teaspoon Cayenne pepper on top of each one. Cover with cold vinegar, tie down securely and store. This cabbage can be eaten within 2 or 3 days.

BLACKBERRY CHUTNEY

2·7 kg/6 lb blackberries
900 g/2 lb apples
900 g/2 lb onions
25 g/1 oz salt
50 g/2 oz dry mustard powder

50 g/2 oz ground ginger
2 teaspoons ground mace
1 teaspoon Cayenne pepper
1 litre/2 pints vinegar
900 g/2 lb light soft brown sugar

Wash the blackberries and put them into a pan. Peel and chop the apples and onions. Add them to the blackberries together with all the remaining ingredients except the sugar. Cook gently for 1 hour. Put through a sieve and add the sugar to the pulp. Cook until thick and pour into jars. Cover as usual.

ELDERBERRY CHUTNEY

675 g/1$\frac{1}{2}$ lb elderberries
1 onion
50 g/2 oz Demerara sugar
250 ml/$\frac{1}{2}$ pint vinegar
15 g/$\frac{1}{2}$ oz ground ginger

A few cloves
1 teaspoon salt
$\frac{1}{4}$ teaspoon pepper
$\frac{1}{8}$ teaspoon mace
50 g/2 oz stoned raisins

Pass berries through sieve, chop the onion finely, and boil with the other ingredients for 15 minutes. Pot as usual.

GREEN TOMATO CHUTNEY (1)

675 g/1$\frac{1}{2}$ lb green tomatoes
450 g/1 lb apples
225 g/8 oz sugar
350 g/12 oz sultanas
100 g/4 oz onions

1 teaspoon salt
25 g/1 oz mixed spice
500 ml/1 pint vinegar
Pinch of dry mustard powder

Use an enamelled pan or casserole. Chop all the ingredients and cook slowly together until the colour deepens; this takes 1½–2 hours. Put into jars, and seal.

GREEN TOMATO CHUTNEY (2)

450 g/1 lb green tomatoes	450 g/1 lb sugar
3 large apples	½ teaspoon Cayenne pepper
3 large onions	1 teaspoon ground cloves
500 ml/1 pint cider vinegar	1 teaspoon ground cinnamon

Peel the tomatoes, slice and put in a bowl with a sprinkling of salt. Allow to stand overnight. Next day, turn into a strong pan, add peeled, sliced apples and onions, vinegar, sugar, Cayenne and spices. Bring to the boil and simmer for about 1 hour until the sugar is dissolved and the fruit and vegetables tender. Turn into warmed jars, allow to cool, then cover tightly and store in a cool, dark place.

PLUM CHUTNEY

900 g/2 lb plums, weighed after stoning	450 g/1 lb light soft brown sugar
450 g/1 lb carrots	25 g/1 oz chopped garlic
500 ml/1 pint vinegar	25 g/1 oz chillies
450 g/1 lb stoned raisins	25 g/1 oz ground ginger
	40 g/1½ oz salt

Mix the plums with minced carrots and vinegar and simmer until soft. Add the other ingredients, and simmer until the mixture is thick. Put into jars and cover tightly.

MINT CHUTNEY

450 g/1 lb sugar	225 g/8 oz red or green tomatoes
500 ml/1 pint vinegar	450 g/1 lb cooking apples
350 g/12 oz mint leaves	2 teaspoons salt
225 g/8 oz sultanas	2 teaspoons made English mustard
6 small onions	

Mince together the onions, apples, tomatoes and mint leaves. The sultanas can be minced or left whole as preferred. Heat the vinegar, and add and dissolve the sugar, salt and mustard. Mix in the minced ingredients and boil for 20 minutes. Bottle and seal.

RHUBARB CHUTNEY

900 g/2 lb chopped rhubarb
900 g/2 lb brown sugar
450 g/1 lb sultanas
25 g/1 oz crushed garlic
25 g/1 oz finely chopped shallots

25 g/1 oz salt
25 g/1 oz bruised root ginger
500 ml/1 pint vinegar
½ teaspoon Cayenne pepper
Grated rind and juice of 1 lemon

Put all the ingredients into a thick pan and boil together until thick and dark brown. Remove the root ginger, and put chutney into pots.

BEETROOT CHUTNEY

900 g/2 lb onions
1·35 kg/3 lb beetroot
500 ml/1 pint vinegar
675 g/1½ lb apples

450 g/1 lb sugar
½ teaspoon salt
1 teaspoon ground ginger

Boil and chop the onions and beetroot. Put into a pan with the vinegar, the peeled and chopped apples, sugar, salt and ginger. Boil to a thick chutney consistency, which will take about 1 hour. Pot as usual.

MRS HAWKYARD'S DRIED FRUIT CHUTNEY

2·25 kg/5 lb apples
250–500 ml/½–1 pint vinegar
1 tablespoon salt
225 g/8 oz stoned dates
225 g/8 oz raisins or sultanas

1 small tablespoon ground ginger
225 g/8 oz onions, minced
450 g/1 lb Demerara sugar
6 chillies

Peel and core the apples. Put the salt, ginger, chopped chillies and sugar into a pan with some of the vinegar. Add the apples and minced onions and bring to the boil. Add the chopped dates and whole raisins or sultanas and simmer until thick and brown, adding more vinegar as required (the apples make a lot of juice, and the chutney should not be runny). Put into warm jars and cover well.

NORWICH APPLE CHUTNEY

1 kg/2½ lb apples	375 ml/¾ pint vinegar
225 g/8 oz onions	1 tablespoon pickling spice
225 g/8 oz light soft brown sugar	½ tablespoon dry mustard powder
100 g/4 oz sultanas	1 teaspoon coriander seeds
15 g/½ oz salt	2 pieces root ginger

Peel the apples and onions. Mince or chop them finely. Simmer with half the quantity of vinegar until tender. Add sugar, sultanas, salt, pickling spice, mustard, coriander seeds, ginger and remainder of the vinegar. Simmer for about 20 minutes until thick. Remove the ginger and turn into heated jars while hot and put on glass lids, if used, firmly. If ordinary jars are used, a cover should be put on to stop the vinegar evaporating, i.e. good corks or a layer of thick, waxed vinegar-proof paper, then a metal lid and clip; the clip can be removed when the chutney is cold.

RIPE TOMATO CHUTNEY

450 g/1 lb ripe tomatoes	8 g/¼ oz salt
225 g/8 oz onions	8 g/¼ oz ground ginger
100 g/4 oz sour apples	Pinch of Cayenne pepper
450 g/1 lb stoned raisins	250 ml/½ pint vinegar
100 g/4 oz light soft brown sugar	

Skin the tomatoes and peel and core the apples. Chop the tomatoes, onions, apples and raisins. Mix all the ingredients and boil to a mash. This will take an hour or more. Put into small jars, cover, and seal when cold.

PICKLED PEARS

2·7 kg/6 lb hard pears   25 g/1 oz cinnamon stick
1·35 kg/3 lb sugar   24 cloves
250 ml/½ pint vinegar   24 peppercorns

Peel the pears and cut in half if they are large. Put them in cold
salted water to keep a good colour. Dissolve the sugar in the
vinegar and add the spices tied in a muslin bag. When hot, add
the pears and simmer gently until the pears are tender but not
broken. Put the pears into warm jars, pour the syrup over, and
cover firmly.

SPICED VINEGAR APPLES

900 g/2 lb apples   500 ml/1 pint vinegar
15 g/½ oz whole cloves   900 g/2 lb sugar
15 g/½ oz stick cinnamon   ½ teaspoon salt
15 g/½ oz whole allspice

Put the sugar, vinegar and salt into a saucepan, with the spices tied
in a muslin bag. Bring to the boil and add the peeled, cored and
sliced apples. Cook gently until the apples are tender, then take
out the fruit, drain carefully and pack into warm jars. Boil the
syrup until it thickens, take out the spice bag, pour over the
apples and seal tightly.

PICKLED BLACKBERRIES

1·35 kg/3 lb blackberries   ½ teaspoon each ground
450 g/1 lb sugar   cinnamon and ground cloves
250 ml/½ pint vinegar

Simmer the vinegar, sugar and spices together for 5 minutes. Add
the blackberries and simmer for 15 minutes. Bottle and seal down
while very hot.

SWEET PICKLED DAMSONS

1·8 kg/4 lb large damsons
500 ml/1 pint vinegar

675 g/1½ lb sugar
25 g/1 oz mixed pickling spice

Prick the damsons with a large needle. Put the vinegar, sugar and spice in a pan and heat until the sugar has dissolved. Add the damsons, cook until soft but not broken, and then lift carefully into jars. Reduce the vinegar to a syrup by boiling, remove the spices and pour the syrup over the fruit. Cover tightly. These are good with poultry or cold meat, particularly goose.

SPICY PICKLED PLUMS

1 kg/2½ lb firm plums
500 ml/1 pint vinegar
675 g/1½ lb sugar
2·5 cm/1 inch cinnamon stick

1 teaspoon cloves
Blade of mace
10 allspice berries

Prick the plums with a needle. Boil the vinegar, sugar and spices and pour over the plums. Leave overnight. Drain off the syrup and boil it for 10 minutes. Pour over the fruit again and leave for 12 hours. Bring to the boil with the plums. Remove the spices and put the plums into hot preserving jars. Boil up the syrup, pour over the plums, and screw on the tops immediately.

PICKLED GOOSEBERRIES WITH GARLIC

900 g/2 lb gooseberries
225 g/8 oz light soft brown sugar
1 litre/2 pints white wine vinegar
1 tablespoon dry mustard

2 whole garlic heads
350 g/12 oz raisins
15 g/½ oz Cayenne pepper

Cook together the gooseberries, sugar and half the vinegar until they are soft. Stir in the mustard, crushed garlic, raisins and Cayenne pepper. Add the remaining vinegar, stir well and put into preserving jars. Seal at once. Keep for 6 months before using.

GOOSEBERRY RELISH

900 g/2 lb gooseberries
350 g/12 oz seedless raisins
450 g/1 lb onions
225 g/8 oz brown sugar
1 teaspoon dry mustard

1 tablespoon ground ginger
2 tablespoons salt
¼ teaspoon Cayenne pepper
2 teaspoons turmeric
500 ml/1 pint vinegar

Top and tail the gooseberries and put them through a mincer with the raisins and the onions. Add the sugar, mustard, ginger, salt, Cayenne pepper, turmeric and vinegar. Bring slowly to the boil, and then simmer for 45 minutes. Put through a coarse sieve. Reheat thoroughly and pour into bottles.

WORCESTERSHIRE SAUCE

500 ml/1 pint brown malt
  vinegar
2 shallots
2 tablespoons anchovy essence

3 tablespoons walnut ketchup
2 tablespoons soy sauce
A little salt

Mix all the ingredients together and put into a bottle. Cork firmly and shake the bottle twice a day for a fortnight. Strain and bottle.

TOMATO SAUCE

1·8 kg/4 lb ripe tomatoes
4 large onions
450 g/1 lb Demerara sugar
25 g/1 oz salt

50 g/2 oz peppercorns
15 g/½ oz cloves
2 teaspoons Cayenne pepper
500 ml/1 pint vinegar

Slice the tomatoes and onions and mix with the other ingredients. Simmer gently for 2 hours, stirring occasionally. Rub through a fine sieve, leaving nothing but spice, seeds and skin in the sieve. Bring to the boil and boil for 5 minutes. Bottle when cold.

SWEET-SOUR PLUM SAUCE

1·8 kg/4 lb plums or damsons	15 g/½ oz each ground ginger,
225 g/8 oz onions	allspice, nutmeg and dry
500 ml/1 pint vinegar	mustard powder
25 g/1 oz salt	225 g/8 oz sugar

Cut up plums and onions and cook with the vinegar, salt and spices for 30 minutes. Sieve, stir in the sugar and bring to the boil. Simmer for 1 hour, stirring occasionally, and bottle while still warm.

Potted products

Potted meats, fish and even vegetables and cheeses were often prepared in country households before the days of refrigerators. 'Potting' under a coating of clarified lard or butter was a useful way of preserving such products for a few days when supplies were plentiful. These 'potted' preserves were put up in very small jars, as they had to be eaten quickly once the seal of fat was broken. The flesh was usually minced or pounded, making them rather like pastes, so they can be sliced and eaten with salad, or can be used on toast or in sandwiches.

Whole game birds were sometimes 'potted' too; but the term only indicated that they had been cooked for a long time in a slow oven just with some butter and their own juices. Thereafter, the recipe might be for a hot pot-roast dish or for a whole bird preserved in fat.

CLARIFIED BUTTER

Place the desired quantity of unsalted butter in a saucepan and place over low heat. Skim off the foam from the surface as the butter heats. One 225 g/8 oz piece of butter will take 15–20 minutes; a larger quantity can take as long as an hour. When the butter becomes very clear, particles of sediment sink to the bottom of the pan, and foam stops rising to the surface, remove it from the heat and strain it through an extremely fine sieve or through several thicknesses of cheesecloth, leaving any excess sediment in the bottom of the pan. Allow the butter to cool to lukewarm before using it. Clarified butter can be stored in the refrigerator for several weeks, or can be frozen and stored for up to 6 months.

POTTED SHRIMPS

450 g/1 lb shrimps, cooked and shelled
300 g/10 oz butter

½ teaspoon ground mace
½ teaspoon ground nutmeg
Pinch of Cayenne pepper

Prepare the shrimps. Put 100 g/4 oz butter into a saucepan, and melt it slowly. Skim off foam and remove butter from heat. Spoon the clear butter into a bowl, and discard the milky solids at the bottom of the pan. Melt the remaining butter over moderate heat. Stir in the spices and add the shrimps. Stir them so they are coated in the butter. Pour into individual dishes or one large one. Pour the clarified butter over them and leave until cold.

POTTED MEAT

Put any kind of cooked meat twice through the mincer, or rub through a sieve; season to taste, not forgetting nutmeg or cinnamon, if liked. Mix well with butter and press into pots; pour melted clarified butter over to preserve it.

POTTED BEEF

450 g/1 lb shin of beef
1 teaspoon salt

⅛ teaspoon pepper
100 g/4 oz clarified butter, melted

Wash and dry the meat and cut into very small pieces. Season and place in a stone jam jar or in a basin; cover with aluminium foil or greased greaseproof paper and stand in a pan of water. Cover the pan and simmer for 2½ hours. Strain the liquid into a bowl and add 75 g/3 oz butter. Mince the meat several times till very fine. Mix with the liquid. Put into a clean jar or bowl and pour over it the remaining melted clarified butter. Keep in a cool place and use within 2 days.

POTTED PIGEON

3 pigeons	Bone stock from pigeons
Worcestershire sauce, if liked	Melted butter
Pepper and salt	

Skin and clean the pigeons. Place in a pan with water to cover and cook till meat begins to leave the bones. Take off fire, remove bones and mince meat finely. Put bones back in pan and boil till water has reduced to 1 cupful. Add all seasonings, moisten with bone stock and a little melted butter. Boil or bake small heatproof pots or jars to sterilize. Press in the meat mixture, and knock out any air pockets. Cover with melted butter, preferably clarified.

POTTED GROUSE

2 old grouse	Clarified butter, melted
1 carrot	Bunch of mixed herbs
1 onion	Salt and pepper
50 g/2 oz streaky bacon	

Slice the carrot and onion, and cut the bacon in neat pieces and fry in butter until golden. Put into a casserole with the herbs and plenty of salt and pepper, and put the grouse on top. Cover with stock and cook at 300°F, 150°C, gas mark 2 for 2½ hours. Remove the carrot. Remove all the bones of the grouse, and put the meat through a mincer, then pound, sieve or process it in a liquidizer. Press into a shallow dish and cover with melted, clarified butter.

POTTED PARTRIDGE

2 partidges   250 ml/½ pint game stock
225 g/8 oz butter

Season the birds inside and out and put a lump of butter in each. Put into a casserole with some good stock and the rest of the butter, cover with a double layer of cooking foil and a lid and cook at 325°F, 170°C, gas mark 3 for 1½ hours. Leave until cold, when the butter will form a seal on top. Do not uncover until they are to be eaten; they will keep for several days.

POTTED RABBIT

1 jointed rabbit	12 allspice
50 g/2 oz butter	6 peppercorns
1 cube sugar	Ground nutmeg to taste
1 onion	225 g/8 oz butter
12 cloves	2 teaspoons Worcestershire sauce

Soak the rabbit joints in salted water for 2 hours and dry well. Put them into a casserole with a tightly-fitting lid, and add 50 g/2 oz butter, sugar, the onion stuck with cloves, allspice, peppercorns, and a good sprinkling of nutmeg. Put on the lid and cook at 300°F, 150°C, gas mark 2 for 3 hours. Cool and remove meat from the bones. Put the meat through the mincer twice and mix with the juices from the casserole, most of the butter and the Worcester-shire sauce. Put into small pots, and cover with a little extra melted butter.

POTTED STILTON

225 g/8 oz butter
900 g/2 lb Stilton
Salt

Powdered mace
Port as required
Clarified butter

Pound the butter and cheese in a mortar. Season with salt and mace, moisten with a very little port and press down well in little pots. Cover with clarified butter.

CHAPTER 12
STORING, SALTING AND SMOKING

Storing vegetables and fruits

ROOT vegetables can be stored in trenches or under straw or sand on a dry floor. Potatoes and turnips take up a lot of space indoors, so they are best stored outside in trenches about 1 m/3 feet wide and 15 cm/6 inches deep. The roots should be piled in triangular heaps about 1 m/3 feet high, covered with straw or earth, leaving a little straw at the top so that moisture escapes. Turnips can also be stored in a heap, simply covered with straw or sand, and so can beetroot. Parsnips can be stored under straw in a cool place, or they can be left in the ground. Carrots are best lifted and stored in a cool place in boxes raised above ground level.

Marrows and pumpkins can be stored in a cool dry place away from frost, or they can be hung in nets. Plenty of stalk should be left on, and it is wise to seal the stalk end with wax.

Let onions dry outside for a week or two, and then store them in an old stocking, or plait them together.

STORING FRUIT AND NUTS

Apples, pears and quinces are best left in an airy place to cool and sweat for a few days before storing permanently. The apple store should be a cool, dark and very slightly moist place such as a shed, cellar or attic which is frost-proof. Store the fruit on trays; inspect it frequently and remove unsound fruit. Pears ripen quickly and need extra care. Special eating apples can be wrapped in waxed paper or in sheets of newspaper before storing in boxes.

Nuts should be removed from their outer husks, and walnuts and almonds need scrubbing. Chestnuts and walnuts can be packed in a crock with salt or dry sand between each layer. Nuts to be used for cooking can be shelled, dried off in a cool oven, and packed into clean glass jars.

Drying fruit and vegetables

Drying is the oldest method of preservation. Apples, dessert pears, grapes, sweet plums, peas, beans, onions, leeks and mush-rooms are all suited to it. They can be dried in the oven, a warm cupboard or a rack over the stove, in a constant gentle heat with a current of air to carry away moisture (this is best obtained by leaving a cupboard or oven door slightly open). Fruit and vege-tables should be spread on oven racks or wire cake trays spread with muslin; this should be scalded before use, or it may scorch during drying. The ideal heat for drying is between 120°F–150°F, 50°C–65°C, as the fruit or vegetables should be dried, *not* cooked or scorched.

APPLE RINGS

Apples should be ripe but not over-ripe. Using a silver or stain-less steel knife, peel and core the apples and cut into rings about 0·5 cm/¼ inch thick. Put into a basin of salt water immediately (use 15 g/½ oz salt to 1 litre/2 pints water) and leave for 10 minutes. The rings should be threaded on a stick which can rest on the runners of an oven, and the rings should not touch each other. Dry at 150°F, 65°C, for some hours. Apples should be like dry chamois leather, moist and pliable. Cool in the air before packing tightly in paper bags, or in dry jars or tins. Store in a dry, dark place.

It is best to soak dried fruit for 24 hours before cooking, and to use the water used to soak them for cooking too; flavour it with a little lemon or vanilla, a clove or a piece of ginger.

DRIED PLUMS

Plums must be ripe. Halve and stone them, or dry them whole. Stretch muslin on sticks to replace oven shelves, and dry plums on these. Dry slowly like apples.

DRIED BEANS

Leave haricot beans on the plants until dry and withered. Pull up plants and hang in an airy shed. Shell the peas and store as for seed. Young French and runner beans can be sliced, blanched for five minutes, drained, and dried in a thin layer.

DRIED MUSHROOMS

Cut the stalks short and peel the mushrooms. Lay them on the oven racks and when they are dried quite stiff, store them away. When preparing them for use, soak them in water and simmer them in a little stock.

DRIED ONIONS AND LEEKS

Peel onions and take away any bad parts, and slice them; lay on muslin on oven racks. Leeks may be cut in strips lengthwise if preferred. Keep them moving about occasionally to help the drying, and when they are quite crisp take them out, and after a little while store them away.

DRIED PEAS

Leave marrowfat varieties on the plants until dry and withered. Pull up the plants and hang in an airy shed. Shell the peas and store as for seed. For young, sugary peas, blanch them for 5 minutes, drain them and shake off excess moisture. Spread out in a thin layer and dry very carefully, without scorching.

Salting and smoking

While it is comparatively easy to salt food at home, smoking is a more complicated business and involves the preparation of a smoke-box. Salting preserves food quite well, but smoking has additional preservative qualities as well as giving the food a special flavour. Foods which can be smoked include eel, salmon, trout, cod's roe, ham and bacon, tongue, turkey, goose, duck and chicken, beef, mutton and home-made sausages; some items need brining before smoking.

The simplest form of smokehouse can be constructed in a 10-gallon drum with the bottom cut out and a replaceable top which has a few holes punched in. This is mostly useful for smoking trout or haddock, suspended over the concentrated source of heat and smoke. Haddock should be split, cleaned and beheaded, rubbed inside and out with salt, and left overnight, then dried in the open air for 3 days. Trout need not be split or beheaded, but the gut should be removed. The fish should then be suspended by the tail on a rod across the top of the drum, and tied with a piece of wire at least 30 cm/1 foot from the fire. The drum should then be up-ended over the fire – best made between bricks on which the drum stands. The heat must be evenly maintained during smoking – which will take from 9 to 12 hours.

In addition to the basic smokehouse, keep a good supply of wood handy. The object of creating the smoke is to make fumes which solidify the albumen in the meat. This halts decomposition; any special flavour is a bonus. The best smoke is produced by slow combustion by hardwood shavings; oak, beech, and hornbeam are excellent, especially with additional flavour provided by juniper and bay. The addition of thyme, sage or heather makes a good variation. Resinous woods should be avoided because they can give an unpleasant flavour to some products.

A slightly more elaborate smokehouse can be constructed for permanent use. This can be a drum or a packing-case which has been made smoke-proof at the joints, standing across a trench. The trench should be about 3 m/10 feet long, 30 cm/1 foot deep and 30 cm/1 foot wide, dug in the direction of the prevailing wind, with old paving stones or sheet iron to roof it over. If the lid of the house is hinged, it will be easier to use, and it should have small holes or a tube inserted as a vent.

To use this type of smokehouse, light a fire at the end furthest from the box, cover with stones or iron sheets, and open the lid of the box. When the fire is red hot, draw it to the end of the trench and put a load of hardwood sawdust between the fire and the box. Leave a little flue space, cover the trench and seal all spaces with earth. The food can be hung across the box and the lid closed and not opened for 48 hours.

The idea is to build up a progressively denser smoke which dries and flavours the food gradually; if the first smoke is too dense, it will form a dry coating on the food which will not then be penetrated by the later smoking. For this type of smoking, the food should be brined first in a strong brine (with enough salt to float a potato). A small fish need only be brined for 20 minutes, but a salmon needs several days, and more elaborate preparation.

The smoking method which is most likely to appeal today is the one using an old-fashioned farmhouse chimney with equipment which can still be used for hams, sausages and other meats. These must be cured first, and are then best left to dry for 2 or 3 days before smoking. The food to be smoked can also be hung above the opening of an old bread oven so that the smoke gently enfolds it.

In the latter case, the temperature should never rise above 90°F, 32°C, at which point the fat melts and the meat is spoiled. The fire should only be smouldering, not flaming. On the first day, the meat should only be smoked for 30 minutes, then rubbed down with pepper, thyme and chopped bay leaves, which will cling to the fat. After cooling and drying for 48 hours, the meat should be smoked again for 1 hour. After further drying for 48 hours, and 1 hour's smoking, a light flavour will be obtained. The meat should then be hung in the chimney for 2 or 3 weeks before being stored in a cool dry place. The meat will lose about one-quarter of its weight in smoking.

The wide chimney can be used for the complete smoking, simply with the exposed meat suspended high up on a bar or on hooks on wire, but the fire will need careful attention throughout. Smoke the meat for about an hour a day, allowing a total of at least 3 weeks for complete smoking.

A better method of smoking is by regulating the smoke-flow; construct a smoking-box for the fireplace, to fit on a wall above the fire. To do this, a sheet of metal has to be fitted across the whole chimney with a piece of piping going through it and the wall into the smoking-box. A second piece of piping should then go out of the top of the box and back into the chimney. Meat in the box needs about 2 hours a day for 8 consecutive days.

Salt cures for ham and bacon

SWEET CURE

This is a sweet pickle for ham or bacon, using a carcass of about 72 kg/8 score lb. Split the carcass, and from each side cut a rounded ham and a round shoulder (fore-ham). De-bone the middle except for the chump end of the loin, which can be used fresh or lightly salted. To make packing easier, the middle may be sub-divided into back and belly. Rub the knuckles with salt, and sprinkle salt on the joints, then pack into a crock. Pour over a pickle (for 6·75 kg/15 lb ham or fore-ham) consisting of 225 g/8 oz block salt, 450 g/1 lb black treacle, 225 g/8 oz brown sugar, 500 ml/1 pint malt vinegar and 1 litre/2 pints old ale, with 1 table-spoon saltpetre. Turn the joints over in the pickle twice daily for the first week, then once daily for 4 weeks. Hang the meat to drain for 24 hours, then encase in clean cotton bags and suspend from hooks. The hams are ready for use in 6 months and do not need soaking before cooking. For 6·75 kg/15 lb bacon, use a pickle of 225 g/8 oz salt, 225 g/8 oz brown sugar, 50 g/2 oz black treacle, 125 ml/¼ pint vinegar and no saltpetre. Pack in crocks and pour over pickle, and turn joints twice daily for 3 weeks. The bacon can be used immediately after curing, or it can be soaked for 1 week with several changes of water before cooking as required.

DRY CURE

This is a dry-cure method for a carcass of 145–180 kg/16–20 score, using 12·7 kg/28 lb salt and 225 g/8 oz saltpetre. Singe the flesh to remove hair and cut the carcass, removing the head, the chine with some of the back meat, and the ribs with a coating of lean meat.

  Clean by sprinkling the flesh side with salt, and rubbing salt into the skin. Leave the sides, flesh side down, to drain for 24 hours, then wipe with a clean cloth. Sprinkle saltpetre on the flesh side of the shoulders and hams. Sprinkle half the salt over the sides, which are placed one on top of the other. After 7 days, sprinkle half the remaining salt on, and put the top side at the bottom. After 7 more days, add remaining salt, and reverse positions of sides. The sides are in cure for about 4 weeks in all.

Wipe off sides after curing, and hang up to dry for 7 days. Store sides whole, or for convenience cut into hams, middles and shoulders before hanging them up in clean cotton bags.

HEAVY CARCASS CURE

This is most suitable for a heavy carcass, which may be cut in three different ways. One method involves removing a chine of 15 cm/6 inches to 20 cm/8 inches wide and salting the 'long side'; the carcass can be simply split; or it may be cut into hams, forehams and middles. The ingredients for curing are 12·7 kg/28 lb salt, 225/8 oz saltpetre and 450 g/1 lb Demerara sugar. Rub saltpetre in first, spreading most thickly on blood patches. Sprinkle meat with salt and pack on a layer of salt in a trough. Place hams on top and every day for a fortnight, sprinkle on salt. When meat is cured, wipe salt off and sprinkle with flour. After being dry for 3 months, pack in a bin containing slaked lime.

CHAPTER 13
THE HERB GARDEN

Most cottages and farm gardens have various herbs growing among the flowers or vegetables, where they can be quickly and easily picked for cooking. A specially-planned herb garden is pleasant, but by no means necessary for the cook; a large tub or a series of pots can provide nearly all the herbs needed in the kitchen. The taller and more decorative herbs can be used in flower borders in the time-honoured country way.

Herbs are easy to grow and not fussy about soil on the whole. The many types of mint, and angelica, like moist soil, and parsley needs a rich soil, while fennel prefers open ground. Many others prefer poor, dry land, but they do like sunshine. Most of the herbs can be grown from seed, but others are best grown from the division of older plants. Where a plant can be grown by both methods, it will be found that root division gives quicker results.

A selection of the following herbs will be found very useful in the kitchen. These herbs are of course best used fresh, as they have a much stronger, fresher flavour; but they can usefully be dried or frozen for winter use.

Drying Herbs   Herbs for drying should be picked just before they come into flower. They are best picked on a dry day before the sun is hot. Remove leaves from the stalks of large varieties, and tie small herbs into sprays. Put on shallow trays in thin layers and leave in a cool oven (125°F, 60°C) or an airing cupboard, or on a cooker rack, until dry. This gives clean freshly-coloured herbs with good flavour. Parsley is not very easy to dry; it should be placed in a hot oven (400°F, 200°C) for 1 minute, and then be finished off in the cool oven or airing cupboard; then it will retain its bright green colour. When the herbs are dry, remove the stems and rub the herbs down with a rolling pin. Put into small tins or jars, and store in a cool, dry place. Dried herbs should be used within a year, sooner if possible.

Freezing Herbs   Wash herbs and pack them in foil or polythene to freeze. Herbs can also be chopped and frozen in ice-cube trays, and then the cubes can be taken out and packed into bags for storage.

Growing and using herbs

ANGELICA

Growing   Seeds germinate slowly and should be kept in moist sand before sowing in August, or should be used straight from the plant.
Main Uses   Candy the stems for decoration and flavouring. Good as a flavour with rhubarb.

BASIL

Growing   Sow the seeds in gentle heat in March, prick off into boxes and then plant in a rich warm border in June. Plants also grow well in pots. This is a tender plant which does not care for cold.

Main Uses   Use with turtle soup, tomatoes, liver.

CARAWAY

Growing   Sow the seeds in autumn or spring. This plant is a hardy biennial. Harvest in July and remove seeds at once.

Main Uses   In cakes and biscuits, and on cabbage.

CHERVIL

Growing   Sow small successions of seed from early spring until autumn, watering carefully in dry weather.

Main Uses   In salads, egg and fish dishes.

CHIVES

Growing   Divide clumps every spring or autumn, and lift and re-plant every two years. Don't let the plant run to flower.

Main Uses   For salads, egg dishes, cream cheese, soups, flavoured vinegar.

CORIANDER

Growing   Sow seeds of this annual plant in April. Cut down the plant when the seeds begin to ripen, leave in a warm place to dry and remove the seeds.

Main Uses   With sweets, curries. Use the leaves in soups and stews.

DILL

Growing Sow seeds in March and thin out plants.
Main Uses Leaves – new potatoes, fish. Seeds – flavoured vinegar, cucumber dishes.

FENNEL

Growing Sow seeds in April or May, but germination is uncertain.
Main Uses Use leaves for fish, salads, vinegar, pickles.

HORSERADISH

Growing Plant single crowns with young roots 15 cm/6 inches long in well-prepared soil trenched with a dressing of rotten manure. Spring plants will give good roots in autumn, which should be lifted and stored in sand.
Main Uses In sauce, flavoured vinegar.

LOVAGE

Growing A large plant which likes a lot of water. Sow plants in the spring (they will need about 1 m/3 feet growing space, and are also tall). Will also grow from fresh seed.
Main Uses The flavour of the leaves which is like hot-spiced celery is good in soups, casseroles, stews.

MARJORAM

Growing Pot and Sweet-Knotted Marjorams are the types most commonly grown; grow from seed. The plant is tender and best grown as an annual.
Main Uses In forcemeats, soups, stews.

MINT

Growing There are dozens of different mints, but round-leaved (Lamb Mint) is best for sauce. Plant in early spring by division of roots in a moist place. Mint roots spread rapidly.

Main Uses In mint sauce, and on new potatoes, jelly.

PARSLEY

Growing Grow from seed in the open ground or in pots. Germination is slow. Plants like a well-drained soil in a semi-shady position.

Main Uses Immensely varied. Our most commonly used garnishing and flavouring herb.

ROSEMARY

Growing Grow from cuttings in well-drained sheltered soil.

Main Uses With lamb, pork.

SAGE

Growing Grow from seed or root division. There are many varieties, but Narrow Silver Leaved and Red Sage make very beautiful plants.

Main Uses Use with pork, goose, duck, sausages, broad beans.

SAVORY

Growing Winter Savory is a perennial, evergreen in winter; but Summer Savory which is an annual raised from seed, has a more subtle flavour.

Main Uses With broad beans.

SWEET BAY

Growing A bush which grows best in dryish half-shady conditions. Bay trees are difficult to get started; they are best propagated by layering. Plants do not like frost, but young plants in pots can be kept in a greenhouse in winter.

Main Uses In soups, stews, fish dishes, egg custards, milk puddings.

TARRAGON

Growing Choose French tarragon which has a better flavour than the Russian variety. Grow from cuttings or root division. The plant does not dry well and is best used fresh.

Main Uses With many foods; a favourite mild seasoning for chicken, fish, sauces, flavoured vinegar.

THYME

Growing There are many varieties of thyme, which may be grown from seed or from root division. Lemon thyme is deliciously refreshing.

Main Uses In forcemeats and stuffings, soups.

Dishes using herbs

HERB VINEGAR

Flavoured vinegars can be made which are delicious for cooking. Place 250 ml/$\frac{1}{2}$ pint of herbs in 500 ml/1 pint of wine vinegar for 4 days to infuse. Tarragon and fennel make particularly good vinegars.

HERB JELLY

Mint jelly is often made, but the same recipe is less often used (though it can be) to produce parsley, sage, thyme or bay-leaf jelly. These are delicious with pork, ham and poultry.

SAGE AND ONION STUFFING

450 g/1 lb onions
Salt and pepper
100 g/4 oz soft white breadcrumbs

2 teaspoons finely-chopped sage
25 g/1 oz butter

Chop the onions and simmer with just enough water to cover them for 10 minutes. Strain and keep the cooking water. Mix the onions with the breadcrumbs, sage, butter, salt and pepper and add just enough water to bind the stuffing. Use for fat meats such as pork, goose and duck.

PARSLEY AND THYME STUFFING

75 g/3 oz soft white breadcrumbs
50 g/2 oz butter
1 tablespoon chopped onion
Grated rind and juice of 1 lemon
Salt and pepper
1 tablespoon chopped fresh
  thyme

½ tablespoon chopped fresh
  parsley
1 tablespoon chopped fresh
  marjoram
1 egg

Melt the butter, and soften the onion in it until golden. Mix with all the other ingredients and use for stuffing chickens, turkey or veal.

HERB SEASONING

Dried orange peel
Dried thyme

Dried marjoram
Dried hyssop

Pound the orange peel to powder. Mix two parts orange peel with one part of each of the herbs. Keep in a well-stoppered jar to use for stuffings, forcemeats and meat loaves.

SWEET HERB SEASONING

50 g/2 oz parsley	25 g/1 oz lemon thyme
50 g/2 oz marjoram	25 g/1 oz basil
50 g/2 oz chervil	25 g/1 oz savory
25 g/1 oz thyme	15 g/½ oz tarragon

Dry the herbs when they are in season and weigh them when they are dried. Rub each one to a fine powder, and sift through a strainer. Mix together and keep in a tightly-stoppered bottle for seasoning.

SEASONING SALT, HOME-MADE

1 teaspoon, mixed dried herbs	25 g/1 oz pepper
15 g/½ oz mixed ground cloves, mace and ginger	25 g/1 oz salt

Mix well together and rub through a sieve. Put into an airtight tin or bottle and keep near the stove. Use sparingly in soups and stews.

ROSEMARY OR LAVENDER SUGAR

Sprigs of fresh rosemary or lavender	Caster sugar

Clean and dry the rosemary or lavender. Put into a screw-topped jar and fill with sugar. Shake well and leave for 24 hours. Shake again and leave for a week before use. Use the sugar in milk puddings of all kinds, or sprinkle on cakes or biscuits.

MIXED HERB BUTTER

100 g/4 oz butter
1 teaspoon chopped fresh parsley
½ teaspoon chopped fresh mint
½ teaspoon chopped fresh chives
¼ teaspoon chopped fresh
 tarragon

¼ teaspoon chopped fresh
 marjoram
Lemon juice

Soften the butter at room temperature until it can be creamed. Blend in the herbs, and add as much lemon juice as the butter will absorb easily. Put into tightly-covered jars and keep in a cool place. Use on bread, toast or sandwiches, or on hot meat or fish.

PARSLEY SAUCE

1 tablespoon butter
1 tablespoon flour
250 ml/½ pint milk or stock

3 tablespoons chopped fresh
 parsley

Melt the butter and work in the flour. Add the milk slowly, and cook gently for 5 minutes. Just before serving, add the chopped parsley. This is a good standard sauce with fish and ham, and the stock from cooking the fish or ham can be used as all or part of the liquid.

FENNEL SAUCE

40 g/1½ oz butter
1 heaped tablespoon chopped
 fennel

25 g/1 oz plain flour
375 ml/¾ pint water
Salt and pepper

Melt 25 g/1 oz butter and cook the fennel in it for ½ minute. Blend in the flour and gradually add the water, beating smoothly over a low heat. Cook gently until the sauce is creamy, season to taste and add the remaining butter. Serve with grilled mackerel and other fish. It does wonders for frozen fillets.

HERB CHEESE

2 tablespoons fresh mixed herbs
2 tablespoons double cream
3 tablespoons dry sherry

100 g/4 oz grated sharp-flavoured
  cheese
Salt and pepper

Choose a good mixture of herbs, such as parsley, sage, thyme, chives and tarragon. Put them with the cream, sherry, cheese, salt and pepper into a thick pan over a low heat, and heat very gently until the mixture is creamy and very pale green in colour. Put into small hot jars and cover with jam pot covers. Keep in a cool place, and use fairly quickly.

HERBED SAVOURY BALLS

75 g/3 oz plain flour
25 g/1 oz shredded suet
½ teaspoon baking powder
1 small onion, finely-chopped

Salt and pepper
1 heaped tablespoon chopped
  mixed herbs

Mix together the flour, suet and baking powder. Add the very finely-chopped onion, salt and pepper and chopped herbs. Mix to a light dough with cold water. Form into small balls and roll them lightly in flour. Put into soup or stew and simmer for 20 minutes.

HERB PIE WITH HAM

225 g/8 oz shortcrust pastry
25 g/1 oz grated cheese
100 g/4 oz cooked ham or
  rindless bacon
2 eggs
250 ml/½ pint milk
1 tablespoon chopped onion

1 teaspoon chopped chives
1 teaspoon chopped parsley
1 teaspoon chopped tarragon
1 teaspoon chopped lovage
1 teaspoon chopped chervil
1 teaspoon chopped marjoram
Salt and pepper

This combination of herbs is a very good one, but of course you can vary the selection to suit what you have to hand. Mix the pastry, including the cheese in it; line a flan ring or pie plate with the pastry. Chop the ham or bacon finely and sprinkle on the pastry base of the pie. Beat together the eggs and milk lightly and add the finely-chopped onion and herbs. Season with salt and pepper and pour into the pastry case. Bake at 400°F, 200°C, gas mark 6 for 35 minutes.

SAGE AND ONION TART

225 g/8 oz shortcrust pastry
3 medium-sized onions
25 g/1 oz butter
125 ml/¼ pint creamy milk
1 egg
1 tablespoon chopped fresh sage

1 teaspoon chopped fresh parsley
100 g/4 oz rindless bacon, chopped
Salt and pepper

Line a pie plate with the pastry. Chop the onions and toss them in the hot butter until soft. Mix with the milk, egg, herbs, chopped bacon and seasoning, and pour into the pastry base. Bake at 400°F, 200°C, gas mark 6 for 35 minutes.

POTATO POT PIE WITH ROSEMARY

900 g/2 lb potatoes
450 g/1 lb onions
Salt and pepper

Rosemary sprigs
50 g/2 oz butter
250 ml/½ pint milk

Peel the potatoes and onions and slice them thinly. Put into a greased casserole in alternate layers, seasoning well with salt and pepper and with very finely-chopped rosemary leaves. Dot with the butter and finish with a layer of potatoes. Pour in the milk. Put on a lid and bake at 350°F, 180°C, gas mark 4 for 1½ hours until the milk has been absorbed. The lid should be removed for the last 15 minutes to brown the top of the potatoes. This pot pie is good with all kinds of meat or poultry.

FISH IN CIDER AND HERB SAUCE

450 g/1 lb fish fillets	Squeeze of lemon juice
Seasoned flour	65 ml/2 fl oz dry cider
Butter	2 tablespoons cream
Mixed fresh herbs, chopped	

Use any filleted fish you like for this dish. Bream, sole, hake and John Dory are all good cooked this way. Dry the fillets and dip them in seasoned flour, using plenty of freshly-ground pepper. Heat a good knob of butter in a flameproof oven-to-table pan and add about a tablespoon of finely-chopped mixed fresh herbs (fennel, parsley, marjoram and basil are good for this). Fry the fish, skin side down, for 3 minutes, then turn the fish and cook for a further 3 minutes. Squeeze on lemon juice, and add the cider. Cover the pan and simmer over very low heat for 10 minutes. Just before serving, take the skin off the fish, and pour on the cream. Serve straight from the hot dish.

HERBED MEAT LOAF

450 g/1 lb spinach	$\frac{1}{2}$ garlic clove
450 g/1 lb lean pork	1 teaspoon salt
100 g/4 oz cooked ham	Pinch of black pepper
1 heaped tablespoon chopped mixed herbs	$\frac{1}{4}$ teaspoon ground nutmeg
50 g/2 oz onion	1 egg

Cook the spinach in as little liquid as possible, drain it and press it dry. Mince the pork finely, and chop the ham in small pieces. Grate the onion and crush the garlic clove. Mix together the spinach, pork, ham, herbs, onion and garlic and season with salt, pepper and nutmeg. Mix well with the egg. Put into a casserole or loaf tin, and cover. Put into a baking tin containing hot water which comes halfway up the dish. Bake at 350°F, 180°C, gas mark 4 for 1 hour. Cool for 24 hours before using.

PICKLED NASTURTIUMS (MOCK CAPERS)

Nasturtium seeds
1 litre/2 pints vinegar
50 g/2 oz salt
12 peppercorns

Piece of horseradish root
2 cloves
4 tarragon leaves

Wash the seeds and leave them to soak overnight in cold water.
Mix the vinegar with salt, peppercorns, horseradish, cloves and
tarragon. Drain the seeds and put them into jars. Cover with the
cold spiced vinegar. Cover tightly and keep for 12 months before
using.

CHAPTER 14
GOOD CHEER

HOME-MADE wines, beers and soft drinks used to be part of every country household's stores. These drinks were made from flowers, fruit, roots, grains and herbs. The normal equipment for the brewing or wine-making consisted of a stoneware crock with a lid; and fermentation was usually started by the old method of spreading yeast on a piece of toasted bread. After fermentation, the liquid was put into wooden casks, and, later, into bottles.

In winter, the home-made beer, cider or wine was often used heated and spiced, to ward off colds and chills. But for children, the treatment for colds was more usually a dose of a fruit or flower-flavoured syrup, diluted with water; this served to soothe a rough throat, and induce sleep, and it unintentionally gave a child the much-needed vitamins stored in the summer fruit.

Lighter drinks, such as barley water and lemonade, were usually made as thirst-quenchers. The same use was made of the wines, beer and cider drunk (often in the form of syllabubs) by the men working in the harvest and hay fields in summer. They were, however, used even more for social occasions of all kinds, as were whey and buttermilk drinks.

Beers, cider and wines

GINGER BEER FROM A 'PLANT'

15 g/½ oz fresh yeast
2 teaspoons ground ginger
2 teaspoons sugar

375 ml/¾ pint water
For ingredients added later, see
   the recipe

Mix all these ingredients. Leave for 24 hours, then feed daily with 1 teaspoon ground ginger and 1 teaspoon sugar. After 7 days, strain through a cloth. Reserve both the liquid and the solid matter in the cloth (which is the 'plant').

To finish the ginger beer, mix the strained liquid with 2·5 litres/ 5 pints cold water, the juice of 2 lemons and 675 g/1½ lb sugar dissolved in 1 litre/2 pints hot water. Mix well, pour into screw-topped (beer or cider) bottles, and leave for a week before using. This makes 4·5 litres/8 pints ginger beer.

Halve the remaining solid (the 'plant') and mix with 375 ml/ ¾ pint water; add another 15 g/½ oz fresh yeast, 2 teaspoons ground ginger and 2 teaspoons sugar. Leave for 24 hours, then feed daily with 1 teaspoon ground ginger and 1 teaspoon sugar for 7 days as before. Strain as before. Repeat the whole process every 2 weeks to keep up a supply of ginger beer.

QUICK GINGER BEER

25 g/1 oz root ginger
450 g/1 lb sugar
25 g/1 oz cream of tartar

Juice and rind of 1 lemon
25 g/1 oz yeast

Put the bruised ginger, sugar, cream of tartar and lemon rind into a bowl. Pour on 4·5 litres/8 pints boiling water, stir well, and leave to stand until cold. Add the lemon juice. Mix the yeast with 65 ml/2½ fl oz cold water and add to the other ingredients. Leave overnight, then bottle in screw-topped bottles. This ginger beer can be used after 48 hours.

HOP BEER

450 g/1 lb malt extract   4·5 litres/8 pints water
25 g/1 oz hops   25 g/1 oz yeast

Boil the malt, hops and water for 1½ hours, adding water to make up the original quantity. Strain through muslin. When the liquid is cool, add the yeast and leave covered for 3 days. Syphon off and bottle. Put 1 lump of sugar in each bottle and cork. This is ready in 7 days.

SIMPLE CIDER

1·35 kg/3 lb cooking apples   900 g/2 lb granulated sugar
6·75 litres/12 pints water   3 lemons

Clean the apples, cut them up and mince them with the cores and skins. Place in an (for preference) earthenware bowl and add cold unboiled water. Leave for 1 week, stirring night and morning. Strain the liquid. Stir in the sugar and add the grated rind and juice of the lemons. Set aside for 24 hours, then strain and bottle tightly in screw-topped bottles. This still cider can be drunk within a few days of making, but tastes even finer if left for a few months.

CIDER

3·5 kg/8 lb apples   Juice of 3 large lemons
9 litres/16 pints boiling water   3·5 kg/8 lb sugar
25 g/1 oz root ginger   125 ml/¼ pint boiling water

Do not use any metal when making this drink. Do not peel the apples, but cut them up roughly. Cover with boiling water and leave for 2 weeks, pressing and crushing the apples well from time to time. Strain the liquid. Add the bruised root ginger, lemon juice and sugar, and stir to dissolve the sugar. Add 125 ml/ ¼ pint boiling water, and then leave to stand for 14 days, removing the scum as it rises. Strain into screw-topped bottles and screw on the tops lightly for 2 days. Tighten the stoppers and keep in a cool, dark, dry place for 2 months.

HERB BEER

Small bunch of mixed herbs	900 g/2 lb sugar
25 g/1 oz hops	15 g/½ oz yeast
9 litres/16 pints water	

Make a good selection of herbs, including parsley, thyme, sage and mint. Put the hops and herbs into the water and boil for 1 hour. Strain on to the sugar and stir until it is dissolved. When the mixture is cool, add the yeast. Leave the liquid to stand for 12 hours, and put it into bottles.

NETTLE BEER

900 g/2 lb young nettles	450 g/1 lb Demerara sugar
4·5 litres/8 pints water	25 g/1 oz cream of tartar
2 lemons, rind and juice	25 g/1 oz yeast

Cut off the nettle roots and discard them. Rinse the tops, drain and boil in the water for 15 minutes. Strain into a bowl containing the lemon peel (remove all white pith) and juice, sugar and cream of tartar. Stir vigorously and cool. Add the yeast and keep the bowl covered with a thick cloth in a warm room for 3 days. Strain, bottle and cork, and keep a week before drinking. This is supposed to be a good drink for cleansing the system in spring and early summer.

BEETROOT BEER

450 g/1 lb beetroot	500 ml/1 pint stout
225 g/8 oz sugar	

Wash the beetroot and slice into a bowl. Sprinkle on the sugar and leave for 24 hours. Strain, add the stout, bottle and cork. This is ready in 7–14 days.

TREACLE ALE

450 g/1 lb golden syrup
225 g/8 oz black treacle
4·5 litres/8 pints water
25 g/1 oz yeast

15 g/½ oz ground ginger (optional)
Rind of 1 lemon (optional)

Melt the syrup and treacle in the boiling water. Cool and add yeast. Cover the bowl with a thick cloth and keep in a warm room for 3 days. Syphon off the liquid without disturbing the yeast deposit, bottle and cork. Keep several days before drinking. If ginger and lemon rind are used, add with the boiling water.

BARLEY WINE

450 g/1 lb barley
450 g/1 lb raisins
450 g/1 lb potatoes

1·8 kg/4 lb sugar
25 g/1 oz yeast

Put the barley and chopped raisins into an earthenware jar. Do not peel the potatoes but cut them into very small pieces or grate them. Add them to the barley and raisins, with the sugar. Pour on 4·5 litres/8 pints hot, but not boiling, water and stir until the sugar has dissolved. Add the yeast and leave for 21 days, stirring every day. Strain and bottle, leaving the corks loose for a week or two. Cork firmly, and leave at least 6 months before use.

HONEY BOTCHARD

25 g/1 oz hops
4·5 litres/8 pints water
1·5 kg/3½ lb honey

25 g/1 oz yeast
1 slice toast

Put the hops into the water and boil them for 30 minutes. Strain the liquid and then stir in the honey. Spread the yeast on both sides of the toast and let it float in the wine. Let it start fermenting, and leave it for 21 days after fermentation has begun. Then skim the wine and pour into bottles. It is ready to drink within a few weeks after bottling.

EASY APPLE WINE

2·7 kg/6 lb apples   900 g/2 lb sugar
4·5 litres/8 pints water

Cut up the apples, including the skins and cores. Cover with the water, and mash and stir frequently for 2 days. Strain the liquid and heat up 500 ml/1 pint of it. Pour this over the sugar. Stir well to dissolve, and then add the rest of the liquid. Leave to stand for 3 days. Skim, strain and bottle, corking lightly at first. Push corks in firmly later.

BEE WINE

1·35 kg/3 lb honey   15 g/½ oz yeast
Peel of 2 lemons   8 g/¼ oz phosphate of ammonia
4·5 litres/8 pints cold water   8 g/¼ oz cream of tartar

Add the honey and lemon peel to the cold water and boil for 30 minutes. Pour into a container and when the mixture has become tepid, add the yeast creamed with a little cold water. Add the phosphate of ammonia and the cream of tartar. Cover the container with a piece of muslin and let it ferment. When the liquid has ceased 'working', cover the container closely. After 6 months, pour into bottles and cork down.

NETTLE WINE

3·5 kg/8 lb young nettles   1·35 kg/3 lb white sugar
50 g/2 oz root ginger   15 g/½ oz yeast
3 lemons, rind and juice   1 slice toast
4·5 litres/8 pints water

Boil the nettles, bruised ginger root, lemon rinds and juice together in the water until a dark green, then strain and add the sugar. Put the yeast on toast, and put it on the wine when it is at blood heat. Allow to ferment. When fermentation has ceased, put into bottles with a few raisins in each one.

ORANGE WINE

12 large juicy oranges   1·35 kg/3 lb sugar
4·5 litres/8 pints boiling water

Wash the oranges and slice them thinly, including the peel. Put into a china basin and pour over boiling water. Cover with a cloth and leave for a week, stirring two or three times a day. Strain the liquid. Heat up 500 ml/1 pint and stir in the sugar until dissolved. Add to the remaining liquid. Pour into bottles and cork lightly. Allow to ferment. Leave until fermentation has ceased, and then seal. This will be ready in 4 months.

POTATO WINE

900 g/2 lb raisins   2 large potatoes, grated
1·8 kg/4 lb granulated sugar   4·5 litres/8 pints hot water
450 g/1 lb clean wheat   25 g/1 oz yeast

Mix the raisins, sugar, wheat and grated potato with the hot water. When cooled to just warm, add the yeast. Set aside in a warm place and allow it to ferment for 3 weeks. Stir it every day. Carefully strain off through a jelly bag into bottles but do not squeeze the bag as this will make the wine cloudy. Seal and store. The wine will clear itself in about 4 weeks and should be fit to use soon afterwards but it will improve with longer keeping.

MEAD

25 g/1 oz dried hops   25 g/1 oz yeast
900 g/2 lb honey   1 slice toast
9 litres/16 pints water

Put the hops and honey into the water and boil slowly for 1 hour. Cool, and when lukewarm add the yeast spread on a piece of toast. Cover and leave for 4 days. Strain through muslin, and bottle. Allow to ferment. Only cork loosely until fermentation has ceased, then cork tightly. Keep for 1 year before using.

SLOE WINE

3·5 kg/8 lb sloes
4·5 litres/8 pints boiling water

50 g/2 oz root ginger
Sugar

The sloes are best picked after a frost. Put them into a bowl and pour on the boiling water. Add the bruised ginger and cover with a piece of muslin. Leave for 3 days, stirring each day. Strain and allow 450 g/1 lb sugar to 1 litre/2 pints of liquid. Stir well, and then bottle and cork lightly. Fermentation will soon start. Leave alone until fermentation ceases. This wine can be drunk after 4 months, but improves with keeping longer.

ELDERFLOWER CHAMPAGNE

4 heads of elderflowers
675 g/1½ lb sugar
2 tablespoons white wine vinegar

4·5 litres/8 pints cold water
2 lemons

Put elderflowers, sugar, vinegar and water into a bowl. Squeeze the lemons and add the juice to the mixture. Cut the lemon skins in quarters and add to the liquid. Leave to stand for 24 hours, stirring occasionally. Strain and bottle into screw-topped bottles. Ready to drink within a few days.

MARROW RUM

1 large firm ripe marrow

Demerara sugar

The marrow should be very, very firm and too tough for cooking or cutting with a kitchen knife. Saw through the stalk end, and scoop out the seeds and pulp. Fill the marrow completely with sugar. Put the top back and tape it tightly in place. Put into a bag made of strong cloth and hang it in a cool dry place. After 2 weeks, fill the marrow again with sugar. Seal the top again and hang up the marrow. After about a month, the sugar will begin to drip. Take the marrow from the bag and make a hole in it where the sugar is starting to drip. Let the liquid run through a muslin-covered funnel into bottles. Cork them lightly. Fermentation will soon start. When it has ceased (in a few weeks) cork firmly. Keep for at least a year before using.

Soft drinks, cordials and syrups

THRIFTY APPLE DRINK

Peelings and cores from 1·8 kg/   1 lemon
   4 lb apples   12 cubes sugar
2·25 litres/4 pints boiling water

Put the peelings and cores in a bowl and pour on the boiling water. Rub the sugar cubes over the rind of the lemon to extract the flavour, and add these to the liquid. Cut the lemon in thin slices and add. Cover and leave overnight. Strain and sweeten. Do not keep.

RHUBARB DRINK

3 sticks rhubarb   225 g/8 oz sugar
1 lemon

Cut the rhubarb in very small pieces and pour on 4·5 litres/8 pints boiling water. Add the lemon cut in thin slices and the sugar. Stir until the sugar has dissolved, and then leave until cold. This is a very refreshing drink on a hot day, but not for keeping.

LEMON BARLEY WATER

100 g/4 oz pearl barley
2 lemons

50 g/2 oz cube sugar
1 litre/2 pints boiling water

Wash the barley and put it into a saucepan. Just cover with cold water and bring to the boil. Boil for 4 minutes and strain off the water. Put the barley into a large jug. Rub off the yellow part of the lemon rind on to the sugar and add this to the barley. Pour on the boiling water. Stir to dissolve the sugar and leave until cold. Stir in the juice of the lemons. Strain into a jug, and chill.

FRESH LEMONADE

4 lemons
900 g/2 lb sugar
1 teaspoon oil of lemon

2 teaspoons tartaric acid
1 litre/2 pints boiling water

Squeeze the lemons over the sugar in a basin. Add the oil and acid. Pour on the boiling water. Stir well to dissolve the sugar and leave until cold. Pour into bottles and cork firmly. Store in a cool place, and dilute with water to taste.

SPICED CIDER DRINK

1 litre/2 pints cider
2 tablespoons honey
2 tablespoons lemon juice

1 teaspoon ground nutmeg
1 teaspoon ground cinnamon

Place all the ingredients in a saucepan and bring gently to the boil. Simmer for 10 minutes. Strain through muslin before pouring into glasses. Garnish with apple slices and lemon slices.

KENTISH CORDIAL

900 g/2 lb damsons
1 litre/2 pints water
450 g/1 lb elderberries

1·8 kg/4 lb sugar
5 drops essence of cloves
A little clear honey

Remove the stones from the damsons, and crack 12 of them. Pour the water over the damsons and cracked stones and leave for 24 hours. Boil for 15 minutes, then strain the liquid over the elderberries. Leave again for 24 hours and bring to boiling point. Add the sugar and simmer for 10 minutes. Take off the heat and add the essence of cloves. Bottle when cold, adding 1 teaspoon clear honey to each 500 ml/1 pint. Good for a cold, diluted with hot water.

SUFFOLK BLACKBERRY CORDIAL

1 kg/2 lb ripe blackberries   450 g/1 lb cube sugar
500 ml/1 pint white vinegar   225 g/8 oz honey

Put the blackberries into an earthenware jar and pour on the vinegar. Leave them to stand for a week, stirring and pressing the blackberries two or three times a day to squeeze out the juices. Strain the liquid into a saucepan and add the sugar and honey, and boil for 5 minutes. Cool completely and pour into dark bottles. Cork well and store in a cool place. Use 1 tablespoon of cordial in a glass of hot water as a good bedtime drink; again, it is very good for relieving a cold.

ELDERBERRY SYRUP

2·25 kg/5 lb ripe elderberries,   Cube sugar
   weighed after stripping   Brandy
500 ml/1 pint water
1 small egg white, lightly
   whipped

The berries should be weighed when they have been stripped from their stalks. Wash them and put them into an earthenware jar with the water. Cover and leave in a very low oven until the fruit is pulpy. Strain through a jelly bag and measure the juice. Allow 450 g/1 lb sugar to each 500 ml/1 pint of liquid. Put the juice in a pan and add the egg white which has been whipped to a light froth. Bring to the boil and remove the scum. Warm the sugar and add to the liquid. Bring to the boil, skimming often, and leave to simmer for 5 minutes. Put into bottles and add 1 teaspoon brandy to each bottle. Seal tightly. Dilute with hot or cold water when used. Another drink very good for colds.

LEMON SYRUP

2 lemons
800 g/1¾ lb cube sugar

500 ml/1 pint boiling water
25 g/1 oz tartaric acid

Peel the lemons very thinly. Add the peel to the cube sugar and pour on the boiling water. Squeeze the juice of the lemons into a basin. Mix the tartaric acid with it, then stir all together. Strain and bottle. Use about 2 tablespoonfuls to a tumbler of water.

RASPBERRY VINEGAR

900 g/2 lb raspberries
1 litre/2 pints white vinegar

900 g/2 lb sugar

Put the raspberries into a bowl and crush well. Put them into a jar with the vinegar, cover with muslin, and leave for a week. Strain the liquid into a saucepan and add the sugar. Heat gently until the sugar has dissolved, then boil rapidly, removing the scum as it rises. Pour into warm bottles and cork well. Dilute with hot or cold water to drink.

VIOLET SYRUP

900 g/2 lb violet heads
1·5 litres/3 pints water

Sugar

Soak the violet heads in the water for 24 hours, keeping them covered. Strain off the liquid and measure it. Allow 450 g/1 lb sugar to each 500 ml/1 pint of liquid. Stir until the sugar dissolves and then bring the liquid slowly to the boil. When it boils, remove it from the heat and cool. Bottle when cold and cork tightly. This is very good for sore throats.

Hot mixed drinks

MULLED ALE

3 eggs
1 litre/2 pints milk
500 ml/1 pint ale

100 g/4 oz caster sugar
A little grated nutmeg

Bring the ale to the boil in a saucepan, then set aside. Beat the eggs, and stir in the milk, pour this mixture into the ale. Add the sugar and nutmeg, and heat slowly, but do not boil. Let it thicken, stirring meanwhile. Serve very hot.

OATMEAL CAUDEL

2 tablespoons oatmeal
500 ml/1 pint hot water
Lemon rind
Pinch of cinnamon

Light soft brown sugar
Blade of mace
500 ml/1 pint ale, heated

Boil the oatmeal in the water with the lemon rind and spices and enough brown sugar to taste. When thick, pour into the heated ale, stirring meanwhile.

MILK POSSET

500 ml/1 pint milk
75 ml/3 fl oz white wine or
  sherry
A squeeze of lemon

A little sugar
Pinch of ground ginger
Pinch of nutmeg

Heat the milk; when it froths add the wine or sherry. Strain and add lemon juice, and sugar to taste. Stir in ginger and nutmeg. Serve hot.

CORNISH EGGY'OT

2 eggs   1 litre/2 pints beer
2 tablespoons sugar

Beat the eggs and sugar together and pour on hot beer. Stir briskly and drink while hot. *Sampson* is made the same way but substituting cider for beer.

TREACLE POSSET

250 ml/½ pint milk   1 tablespoon golden syrup, or
                                dark treacle

Bring the milk to the boil and pour it over the syrup or treacle in a jug; stir well and serve very hot.

HOT CHRISTMAS PUNCH

12 cubes sugar   4 tablespoons water
2 oranges   2 lemons
8 cloves   1 litre/2 pints cider
1 level teaspoon ground nutmeg 75 ml/3 fl oz rum
1 stick cinnamon   75 ml/3 fl oz brandy

Rub the sugar over the rind of one of the oranges to remove the zest. Cut this orange in halves, squeeze out the juice and put into a pan with the sugar. Cut the other orange into eight sections, stick a clove into the skin of each section and then sprinkle with the nutmeg. Add to the pan with the cinnamon, water and rind of the lemons, cut into strips. Heat gently until the sugar dissolves and then simmer for 5 minutes. Leave to cool until needed. Remove the cinnamon, pour in the cider and heat until really hot, but not boiling. Add the rum and then the brandy and heat again for a minute. Divide the orange sections and lemon rind between eight glasses, add the hot cider and serve at once.

Cold mixed drinks

HIPPOCRAS

225 g/8 oz light soft brown sugar   8 g/¼ oz cardamom
25 g/1 oz cinnamon   Pinch of Cayenne pepper
15 g/½ oz ginger   1 litre/2 pints red wine

Stir the sugar and spices into the wine and leave it to stand until it clears completely. Pour off the clear liquid into a bottle. This is a good drink after a rather heavy meal. The spicy dregs can be used to add savour to stews and soups.

CORNISH SPICED ALE

1 litre/2 pints ale   ½ teaspoon ground nutmeg
4 cloves   1 teaspoon sugar
Pinch of mixed spice   2 large apples

Heat the ale slowly but do not boil. Add the cloves and other spices, and the sugar. Peel and slice the apples and add them to the ale. Leave in a warm place to infuse for 10 minutes and strain. Serve with a piece of apple in each tankard.

CHAPTER 15
FESTIVAL FOOD

THE country year's labour has always been broken from time to time by festivals noted for special seasonal dishes. Many of these feast days have their origins far back in history, in ancient pagan worship of the changing seasons and weather. These were later taken over by the early Christian church, and their feast-day foods with them. For instance, in Lancashire, a cake now associated with All Souls' Day on 2 November used also to be known as a 'Har Cake', so named for the Norse god Odin or 'Har'.

Other feasts, with their special suppers or cakes, marked the times when vital seasonal tasks were completed; sheep-shearing was one; the in-gathering of the harvest was another, when the annual Michaelmas goose was roasted.

Many of our favourite old buns and cakes were originally specially baked for these occasions, but the association is now forgotten. Such cakes include Sally Lunns, which were baked for Good Friday.

Shrewsbury Cakes, Tansy Cakes, Johnny Cakes, Popovers and Pikelets were all served during Lent or at Easter, so were fruit-filled pastries such as Cumberland Cakes, Banbury Cakes and Eccles Cakes.

Sometimes, however, our cakes, gingerbreads and pies record, by their names or shapes, the reason why they are made on special days. Some gingerbread moulds, for instance, record the story of an old event long past or of an act of charity; in both cases, money was left in trust long ago to provide the annual hand-out, and is still used for the same purpose.

Fritters, cakes and pies

PATELEY FRITTERS

20 g/¾ oz yeast	½ teaspoon grated lemon rind
500 ml/1 pint milk	1 tablespoon sugar
350 g/12 oz plain flour	Pinch of salt
25 g/1 oz lard	Pinch of ground cinnamon
75 g/3 oz currants	1 large apple
40 g/1½ oz raisins	

These fritters come from Yorkshire and were traditionally eaten on Ash Wednesday. The first four days of the week which signalled Lent or Shrovetide all had their own names and special foods. Collop Monday was celebrated with eggs and collops (thick slices of meat); this was followed by Shrove or Pancake Tuesday, Fritter or Frutas Wednesday, and Bloody Thursday (when black puddings were eaten).

Mix the yeast with a little warm milk and leave it to start working. Put the flour into a warm bowl. Melt the lard in the remaining milk, heated to lukewarm. Put the yeast into the centre of the flour, and add the lard and milk mixture. Leave for 5 minutes, and then add the currants, raisins, lemon peel, sugar, salt and cinnamon. Peel the apple and chop it finely. Add to the mixture and beat all the ingredients to a stiff batter. Leave in a warm place for 1 hour to rise. Put large spoonfuls of the batter into hot dripping or lard and fry until golden. Turn each fritter and cook the other side until golden.

KENTISH LENTEN PIES

450 g/1 lb plain flour	100 g/4 oz butter
2 teaspoons baking powder	175 g/6 oz lard

Filling:

1 litre/2 pints milk	100 g/4 oz butter
2 bay leaves	Pinch of mixed spice
4 tablespoons ground rice	2 eggs
100 g/4 oz sugar	1 tablespoon currants

Make a pastry with the flour, baking powder, butter and lard, and enough cold water to make a firm dough. Line large patty tins with this pastry. Reserve 125 ml/¼ pint milk, and boil the rest with the bay leaves. Mix the remaining milk with the ground rice, and add this mixture to the boiling milk. Cook for 3 minutes. Add the sugar, butter and spice and leave to cool to lukewarm. Add the beaten eggs and pour the mixture into the pastry-lined tins. Sprinkle with currants and bake at 375°F, 190°C, gas mark 5 for 30 minutes. Eat hot or cold. These were eaten only in Lent, and were sometimes known as 'pudding pies'.

PALM SUNDAY FIG CAKE

175 g/6 oz dried figs	Pinch of salt
175 g/6 oz plain flour	65 g/2½ oz caster sugar
½ teaspoon baking powder	65 g/2½ oz butter

Chop the figs roughly and simmer in just enough water to cover them until they are tender. Leave to cool. Mix together the flour, baking powder, salt and sugar, and rub in the butter. Mix to a batter with the cooled figs and cooking water. Pour into a greased and floured 17·5 cm/7 inch round cake tin, and bake at 375°F, 190°C, gas mark 5 for 45 minutes.

GOOD FRIDAY HOT CROSS BUNS

225 g/8 oz plain flour
Pinch of salt
¼ teaspoon mixed spice
125 ml/¼ pint milk
15 g/½ oz yeast

50 g/2 oz butter
40 g/1½ oz caster sugar
1 egg
75 g/3 oz currants
15 g/½ oz finely-chopped peel

Sieve the flour, salt and spice in a mixing bowl. Warm milk to blood heat. Add yeast and butter, stir until dissolved, mix in sugar and beaten egg. Pour on to the flour, and beat until smooth. Turn on to a floured board, work in the currants and peel, and knead well. Put in a buttered bowl, sprinkle with flour, cover with a clean cloth, and put in a warm place to rise for 1½ hours or until the mixture has doubled its bulk. Knock down with the hand and leave to rise as before for 30 minutes. Knead the dough and shape into eight rounds. Put on two greased baking sheets and on each bun put a paste cross made with flour and water dough. Prove in a warm place until nearly doubled in size (about 15 minutes). Bake at 425°F, 220°C, gas mark 7 for 15 minutes. While still hot, brush with a glaze made by boiling 1 tablespoon sugar in 1 tablespoon milk.

SIMNEL CAKE

Marzipan:

450 g/1 lb ground almonds
450 g/1 lb icing sugar
½ teaspoon almond essence

1 tablespoon lemon juice
4 egg yolks

Cake:

175 g/6 oz butter
175 g/6 oz Demerara sugar
3 eggs
225 g/8 oz self-raising flour
1 level teaspoon nutmeg
1 level teaspoon cinnamon
1 level teaspoon mixed spice
Pinch of salt

450 g/1 lb currants
225 g/8 oz sultanas
100 g/4 oz mixed peel
Milk to mix
Jam
Beaten egg to glaze
Glacé icing

Mix the marzipan ingredients to a stiff paste and knead well; divide into three and roll out two of the pieces into circles 20 cm/ 8 inches in diameter. Put aside with the rest of the marzipan. To make the cake, cream butter and sugar together until light and fluffy, then beat in the eggs one at a time. Sieve the flour, spices and salt together and add to the mixture; finally add the dried fruit. If the mixture is a little stiff, add enough milk to give a dropping consistency. Put half the cake mixture into a greased and lined 20 cm/8 inch cake tin, then put in one circle of marzipan and cover with remaining cake mixture. Bake at 300°F, 150°C, gas mark 2 for 3½ hours. Allow to cool. Brush the top of the cake with a little warm jam, and put on the second circle of marzipan; press down well. Make twelve small balls from the remaining marzipan, and arrange these round the edge. Brush lightly with a little egg and put the cake into a hot oven or under the grill for a few seconds to glaze lightly. Fill the centre with a little white glacé icing and decorate.

Originally, the Simnel cake was taken home by servant girls on 'Mothering Sunday' (the fourth Sunday in Lent) as a present for their mothers. It was made with figs, the fruit symbolizing 'fruitfulness in offspring'.

Only later did it become a traditional Easter-time cake. The balls of marzipan symbolize the number of Christ's disciples.

SEDGEMOOR EASTER CAKE

225 g/8 oz plain flour	½ teaspoon mixed spice
100 g/4 oz butter	½ teaspoon ground cinnamon
100 g/4 oz caster sugar	1 egg
100 g/4 oz currants	2 tablespoons brandy

Rub the butter into the flour and stir in the sugar, currants, spice and cinnamon. Beat the egg with the brandy and mix with the dry ingredients. Roll out 1·25 cm/½ inch thick, cut into rounds and bake at 350°F, 180°C, gas mark 4 for 20 minutes.

EASTER BISCUITS

75 g/3 oz butter
75 g/3 oz caster sugar
1 egg yolk
Pinch of mixed spice

175 g/6 oz plain flour
50 g/2 oz currants
15 g/½ oz candied chopped peel
Milk to mix

Glaze:

1 egg white

Caster sugar

Cream the butter and the sugar until light and fluffy. Add the egg yolk and work into the spice and flour. Add the fruit and peel and enough milk to give a stiff dough. Roll out thinly on a floured board and cut into shapes with a cutter. Put on to a greased baking sheet and bake at 400°F, 200°C, gas mark 6 for 15 minutes. After 10 minutes, brush with egg white and sprinkle with caster sugar.

GLOUCESTERSHIRE WHITE POT

1 litre/2 pints milk
2 eggs
1 tablespoon plain flour
1 tablespoon dark soft brown
  sugar

2 tablespoons black treacle or
  golden syrup
15 g/½ oz butter
100 ml/4 fl oz water

Mix the eggs, flour, sugar and treacle together with a little cold milk. Bring the rest of the milk to the boil and pour it on to the mixture, stirring well. Put in oven dish and dot with butter. Pour the cold water in the middle without stirring. Bake at 325°F, 170°C, gas mark 3 for 2 hours. This is a traditional dish for Whitsun, but is used for other festivals too.

FIDGET PIE

450 g/1 lb potatoes
450 g/1 lb apples
225 g/8 oz bacon

Salt and pepper
Stock
225 g/8 oz shortcrust pastry

Peel and slice the potatoes and apples. Cut the bacon into small pieces. In an ovenware dish, put a layer of potato slices, then a layer of bacon and a layer of apples. Season the layers with salt and pepper. Repeat the layers until the dish is full, and then moisten with a little stock. Cover with pastry. Bake at 400°F, 200°C, gas mark 6 for 1 hour. This pie was often eaten at harvest suppers. Neck of lamb can be substituted for the bacon.

CREED WHEAT AND FRUMENTY

225 g/8 oz wheat grains	50 g/2 oz currants
Pinch of salt	Pinch of nutmeg
1·5 litres/3 pints water	50 g/2 oz sugar
1 litre/2 pints milk	2 eggs (optional)
50 g/2 oz raisins	Garnish (see recipe)

Put the wheat and salt into 1·5 litres/3 pints water in a casserole. Put into a very low oven and leave overnight to simmer until there is no water left. The wheat will then be 'creed'. Leave until needed. Then add the milk and dried fruit, together with the nutmeg and sugar, and cook gently on the hob or in the oven for 2 hours. Some recipes also include 2 beaten eggs just before the frumenty is ready. Serve with sweetened whey, chopped fresh fruit, or with rum or brandy and cream.

In Wiltshire, this used to be eaten on Mothering Sunday in Lent, and the 'creed' wheat could be bought ready for the dish. In Lincolnshire, it was served hot or cold at sheep-shearing time, and at harvest suppers. In Yorkshire, it was a traditional Christmas Eve or Twelfth Night dish. It is also known as Furmenty and Firmity, and a 'firmity tea' was often served to Lincolnshire children to celebrate sheep clipping.

SHEARING CAKE

225 g/8 oz plain flour	2 teaspoons caraway seeds
100 g/4 oz butter	Ground nutmeg
175 g/6 oz light soft brown sugar	125 ml/¼ pint milk
Rind of ½ lemon	1 egg
1 teaspoon baking powder	

Rub butter into the flour until the mixture is like fine bread-crumbs. Stir in the sugar, lemon, baking powder, caraway seeds and a good pinch of nutmeg. Mix in the milk and lightly-beaten egg. Line a greased cake tin with buttered paper, and put in the mixture. Bake at 350°F, 180°C, gas mark 4 for 1 hour. This was served to celebrate sheep-shearing time.

HARVEST BETSY CAKE

225 g/8 oz barley flour	100 g/4 oz caster sugar
225 g/8 oz plain flour	2 teaspoons golden syrup
1½ teaspoons baking powder	250 ml/½ pint milk
½ teaspoon salt	225 g/8 oz sultanas
100 g/4 oz butter	

Sift the two kinds of flour together with baking powder and salt. Cream butter and sugar, and add syrup. Add the flour mixture and the milk alternately, then fold in the sultanas. Put into a buttered 17·5 cm/7 inch cake tin, and bake at 350°F, 180°C, gas mark 4 for 1½ hours.

KATT PIES (MUTTON OR LAMB)

450 g/1 lb plain flour	225 g/8 oz currants
225 g/8 oz shredded suet	225 g/8 oz brown sugar
Pinch of salt	Salt and pepper
225 g/8 oz minced mutton or lamb	

The pastry for this dish is made like hot-water pastry for raised pies. Put the suet into 125 ml/¼ pint water and bring to the boil. Boil for 2 minutes and mix into the flour with a good pinch of salt. Cool slightly and mould into pies about 10 cm/4 inches in diameter, leaving enough for lids. Arrange layers of meat, currants and sugar in the pastry cases, seasoning them well. Top with thin rounds of pastry and bake at 425°F, 220°C, gas mark 7 for 30 minutes. Eat the pies hot. This is a Welsh dish, made for 12 November, Templeton Fair Day, for the past 200 years.

HEREFORD BRANDY SNAP

75 g/3 oz butter	½ teaspoon ground ginger
100 g/4 oz sugar	1 teaspoon brandy (optional)
100 g/4 oz black treacle	Squeeze of lemon juice
100 g/4 oz plain flour	

Melt the butter, sugar and treacle together, and leave them until cold. Stir in the flour, ginger, brandy (if used) and lemon juice and mix very thoroughly. Drop in teaspoonfuls on to a well-greased tin. Bake at 350°F, 180°C, gas mark 4 for 10 minutes until golden. Cool briefly, then roll quickly round the handle of a wooden spoon before they 'set'. Brandy snaps used to be known as 'jumbles', and even earlier as 'gaufres' or wafers. They were traditionally sold at fairs. This recipe was used for the brandy snaps sold at the Hereford Annual May Fair.

SHROPSHIRE SOUL CAKES

1·35 kg/3 lb plain flour	2 eggs
225 g/8 oz butter, softened	1 teaspoon ground allspice
225 g/8 oz sugar	Milk
25 g/1 oz yeast	

Sift the flour and rub in the slightly softened butter. Work the yeast with a teaspoon of sugar until it is creamy. Mix the flour with the eggs, yeast and enough milk to make a light dough. Leave to rise in a warm place for 30 minutes. Work in the sugar and spice and form into flat buns. Leave in a warm place for 15 minutes, and then bake at 425°F, 220°C, gas mark 7 for 15 minutes. These were distributed on All Souls' Day (2 November) until about 1850. In parts of Cheshire and Shropshire, children still go 'souling' at the end of October, singing from house to house and collecting money.

SHROPSHIRE SPECIAL CAKES

100 g/4 oz ground rice	100 g/4 oz caster sugar
100 g/4 oz plain flour	100 g/4 oz butter
Pinch of caraway seeds	2 eggs

Mix together the ground rice, flour and caraway seeds. Cream the butter and sugar, and work in the flour mixture. Beat the eggs well and gradually add them to the mixture to make a firm dough. Roll out like pastry and cut in circles about 12·5 cm/5 inches across. Bake at 375°F, 190°C, gas mark 5 for 15 minutes. This is another version of the cakes distributed on All Souls' Day.

NORTH COUNTRY PARKIN

175 g/6 oz plain flour	175 g/6 oz black treacle
1 teaspoon salt	150 g/5 oz butter or dripping
1 teaspoon ground ginger	100 g/4 oz dark soft brown sugar
2 teaspoons ground cinnamon	125 ml/¼ pint milk
1 teaspoon bicarbonate of soda	1 egg
300 g/10 oz medium oatmeal	

Sift together the flour, salt, spices and soda. Add the oatmeal and toss lightly, to mix. Warm the treacle, butter, sugar and milk together until the butter has melted. Cool slightly, add egg and beat well. Pour into the centre of the dry ingredients and stir rapidly until smooth. Turn into a greased and lined 17·5 cm/ 7 inch square tin. Bake at 350°F, 180°C, gas mark 4, for 1 hour. Store in an airtight tin for at least 2 weeks before using.

Every part of the North Country makes its own special parkin. Some are quite dry, others very moist and sticky. Parkin is still eaten on Bonfire or Guy Fawkes Night, 5 November. But it is much more ancient than the Guy Fawkes plot; in fact it is associated with old pagan fire-worship and the feast marking the beginning of winter on 2 November. Because of this, Lancashire parkin used to be called 'Harcake' or 'Soul Hars Cake' when that date came to commemorate the Feast of All Souls.

SPECIAL PARKIN FOR GUY FAWKES NIGHT

450 g/1 lb fine oatmeal
225 g/8 oz plain flour
100 g/4 oz dark brown sugar
2 teaspoons ground ginger

1 teaspoon baking powder
225 g/8 oz black treacle
75 g/3 oz melted butter or
   dripping

This is a rich dark gingerbread which should be soft and sticky, and is very good eaten with a piece of cheese. Keep it for several weeks to mellow before eating, if possible in an old-fashioned bread crock. Mix all the dry ingredients together, make a well in the centre and pour in the treacle and melted butter. Beat thoroughly and bake in a buttered rectangular tin at 325°F, 170°C, gas mark 3 for 1½ hours.

BEDFORDSHIRE WIGS

450 g/1 lb black treacle
100 g/4 oz butter
175 ml/7 fl oz milk
450 g/1 lb plain flour

100 g/4 oz sugar
1 teaspoon bicarbonate of soda
2 teaspoons ground ginger
15 g/½ oz caraway seeds

Melt the treacle and butter together in a thick saucepan. When the mixture is hot, stir in the milk. Put all the other ingredients into a bowl and make a well in the centre. Stir in the syrup mixture and blend thoroughly together. Pour into shallow round tins or one large tin, and bake at 350°F, 180°C, gas mark 4 for 30 minutes. The mixture will rise over the edge of the tins so that the thick rim looks like the curl of a wig. These were eaten on St Katherine's Day, 25 November. St Katherine was the patron saint of lace-makers, and her day was considered in the county to herald the beginning of winter. Her feast was observed in many parts of the country. Somerset had Catten Cakes, which were wheels of spiced pastry with currants. St Katherine was martyred on a wheel, so she is also commemorated by firework Catherine wheels.

CAROL-SINGING OR PEPPER CAKE

675 g/1½ lb plain flour
225 g/8 oz butter
225 g/8 oz dark soft brown sugar
25 g/1 oz ground cloves

675 g/1½ lb black treacle
4 eggs
1 teaspoon bicarbonate of soda
A little milk

Rub the butter into the flour until the mixture is like fine bread-crumbs. Stir in the sugar and cloves. Add the treacle and well-beaten eggs, and the bicarbonate of soda mixed with a little milk. Pour into a well-greased roasting tin and bake at 325°F, 170°C, gas mark 3 for 1¾ hours. This Yorkshire cake was often called 'Pepper Cake' and was given to carol singers at Christmastide.

SPECIAL CHRISTMAS CAKE

300 g/10 oz butter
150 g/5 oz caster sugar
150 g/5 oz light soft brown sugar
5 eggs
350 g/12 oz plain flour, sifted
Pinch of salt
½ teaspoon ground nutmeg
¾ teaspoon ground cinnamon
225 g/8 oz currants

225 g/8 oz sultanas
225 g/8 oz seedless raisins
100 g/4 oz glacé cherries
  (quartered)
100 g/4 oz chopped candied peel
1 lemon
100 g/4 oz chopped walnuts
2 tablespoons brandy or sherry

Grease and line a 20 cm/8 inch cake tin, and tie a band of brown paper round the outside. Cream together the butter and sugars till light and fluffy. Beat the eggs well and add gradually to the butter and sugar, together with a little of the sifted flour and spices. Fold in the rest of the flour, salt, fruit, peel, nuts, grated rind and juice of the lemon, brandy or sherry. When evenly mixed, turn into the prepared tin and make a slight hollow in the centre. Bake at 300°F, 150°C, gas mark 2 for 2 hours, then reduce heat to 275°F, 140°C, gas mark 1 for 2 hours. Cover top with a sheet of paper if getting too brown. Keep for 3 weeks before cutting. This makes a lovely moist cake.

MISS PEDELTY'S CHRISTMAS CAKE

225 g/8 oz butter
225 g/8 oz Demerara sugar
5 eggs
300 g/10 oz plain flour
50 g/2 oz ground almonds
225 g/8 oz sultanas
225 g/8 oz currants
100 g/4 oz peel

100 g/4 oz glacé cherries
50 g/2 oz chopped almonds
1 teaspoon mixed spice
1 grated orange rind
1 grated lemon rind
40 ml/1½ fl oz rum
125 ml/¼ pint milk

Mix like the previous cake and bake for 2½–3 hours at 325°F, 170°C, gas mark 3. This makes a nice Christmas cake which will keep moist for a long time.

MOIST CHRISTMAS PUDDING

100 g/4 oz carrots (after peeling)
100 g/4 oz potatoes (after peeling)
100 g/4 oz finely-chopped suet
100 g/4 oz currants
100 g/4 oz sultanas

50 g/2 oz candied peel
50 g/2 oz plain flour
50 g/2 oz soft white breadcrumbs
50 g/2 oz brown sugar
1 tablespoon black treacle

Boil the carrots and potatoes until tender. Drain and mash them well while still hot. Add all dry ingredients and treacle, and mix well. Put in a buttered basin, cover with greaseproof paper and cloth. Boil for 6 hours. Re-boil for 2 hours just before using, if stored, but eat within 2–3 weeks of making.

RICH CHRISTMAS PUDDING

100 g/4 oz plain flour
50 g/2 oz soft white breadcrumbs
2 large eggs
1 teaspoon mixed spice
1 teaspoon ground nutmeg
1 teaspoon ground cinnamon
100 g/4 oz shredded suet
100 g/4 oz light soft brown sugar
100 g/4 oz grated apple
1 small grated carrot
100 g/4 oz mixed candied peel

100 g/4 oz chopped blanched
  almonds
125 ml/¼ pint beer, ale or milk
100 g/4 oz currants
225 g/8 oz raisins
100 g/4 oz sultanas
50 g/2 oz chopped prunes or
  dried apricots
Grated rind and juice of ½ lemon
Grated rind and juice of ½ orange
1 tablespoon black treacle

Mix all the ingredients together, stir well and leave overnight if possible. Place in two basins and cover with greaseproof paper and a floured cloth. Steam or boil for 8 hours. Wrap very securely and store until required. Then re-boil for 2 hours. Serve with brandy butter or Cumberland Rum Butter.

CHRISTMAS EVE WIGS

75 g/3 oz butter
225 g/8 oz self-raising flour
25 g/1 oz caster sugar
25 g/1 oz chopped mixed peel

2 teaspoons caraway seeds
1 egg
A little milk

Rub butter into flour, add sugar, peel and caraway seeds. Mix to a soft dough with egg and a little milk. Put into greased patty-pans and bake at 425°F, 220°C, gas mark 7 for 20 minutes. The mixture rises and curls over to resemble a wig. Eat with mulled elderberry wine, or dip in ale.

WELSH CHRISTMAS FRUIT LOAF

225 g/8 oz mixed dried fruit	175 ml/7 fl oz hot strained tea
25 g/1 oz chopped peel	225 g/8 oz plain flour
50 g/2 oz glacé cherries	½ teaspoon baking powder
100 g/4 oz light soft brown sugar	50 g/2 oz butter
Grated rind of 1 lemon	1 egg
Grated rind of 1 orange	

Steep the fruit, chopped peel, quartered cherries, orange and lemon peel and sugar overnight in the hot tea. Sieve flour and baking powder. Rub in the butter. Beat the egg; add egg and the steeped mixture to the dry ingredients. Turn the mixture into a greased and lined loaf tin. Bake at 350°F, 180°C, gas mark 4 for 1 hour. Keep for 1 day before cutting.

GOD'S KITCHELS

450 g/1 lb puff pastry	1 teaspoon ground nutmeg
225 g/8 oz currants	50 g/2 oz ground almonds
75 g/3 oz chopped candied peel	50 g/2 oz butter
½ teaspoon cinnamon	

These cakes were made in Suffolk during the twelve days of Christmas, from 25 December to 6 January, and were specially kept for visiting godchildren, as this was the one time of the year when they were certain to pay a visit to their godparents. There used to be a saying 'Ask me a blessing and I will give you a kitchel.'

Divide the pastry into two pieces and roll out each piece to a thin square. Mix the currants, peel, spices and almonds and stir into the melted butter. Spread this filling evenly on to one piece of pastry to within 1·25 cm/½ inch of the edge. Moisten the edge with water and press on the second piece of pastry. Press the edges together well. With the back of a knife, mark the top of the pastry into 5 cm/2 inch squares without cutting through the filling. Bake at 425°F, 220°C, gas mark 7 for 25 minutes. Sprinkle with caster sugar and divide into small cakes, where marked, while still warm.

Other dishes

Most of the cakes mentioned at the beginning of this chapter are not included in this book because they are so familiar. But recipes for many others are given in various parts of the book as well as in this chapter. The Berwick May Day Tarts are one example, and the Harvest Betsy Cake is another.

Other dishes besides breads and cakes are associated with some of our festivals. Boar's Head was originally served on Twelfth Night, for instance. Hare Pie is still eaten at Hallerton in Leicestershire on Easter Monday. A Cockle and Mussel Feast is held at Clitheroe in Lancashire to mark the election of the Mayor each year: and grilled trout is the traditional dish served to commemorate Sir Francis Drake's bringing water to Plymouth. In some areas, flummery is put outside the back door on Midsummer Eve 'for the fairies'.

CHAPTER 16
LOCAL DISHES

LOCAL dishes originated in very early times, among tribes and groups of invaders with different customs. They developed individual features because communications were poor and very few people could travel away from their immediate neighbourhood. The raw materials available to country people were very similar, however, so that almost (but not quite) identical dishes appear in different parts of the country.

They developed almost identical traits, too, because even when the ingredients did differ, the cooking methods were similar. For instance, the West Country mackerel and pilchards were cooked in cider or vinegar with spices in the same way as the East Anglian herrings. In the same way, the plain baked goods made of flour and fat with a few currants or a little spice were cooked on a heated griddle over the fire everywhere before ovens came into common use. Because Britain had plenty of timber, stews and boiled puddings were the commonest cooked foods everywhere, for many centuries.

None the less, almost every region has developed its own

recipes, and these are still treasured by countrywomen and are held with pride to be the best.

Local recipes from many different areas are included in every part of this book, but it is not always easy to track down their regional homes since cooking methods and the pace of life have changed in modern times. For one thing, people are more mobile now, and are not restricted to local dishes, so they tend to forget them. The local cakes, pies, biscuits and sweetmeats have kept their identity longest. They still have their own marked features and, more than most other foods, are still made at home and appear in local shops. The following recipes show how country-women in different parts still use flour, sugar, fat, dried fruits and spices, and the local meat, to produce their own local specialities.

Sweet baked goods and sweetmeats

CORNISH FAIRINGS

450 g/1 lb plain flour
225 g/8 oz Demerara sugar
150 g/5 oz butter
50 g/2 oz lard
100 g/4 oz candied lemon peel

Pinch of mixed spice
225 g/8 oz golden syrup
15 g/½ oz bicarbonate of soda
Pinch of tartaric acid
1 teaspoon ground ginger

Rub the butter and lard into the flour. Mix the spices and sugar. Put the syrup into a bowl. Bring the soda to the boil in 2 tablespoons water in a saucepan and add this to the syrup. Do the same with the tartaric acid until it froths and then mix all the ingredients into the flour, together with the lemon peel cut very finely. Mix to a soft paste and roll out into 2·5 cm/1 inch thick strips. Cut these in pieces 2·5 cm/1 inch long. Put on to a greased tin, leaving room for the biscuits to spread. Bake at 350°F, 180°C, gas mark 4 for 30 minutes.

CORNISH HEAVY CAKE

675 g/1½ lb plain flour	15 g/½ oz sugar
100 g/4 oz butter or cream	1 teaspoon salt
100 g/4 oz beef dripping	½ teaspoon grated lemon peel
350 g/12 oz currants	

Mix the butter or cream and the dripping in to the flour without breaking it up too finely. Add the other ingredients and mix to a stiff dough with a little water. Roll out on a board and then roll up the dough again. Leave for an hour and roll out the dough into a circle about 1·25 cm/½ inch thick. Cut across with a knife very lightly into fair-sized squares. Bake at 400°F, 200°C, gas mark 6 for 25 minutes.

CUMBERLAND CURRANT PASTY

225 g/8 oz plain flour	75 g/3 oz butter
50 g/2 oz lard	Pinch of salt

Filling:

175 g/6 oz currants	50 g/2 oz butter
¼ teaspoon cinnamon	50 g/2 oz light soft brown sugar
½ teaspoon allspice	Grated rind of 1 lemon
Pinch of ground mace	

Make pastry with the flour, fats and salt, but do not rub in the fat too much as the pastry should be rather flaky. Roll half the pastry to fit a square or rectangular baking tin. Mix all the filling ingredients and heat them over a gentle heat until the butter has melted and the ingredients can be well mixed together. Spread this filling on the pastry. Damp the edges of the pastry and cover with the remaining piece. Prick the top. Bake at 400°F, 200°C, gas mark 6 for 10 minutes. Reduce the heat to 350°F, 180°C, gas mark 4 for 30 minutes. Cut in squares to serve.

CUMBERLAND RUM BUTTER

100 g/4 oz butter	225 g/8 oz dark soft brown sugar
¼ teaspoon ground nutmeg	65 ml/2½ fl oz rum

Cream the butter and work in the nutmeg and the sugar, gradually adding a few drops of rum at a time until it is all finished. The mixture should be smooth and creamy. This sweet butter was made in Cumberland and Westmorland and put into a bowl to use at christenings. It was eaten by everyone who visited the new baby, traditionally spread on oatcakes, but sometimes on biscuits or bread. The woman who first cut into the bowl was supposed to be the next one who would prepare a similar dish, and butter made for a boy's birth was said to be more infectious than that made for a girl. Sometimes the bowl was hidden, and young people came to the house to search for it and eat the contents. The empty bowl was then used for a collection of money for the baby.

DERBYSHIRE BAKEWELL PUDDING

225 g/8 oz plain flour	100 g/4 oz butter
225 g/8 oz butter	100 g/4 oz sugar
½ teaspoon lemon juice	5 drops almond essence
4 egg yolks	4 tablespoons raspberry jam
2 egg whites	

Make puff pastry using the flour, 225 g/8 oz butter, lemon juice and cold water to mix. Line a pie plate with the pastry and spread with raspberry jam. Beat the egg yolks and whites together. Melt 100 g/4 oz butter and mix this with the eggs, adding the sugar. Beat for 10 minutes and add the essence. Pour into the pastry case and bake at 400°F, 200°C, gas mark 6 for 30 minutes.

DEVONSHIRE FLATS

200 ml/8 fl oz Devonshire cream   225 g/8 oz sugar
450 g/1 lb plain flour   Milk
1 egg

Rub the cream into the flour. Beat the egg into the mixture and add the sugar. Mix thoroughly with a little milk to make a smooth dough. Roll out very thinly and cut into rounds. Sprinkle with a little sugar and bake at 375°F, 190°C, gas mark 5 for 10 minutes.

DURHAM PIKELETS

225 g/8 oz plain flour   Pinch of bicarbonate of soda
40 g/1½ oz sugar   Buttermilk or sour milk
Pinch of salt

Mix the flour, sugar and salt. Make a well in the centre and pour in enough milk to make a batter with the consistency of thick cream. Dissolve the bicarbonate of soda in a little water and add to the batter. Beat well and fry on a griddle or in a frying pan with lard until golden brown on both sides. Spread with butter and serve hot.

LANCASHIRE GOOSENARGH CAKES

450 g/1 lb plain flour   1 teaspoon caraway seeds
Pinch of salt   1 teaspoon ground coriander
350 g/12 oz butter   50 g/2 oz sugar

Mix the flour and salt and rub in the butter. Mix to a smooth dough and roll out about 0·5 cm/¼ inch thick. Cut into 5 cm/2 inch rounds and sprinkle with the spices and sugar. Leave overnight. Bake at 300°F, 150°C, gas mark 2 for 45 minutes until firm but still pale. Sift on a little more sugar as they cool.

GRANTHAM GINGERBREAD (LINCOLNSHIRE)

225 g/8 oz plain flour
1 teaspoon baking powder
100 g/4 oz butter

100 g/4 oz sugar
1 egg
25 g/1 oz ground ginger

Cream the butter and sugar and beat in the egg yolk. Sift together the flour, baking powder and ginger and add to the butter mixture. Whip the egg white stiffly and fold into the mixture. Put into a tin lined with greased paper and bake at 350°F, 180°C, gas mark 4 for 40 minutes. This is a white gingerbread and should remain pale.

NORFOLK BIFFINS

Biffins are red-cheeked apples which are dried out very slowly. Choose apples which have no blemishes and put them on clean straw on a wire cake rack. Cover them well with more straw. Put into a very low oven for 5 hours. Take them out and press them very gently to flatten them slightly without breaking the skins. Return them to the oven for 1 hour and take them out and press them again. When they are cold, coat them lightly with sugar which has been melted over a low heat without colouring.

NORFOLK DUMPLINGS

15 g/½ oz yeast
1 teaspoon caster sugar
125 ml/¼ pint hot water

2 tablespoons milk
450 g/1 lb plain flour

If the sugar is left out of the recipe, these dumplings can be served with meat and gravy.

Cream the yeast and the sugar. Pour the milk and water over the yeast. Put the flour into a basin and pour in the liquid. Mix well and leave to rise in a warm place for 2 hours. Knead the dough well and form into dumplings. Leave them to stand for 10 minutes. Put into a saucepan of boiling water and boil for 20 minutes. Serve hot with melted butter and sugar.

WESTMORLAND THREE-DECKERS

450 g/1 lb shortcrust pastry	Demerara sugar to taste
450 g/1 lb plums, apples or blackberries	

Line a round flat tin with a layer of shortcrust pastry. Put half the fruit on this and sprinkle with sugar. Cover with another layer of pastry, then more fruit and sugar and then top with pastry. Bake at 375°F, 190°C, gas mark 5 for 1 hour; serve topped with sugar.

YORKSHIRE FAT RASCALS

450 g/1 lb plain flour	Pinch of salt
225 g/8 oz butter	100 g/4 oz currants
25 g/1 oz light soft brown sugar	Milk and water mixed

Rub the butter into the flour. Add the sugar, salt and currants and mix to a firm dough with a little milk and water mixed. Roll out 1·25 cm/½ inch thick and cut into 6·25 cm/2½ inch rounds. Dust with a little caster sugar and bake at 350°F, 180°C, gas mark 4 for 20 minutes.

FOCHABERS GINGERBREAD (SCOTLAND)

225 g/8 oz butter	Pinch of ground cinnamon
100 g/4 oz sugar	100 g/4 oz currants
225 g/8 oz black treacle	100 g/4 oz sultanas
2 eggs	75 g/3 oz chopped candied peel
450 g/1 lb plain flour	75 g/3 oz ground almonds
15 g/½ oz ground ginger	1 teaspoon bicarbonate of soda
25 g/1 oz mixed spice	250 ml/½ pint beer
Pinch of ground cloves	

Cream the butter and sugar. Add the slightly warmed treacle. Add the lightly beaten eggs and beat the mixture well. Mix the flour with the spices, dried fruit and almonds. Dissolve the bicarbonate of soda in the beer and gradually mix all the ingredients together. Put into a large greased cake tin at 325°F, 170°C, gas mark 3 for 2 hours.

DONCASTER BUTTERSCOTCH (YORKSHIRE)

450 g/1 lb brown sugar
250 ml/½ pint milk

175 g/6 oz butter
Pinch of cream of tartar

Melt the sugar in the milk over a low heat. Add the butter and cream of tartar and boil until a little dropped into cold water forms a hard ball. Pour into a greased tin and mark into squares with a knife just before the toffee hardens.

EDINBURGH ROCK (SCOTLAND)

450 g/1 lb cube sugar
Pinch of cream of tartar
250 ml/½ pint water

Flavouring and colouring
(lemon, vanilla, raspberry,
rose, ginger or orange)

Crush the sugar and put it into a saucepan with the water. Bring to the boil and add the cream of tartar. Continue boiling without stirring until a little dropped in cold water forms a hard lump. Put in the required flavouring and colouring and pour on to a marble slab. As the mixture cools, push the edges to the middle with a buttered knife. Dust with a little icing sugar and pull until the sugar looks dull. Cut it into pieces with a pair of scissors. Leave it to stand in a warm place for a day until it is powdery and soft.

Plain and savoury dishes

CHESHIRE PORK PIE

675 g/1½ lb pork
450 g/1 lb apples
Salt and pepper
Ground nutmeg

25 g/1 oz sugar
125 ml/¼ pint cider
25 g/1 oz butter
225 g/8 oz shortcrust pastry

Cut the pork into small pieces. Peel and core the apples and cut them into slices. Arrange the pork and apples in a pie dish in layers, seasoning well with salt and pepper, nutmeg and sugar. Pour in the cider and top with the butter. Cover with pastry and bake at 400°F, 200°C, gas mark 6 for 15 minutes. Reduce the heat to 375°F, 190°C, gas mark 5 and cook for 45 minutes.

CORNISH UNDERROAST

900 g/2 lb shin beef   Salt and pepper
225 g/8 oz ox kidney   500 ml/1 pint stock
450 g/1 lb onions   Potatoes
25 g/1 oz plain flour

Cut the beef and kidney into very small pieces. Slice the onions. Toss the meat in flour and season well. Fry the meat and onions in a meat tin with a little dripping until the meat has changed colour. Pour on the stock and leave to simmer while the potatoes are prepared. Peel the potatoes and cut them into pieces about the size of an egg. Put them all over the meat, half below and half above the gravy line like icebergs. Cook at 325°F, 170°C, gas mark 3 for 2 hours until the potato tops are brown and the bottoms soaked in gravy.

DEVONSHIRE LEEK PIE

225 g/8 oz shortcrust pastry   Salt and pepper
6 large leeks   75 ml/3 fl oz single cream
250 ml/½ pint milk

Roll out the pastry to make a 'lid' for the pie dish. Wash and trim the leeks and cut the white part (and a little of the green) into 2·5 cm/1 inch pieces. Put into the milk with salt and pepper, and simmer gently until the leeks are just tender. Pour into the pie dish and add the cream. Cover with the pastry, and bake at 400°F, 200°C, gas mark 6, for 30 minutes. Serve with cold meat.

Variation

For Devonshire Turnip Pie, substitute 450 g/1 lb young turnips for the leeks. Make as above.

LANCASHIRE BRAWN

½ salted pig's head	Strip of lemon peel
1 pig's tongue	12 peppercorns
1 pig's heart	Blade of mace
6 cloves	125 ml/¼ pint vinegar

Simmer the pig's head with tongue and heart and all seasonings except the vinegar for 4 hours in water to cover. Remove meat, and cut half in chunks. Mince the rest of the meat. Strain the stock and return the meat to the saucepan. Pour over the stock and vinegar, bring to the boil, and pour into basins. Leave to set.

MELTON MOWBRAY PIE (LEICESTERSHIRE)

675 g/1½ lb flour	1 egg
Pinch of salt	900 g/2 lb pork
450 g/1 lb lard	Salt and pepper
125 ml/¼ pint milk and water mixed	Stock from meat trimmings and bones

Sift the flour and salt and rub in half the lard. Boil the remaining lard with the milk and water. When it is boiling, pour half of the liquid into the flour and stir well. Add the beaten egg and then the remaining hot liquid. Knead the dough and leave to stand for a few minutes. Using two thirds of the pastry, line a mould or tin, or raise the pastry with the hands over a wooden mould or jam jar and tie a double piece of greaseproof paper round it. Cut the meat into small dice and fill the pastry case, seasoning the meat well with salt and pepper. Cover with the remaining pastry and brush well with beaten egg which contains a pinch of salt. Bake at 400°F, 200°C, gas mark 6 for 20 minutes. Lower the heat to 350°F, 180°C, gas mark 4 and continue cooking for $1\frac{1}{2}$ hours. It is best to make the stock from the meat trimmings and bones the night before and let it set into a jelly. The addition of a pig's trotter will make the jelly set more firmly. When the pie is lukewarm, heat the stock until melted and pour it carefully into the pie through a hole in the lid. Leave until cold and firm before eating.

NORFOLK BEEF PUDDING

225 g/8 oz self-raising flour
75 g/3 oz shredded suet
Pinch of salt

350 g/12 oz stewing steak
1 shallot
Salt and pepper

Make up a suet crust with the flour, suet, salt and enough water to make a firm dough. Roll it out and put it on to a piece of greased foil or greaseproof paper. Cut up the meat and shallot finely and put them on to the suet pastry. Sprinkle with water and season with salt and pepper. Roll up the pastry and tie up in a cloth and steam for $3\frac{1}{2}$ hours.

NORTHUMBERLAND PAN HAGGERTY

450 g/1 lb potatoes
225 g/8 oz onions
A little dripping

100 g/4 oz grated cheese
Salt and pepper

Peel the potatoes and the onions. Cut them in very thin slices and dry the potatoes in a cloth. Heat the dripping and put in a layer of potatoes, then onions, then cheese and another layer of potatoes. Season the layers with salt and pepper. Fry gently until nearly cooked through. Turn in the pan to brown the other side, or brown the top under a grill.

SCOTCH MUTTON PIES

100 g/4 oz beef dripping
250 ml/½ pint water
450 g/1 lb plain flour
1 teaspoon salt

350 g/12 oz lean mutton
Salt and pepper
Grated nutmeg
Gravy

Put the dripping into a pan with the water and bring it to the boil. Sieve the flour and salt together and stir in the hot liquid. Mix well to form a firm dough. Put one-third of the pastry on one side and use the rest to line six pie dishes. Cut the meat into very small pieces and season with salt and pepper and nutmeg. Put the meat into the pastry cases and cover with the remaining pastry. Wet the edges and press them down firmly. Cut a small hole in the centre of each lid. Bake at 375°F, 190°C, gas mark 5 for 40 minutes. Pour a little hot gravy into the pies and serve hot.

NORTHUMBERLAND SINGIN' HINNIES

450 g/1 lb plain flour
½ teaspoon cream of tartar
¼ teaspoon bicarbonate of soda
Pinch of salt

175 g/6 oz currants
100 g/4 oz lard
100 g/4 oz butter
A little milk

Sift the flour with the cream of tartar, bicarbonate of soda and salt. Rub in the lard and butter and stir in the currants. Make into a stiff dough with a little milk. Shape into a round and roll out to 1·25 cm/½ inch thickness. Rub a girdle or frying pan with a little fat. Put on the dough and cook until brown underneath. Turn the cake carefully to brown the other side. Turn once again to make sure it is hot right through. Cut into pieces, split and butter and serve hot.

NORTHUMBERLAND BACON CAKE

450 g/1 lb plain flour	225 g/8 oz cold boiled streaky
225 g/8 oz lard	bacon
1 teaspoon baking powder	

Put the flour into a bowl and rub in the lard until the mixture is like fine breadcrumbs. Add the baking powder and mix well, and then add enough cold water to make a firm pastry. Roll the pastry out into a circle. Cut the bacon into thin slices and cover half the pastry completely. Fold over the other half of the pastry and roll it gently to exclude all air. Prick the pastry all over with a fork and pinch the edges together. Put on to a baking sheet and bake at 375°F, 190°C, gas mark 5, for 40 minutes. This is a favourite mid-morning snack for hungry workers. The cold bacon was often used for breakfast and the remains made into a bacon cake.

SAMPHIRE

Samphire is a fleshy plant which grows on salt marshes, and it is particularly popular in Norfolk. It is best eaten hot with butter like asparagus. Simply wash the samphire well and boil it in fresh water for 10 minutes. Pour over hot melted butter, and suck it like asparagus. Samphire can be blanched for 2 minutes and frozen for later use, and makes an excellent first course before meat or fish. In the eighteenth century it used to be pickled in a mixture of white wine vinegar and salt brine.

YORKSHIRE PAN PIE (BEEF)

1 tablespoon dripping	2 leeks
1 large onion	Salt and pepper
225 g/8 oz stewing steak	75 g/3 oz self-raising flour
3 carrots	40 g/1½ oz shredded suet
2 tomatoes	

Melt the fat in a saucepan. Chop the onion finely and cut the meat into cubes. Fry the onion and the meat until golden. Slice the carrots, tomatoes and leeks, and add them to the saucepan. Add just enough water to cover and simmer for 30 minutes. Season well with salt and pepper and continue cooking gently for 15 minutes. Mix together the flour and suet with a pinch of salt and enough cold water to make a firm dough. Form this dough into a circle slightly smaller than the saucepan. Put this on top of the meat and vegetables. Put on the lid and cook gently for 1 hour.

INDEX

MORE ABOUT PENGUINS
AND PELICANS

For further information about books available from Penguins please write to Dept EP, Penguin Books Ltd, Harmondsworth, Middlesex UB7 0DA.

In the U.S.A.: For a complete list of books available from Penguins in the United States write to Dept CS, Penguin Books, 625 Madison Avenue, New York, New York 10022.

In Canada: For a complete list of books available from Penguins in Canada write to Penguin Books Canada Ltd, 2801 John Street, Markham, Ontario L3R 1B4.

In Australia: For a complete list of books available from Penguins in Australia write to the Marketing Department, Penguin Books Australia Ltd, P.O. Box 257, Ringwood, Victoria 3134.

Other cookery handbooks from Penguin

SPANISH REGIONAL COOKERY
Anna MacMiadhacháin

Anna MacMiadhacháin has travelled extensively through Spain and collected over three hundred recipes for this handbook. They reveal that the true Spanish cuisine, found in country villages and tucked-away cafés, is a subtle blend of imagination and individuality, and that each region produces food of considerable distinction – a far cry from the typical tourist menu at a holiday resort.

MASTERING THE ART OF FRENCH COOKING
VOLUMES 1 AND 2
Simone Beck, Louisette Bertholle, Julia Child

'The most instructive book on fine French cooking yet written in the English language' – Elizabeth David

A practical guide to *haute cuisine*, with hundreds of clear and precise recipes for cooking in the classic French style.

'Essential reading for anyone wishing to produce ambitious and entertaining dishes in the French manner' – *Wine and Food*

'Has been described as being the best book about French cooking in English . . . I agree' – Ambrose Heath in the *Guardian*

More cookery handbooks from Penguin

THE COOKERY OF ENGLAND
Elisabeth Ayrton

'Both a history of English food, from the days when we were esteemed better cooks than the French, and a book of recipes that will extend the repertoire of the Cordon Bleu cook without being too extravagant or too complicated for the novice . . . this is a lovely book which could restore pride to our English kitchens' – *The Times Literary Supplement*

A TASTE OF THE COUNTRY
Pamela Westland

'A garden is a lovesome thing, God wot' – and all the lovelier for providing such a wealth of good food on our back doorsteps.

An ardent advocate of home produce, Pamela Westland has assembled a variety of suggestions and recipes for dealing with the fruits of your labours. She begins by listing the crops you can grow and how to deal with them, and includes mouthwatering recipes for jams, jellies and chutneys. She devotes a chapter to home brewing and wine-making, and demonstrates how cheap, simple and versatile yogurt is. She gives a wide choice of breads, cakes and buns to try, and finally discusses the best ways to store the lot in a home freezer.

THE PENGUIN BOOK OF JAMS PICKLES AND CHUTNEYS
David and Rose Mabey

An excellent book; practical, personal and suggestive, every recipe's clearly the result of real experience and written with great charm' – *The Times*

Jane Grigson in Penguin

JANE GRIGSON'S VEGETABLE BOOK

Written with all the author's customary warmth and erudition, here is a modern kitchen guide to the cooking of vegetables, from the well-beloved cabbage and parsnip to the more exotic chayote and Chinese leaf.

FISH COOKERY

There are over 50 species of edible fish; and Jane Grigson feels that most of us do not eat nearly enough of them. If anything will make us mend our ways, it is this delightful book with its varied and comprehensive recipes, covering everything from lobster to conger eel, from sole to clam chowder. Many of her dishes come from France, others are from the British Isles, America, Spain, Italy – any country where good fish is cooked with loving care and eaten with appreciation.

CHARCUTERIE AND FRENCH PORK COOKERY

Ever since Charles Lamb stated that there was no other taste comparable to that of roast pork, the pig has never looked back. And it is hoped that this book – the first of its kind – will further its popularity in the English kitchen. Together with a guide to *charcuterie* and a host of French pork dishes, it gives new and unusual information on the history and growth of this art. Certain to delight both adventurous housewife and diffident traveller to France, this book allows you to make a true pig of yourself.

GOOD THINGS

Bouchées a la reine, civet of hare, Mrs Beeton's carrot jam to imitate apricot pre-serve, baked beans Southern style, wine sherbet . . .

These are just a few of the delicious and intriguing dishes in *Good Things*: Jane Grigson is a firm believer in the pleasure food gives. Echoing the great chef Carême – 'from behind my ovens, I feel the ugly edifice of routine crumbling beneath my hands' – she emphasizes the delights and solaces of a truly creative activity.

and

ENGLISH FOOD
THE MUSHROOM FEAST

Elizabeth David in Penguin

Elizabeth David is well known for the infectious enthusiasm with which she presents her recipes.

'She has the happy knack of giving just as much detail as the average cook finds desirable; she presumes neither on our knowledge nor on our ignorance' – Elizabeth Nicholas in the *Sunday Times*

FRENCH COUNTRY COOKING

Some of the splendid regional variations in French cookery are described in this book.

FRENCH PROVINCIAL COOKING

'It is difficult to think of any home that can do without Elizabeth David's *French Provincial Cooking* . . . One could cook for a lifetime on the book alone' – *Observer*

MEDITERRANEAN FOOD

A practical collection of recipes made by the author when she lived in France, Italy, the Greek Islands and Egypt, evoking all the colour of the Mediterranean but making use of ingredients obtainable in England.

ITALIAN FOOD

Exploding once and for all the myth that Italians live entirely on minestrone, spaghetti and veal escalopes, this exciting book demonstrates the enormous and colourful variety of Italy's regional cooking.

SUMMER COOKING

A selection of summer dishes that are light (not necessarily cold), easy to prepare and based on the food in season.

SPICES, SALT AND AROMATICS
IN THE ENGLISH KITCHEN

Elizabeth David presents English recipes which are notable for their employment of spices, salt and aromatics. As usual, she seasons instruction with information, explaining the origins and uses of her ingredients.

ENGLISH BREAD AND YEAST COOKERY

Here are breads of all colours and flavours; wholemeal, white, wheatmeal, barley, rye and oatmeal. There are many of our delicious spiced breads, like bara birth and saffron cake; yeast buns such as Chelsea, Bath and Hot Cross; leavened pancakes, muffins, crumpets, pikelets and oatcakes are all described with Mrs David's usual vigour and originality.